BUSINESS FUNDAMENTALS

ESSENTIAL CONCEPTS ALL LAWYERS NEED TO KNOW

■ ■ ■

by

Dwight Drake

University of Washington School of Law

AMERICAN CASEBOOK SERIES®

WEST ACADEMIC PUBLISHING

Mat #41680191

American Casebook Series is a trademark registered in the U.S. Patent and Trademark Office.

© 2014 LEG, Inc. d/b/a West Academic
    444 Cedar Street, Suite 700
    St. Paul, MN 55101
    1-877-888-1330

West, West Academic Publishing, and West Academic are trademarks of West Publishing Corporation, used under license.

Printed in the United States of America

ISBN: 978–1–62810–337–3

To Der, B, Dene, Jar
No dad could wish for anything better

*

PREFACE

This short book has one objective: to enhance the business and financial training of law students. It introduces students to select foundational topics that usually fall outside the scope of a traditional course on business organizations or corporations. The premise of the book is that these topics can enrich such a course by expanding its relevance, broadening the business literacy of the students, and complementing the entity and doctrinal concepts covered in the course. Although structured as a supplement and designed for students who have not had any significant business training, the book will advance the professional development of any student, even the more business-savvy student, by promoting a deeper understanding of the business world and an enhanced ability to interface with business owners and executives and those who serve the business community.

The book's emphasis is on real-world relevance and promoting awareness and a basic understanding (not expertise) of select foundational business concepts. Care has been taken to be concise, not overcomplicate the discussions, and limit the scope of topics. The topics covered in the book will promote student development in six important ways:

1. Students will have a better understanding of core business differences and how businesses are classified and characterized. At the most basic level, such an understanding will help any person communicate and work with others and better comprehend the significance of business trends and developments. The importance of understanding core business differences escalates for the lawyer who wants to assist business owners or executives at any level. It is a prerequisite to developing the capacity to meaningfully assist clients in the processes of identifying and prioritizing specific business objectives.

2. Students will have a better understanding of core accounting concepts and financial statements, the scorecards of business. Financial statements routinely surface in all types of legal transactions, disputes and challenges. A lawyer need not master the art of debits and credits. But a lawyer should know how to read financial statements and understand core concepts that underlie financial statements, the components of the core financial statements, how the statements relate to one another, how key transactions impact financial statements, and the role and limits of financial statement safeguards.

3. Students will be introduced to core quantitative concepts often associated with financial literacy: performance measures and ratios; business debt leveraging concepts and techniques; time-value-of-money concepts; business valuation basics; and elementary microeconomics concepts that are often used to justify or explain a specific event, decision, or course of action. These topics are presented in a concise, understandable manner to facilitate use in a law school course on business organizations. The short discussions focus on core concepts,

avoid nonessential complexities, use illustrative examples, and incorporate problems that test student comprehension.

4. Students will be introduced to the challenges of funding a business enterprise: going public realities and processes; how stock markets work and the related lingo and common trading strategies; start-up capital funding sources; and the importance of securities law registration exemptions and related dangerous misconceptions. Capital is a key prerequisite for success in nearly all businesses. A lawyer should have an awareness of the practical and legal challenges of capital formation and how markets function.

5. Students will have a better understanding of the role of business taxes throughout the world, the challenges of transfer pricing, and rudimentary concepts of C corporations, S corporations, partnership-taxed entities, and self-employment and payroll taxes. A simple Q&A format is used to explain these basics. The hope is that professors will share my view that a study of business organizations is incomplete without an introduction to the rudimentary concepts of business entity taxation and that such concepts deserve a few days of attention in the business organizations course. The discussion in this book will not create any level of expertise, but it will provide a very useful awareness and understanding of foundational concepts.

6. Students will be introduced to the 16 business factors and collateral consequences that impact the all-important choice-of-entity decision for a business. Five example scenarios are used to illustrate and explain these factors and collateral consequences. The choice-of-entity context is an excellent vehicle to teach these core business factors.

The book includes 18 mini-case-study student problems that enable students to analyze and apply the substance of what they are reading to specific fact situations. There are a variety of different ways these student problems can be used to improve the educational process. A professor-only website includes suggestions for using the student problems and PowerPoint slides that provide answers to the student problems.

I thank the University of Washington School of Law for allowing me to teach business and tax courses, the University of Washington Executive MBA Program for giving me the opportunity to teach corporate executives for many years, and attorney Michael Heatherly for his assistance with the manuscript. Above all, I am grateful for the many business owners, executives and professionals who I have had the opportunity to work with and serve for over four decades.

DWIGHT DRAKE
Fall City, Washington
June 2014

SUMMARY OF CONTENTS

———

TABLE OF CONTENTS

———

CHAPTER 1

Classifying and Characterizing Businesses

––––––––––

A. THRESHOLD CHALLENGE

A lawyer needs to appreciate the breadth of the word "business." The term encompasses a huge range of enterprises that differ in many respects. The differences are important. For any lawyer, a threshold challenge is to have an understanding of core business differences. At the most basic level, such an understanding will help any person communicate and work with others and better comprehend the significance of developments and trends that are reported daily.

The importance of understanding core business differences escalates for the lawyer who wants to assist business owners or executives at any level. It is a prerequisite to developing the capacity to meaningfully assist clients in the processes of identifying and prioritizing specific business objectives. And it is that capacity that is often the difference between good and mediocre (or worse) legal services.

Many business owners and executives, even some of the brightest, are incapable of identifying and articulating specific objectives without the aid of a knowledgeable advisor. They often need help in understanding the significance of an issue and eliciting facts and considerations that will impact the identification of their specific objectives relative to the issue. Then a prioritization challenge often surfaces because of conflicts and inconsistencies triggered by competing business objectives. It's a balancing analysis that requires an understanding of the strategic options and trade-offs. In nearly every situation, this understanding is impossible without the knowledgeable input of a legal advisor who understands the uniqueness of the business. The biggest mistake a legal advisor can make is to assume that businesses are essentially the same and owners and executives share the same basic objectives and require the same essential structural plans. Business is never a "one-size-fits-all" game.

This opening chapter focuses on core business differences by explaining owner and entity differences, illustrating different ways businesses are characterized and contrasted, and describing the tool used by a business to explain how and why it is unique. This is not a comprehensive discussion of all significant business differences; it's hard to imagine what such a discussion would entail. The hope is that this short, introductory discussion will provide a useful starting point and foundation for what follows in later chapters and help narrow knowledge gaps between business novices and more business-savvy students.

One important, fundamental business difference needs to be indentified up front. It's the difference between for-profit businesses and non-profit businesses. The former are organized, funded, and operated with a goal of generating a profit for the owners. As we will see, a for-profit enterprise usually has other important stakeholders, including employees, creditors, vendors, communities, taxing authorities and more, but the ever-present driving force (for good or bad) is the profit motives of the owners.

A non-profit business has no owner profit motive. It is organized, funded, and operated to accomplish specifically-identified community or charitable objectives. Although it lacks profit-seeking owners, it can raise capital, own property, employ people, perpetually exist, and operate on a grand scale. Virtually every state has a statutory scheme that authorizes the creation and governs the operation of non-profit entities. And, of course, important provisions of the Internal Revenue Code exempt qualifying non-profit organizations from the federal income tax[1] and specify requirements for donors to receive an income tax charitable deduction for amounts contributed to a charitable entity.[2]

This book is focused only on for-profit businesses. It's not that non-profits are not important; they play vitally important roles in every community. They are just outside the scope of this effort.

B. OWNER DIFFERENCES

Businesses differ based on the type, mix, and number of their owners. Following are brief descriptions of nine business owner classifications. These classifications are not perfect; overlaps, exceptions and omissions regularly surface in the real world. But they work for purposes of explaining different owner expectations and illustrating and analyzing the different and competing objectives that often must be addressed in evaluating options for resolving a specific business challenge. The first eight relate to the 27 million privately owned businesses in America that represent more than 99 percent of all employers, historically produce 65 percent of all net new jobs, and produce 16.5 times more patents per employee than their public company counterparts.[3]

1. SINGLE-OWNER ENTITIES

A single-owner entity is a true soloist. No partners. No co-shareholders. It may be a corporation, a limited liability company, or a sole proprietorship. Whatever the form, the planning focus is on a single owner. The soloist has no need for buy-sell agreements, control strategies, or the complexity of Subchapter K (the partnership provisions) of the Internal Revenue Code. But he or she must

---

1. See, generally, I.R.C. §§ 501 through 505.
2. I.R.C. § 170.
3. See "Small Business Fact Sheet," U.S. House of Representatives Committee on Small Business (May 21, 2013).

still be concerned about entity forms and structures, motivating and retaining key employees, funding and growing the enterprise, developing exit and transition strategies, controlling and managing risks, taxes, and other critical challenges. The business and planning challenges usually are easier only because they are lonelier; there is no need to grapple with the competing objectives and perspectives of co-owners. The focus is always on the hopes, dreams, and risks of a single individual.

2. EMPLOYEE-OWNED ENTITIES

These businesses are owned by individuals who work fulltime for the business. The owners toil in their businesses every day. To them, the business is much more than an investment; it is their job, their career, and often their sole or primary means of support. They cherish the independence of working for themselves. They long for stability; above all, the business must continue to provide the owners their needed cash flows. The owners know that if the business folds, they likely will end up working for another or standing in an unemployment line.

Among the owners, there often is a "democracy" spin on control issues, with minority rights being protected only on the most sensitive issues. The admission of a new owner is a carefully controlled event because any new owner will become a true day-to-day colleague who will have the capacity to directly impact the success of the business. When one leaves the group, the survival and health of the ongoing entity always trumps the interests of the departing owner.

3. INVESTOR-OWNED ENTITIES

These organizations are owned by investors who do not work for the business. The owners often are heavily involved in the highest-level management decisions while others sweat out the day-to-day challenges of the business. For most investors, the business is not their primary or sole means of support; it's an investment. They are looking for a return on that investment – the sooner the better. Compared to employee owners, investors usually are less risk averse and less concerned with the identity of their co-owners or ownership changes.

4. HYBRID ENTITIES

The hybrid organization has both employee-owners and investor-owners. Often it is the most difficult organization for planning purposes. The employee-owners usually put their careers, but not their checkbooks, on the line. They want to do all in their power to protect their paychecks for the long run and control the operations of the business. The investors are concerned about the money they have at risk and the potential of having to put up more if things don't go as planned. They want equity growth and the flexibility to exit and cash out at the most opportune time.

5. DOMINANT-OWNER ENTITIES

This organization has one majority owner and a few small minority owners. The dominant owner may be an employee-owner or an investor-owner. The minority owners are usually employees. The dynamics are very different with this type of enterprise. In almost every situation of this type, the dominant owner will want and expect special treatment. It's not about democratic votes or minority rights.

From the dominant owner's perspective, real damage can be done by trying to create a level playing field to treat all the owners the same. The dominant owner usually will want exclusive control rights that can be passed onto chosen successors and special buy-out rights and liquidity protections to ensure that his or her position always can be preserved. Often the minority owners maintain their equity interests at the will of the dominant owner, who possesses broad rights to terminate and buy out their interests at any time.

6. *FAMILY-DOMINATED BUSINESSES*

Many businesses are owned and controlled by a single family. All planning issues are complicated by estate planning challenges and the dynamics among the family members. Usually the parents have family objectives that take priority over business issues, and often the children have special agendas. In many cases, the objectives of children who work in the business collide with objectives of the "outside children." Liquidity issues often are magnified by estate tax realities. Control issues usually are impacted by family considerations unrelated to the business.

Family-dominated businesses compose more than 80 percent of U.S. enterprises, employ more than 50 percent of the nation's workforce, and account for the bulk (some estimate as much as 64 percent) of America's gross domestic product.[4] Although more than 80 percent of senior family owners claim that they want the business to stay in the family, less than 30 percent acknowledge having a transition plan.[5] The result is that most family businesses remain in the family, but at a dear cost. Best estimates are that less than 30 percent of family dominated businesses survive a second generation, and the survival rate is even uglier for those businesses that make it to generation three.[6]

Although many successful family business owners enjoy a net worth that rivals or exceeds that of other well-heeled clients, the planning dynamics usually are much different when a family business takes center stage. In a recent survey, a startling 93 percent of senior business owners acknowledged that the business is their primary source of income and security.[7] With little or no diversification, everything gets tougher. And more often than not, business and planning challenges are further complicated by strong emotional ties to the business as

---

4. See generally R. Duman, "Family Firms Are Different," Entrepreneurship Theory and Practice, 1992, pp. 13–21; and M. F. R. Kets de Vries, "The Dynamics of Family Controlled Firms: The Good News and the Bad News," Organizational Dynamics, 1993, pp. 59–71; W. G. Dyer, Cultural Change in Family Firms, Jossey–Bass, San Francisco, 1986; and P. L. Rosenblatt, M. R. Anderson and P. Johnson, The Family in Business, Jossey–Bass, San Francisco, 1985; Arthur Anderson/Mass Mutual, American Family Business Survey, 2002.

5. Family to Family: Laird Norton Tyee Family Business Survey 2007, page 5. The survey also indicated that (1) only 56 percent of the respondents have a written strategic business plan, (2) nearly 64 percent do not require that family members entering the business have any qualifications or business experience, and (3) 25 percent do not believe that the next generation is competent to move into leadership roles.

6. J. I. Ward, Keeping the Family Business Healthy, Jossey–Bass, San Francisco, 1987. This study suggests that the survival rate to generation three is less than 15 percent.

7. Family to Family: Laird Norton Tyee Family Business Survey 2007, page 5 (Executive Summary).

well as historical perceptions regarding essential bonds between the family and the business.

7. PERSONAL SERVICE ORGANIZATIONS

These are organizations that generate income by their owners providing services in fields such as healthcare, law, engineering, accounting, actuarial science, performing arts and consulting. It's actually a type of employee-owned organization that warrants its own classification for a few reasons.

First, the owners are the instruments of production of the business; their talents generate the fees that drive everything. The owners are well educated, independent and have the flexibility to make a move at any time. Typically, their large incomes are exceeded only by their larger egos. As a result, these organizations tend to be fragile. Their existence is tied to professional talent that can die, become disabled, or just decide to walk if an ego is bruised. Transitions in and out always are a challenge. Often new blood must be recruited to replenish or expand the talent base.

Second, professional service corporations have been a popular target of Congress. The have their own tax provisions, most of which are not friendly.[8] These include a unique tax avoidance and evasion provision that empowers the government to allocate income, deductions, credits and exclusions between a personal service corporation and its employee-owners.[9] There are severe limitations on a personal service corporation's ability to defer earnings by using a fiscal year.[10] But perhaps the harshest provision is the tax rate structure. Unlike all other C corporations, even other employee-owned organizations, a personal service corporation cannot benefit from the favorable graduated corporate tax rate structure that starts at 15 percent. All income accumulated in a personal service corporation is taxed at the maximum corporate rate of 35 percent.[11]

8. EMERGING PUBLIC COMPANIES

Only a tiny fraction of businesses will ever consider "going public" – having their stock owned and regularly traded by a large number of public shareholders. All other closely held businesses are just too small or not suited for public ownership and the associated regulatory hassles and horrendous expenses. But for those select few that are destined for the big time, going public is the ballgame; it is their mission, their purpose, and a prerequisite to their success. Their closely held status is merely preparatory to their real life as a public company. Typically, these companies are developing and preparing to exploit

---

8. The exception is the right afforded qualified personal service corporations to use the cash receipts and disbursements method of accounting under I.R.C. § 448(b). Any other corporation (unless in the farming business) may not use the cash method of accounting once its annual gross receipts hit $5 million.

9. I.R.C. § 269A. Allocations may be made when the services of the personal service corporation are performed for another corporation, partnership or entity, as is the situation where a professional uses a corporation to hold his or her interest in a broader organization of professionals.

10. I.R.C §§ 441(i). Use of an accounting period other than a calendar year is permitted only upon a showing of a business purpose for the different accounting period. The desire to defer income is not such a valid business purpose. A personal service corporation may adopt a fiscal year with a deferral period of no more than three months under I.R.C. § 444(b)(2), but in such event, the corporation is required to comply with the minimum distribution requirements of I.R.C. § 280H, which eliminate most deferral benefits.

11. I.R.C. § 11(b)(2).

intellectual property rights and are financed and controlled by professional investment funds. All planning is focused on the unique objectives of the deep pockets that are writing the checks and calling the shots in preparation for the big day when the public is invited to the party.

9. PUBLIC COMPANIES

Stocks of these companies are traded daily and available to the public. These are the largest companies, those that populate the pages of the Wall Street Journal. Their primary challenges are building shareholder value and income streams that, in the eyes of all, are viewed as solid and growing. A strong public image is supreme. Staying out of trouble with the SEC and other regulators is a must. Competitive intelligence and strategic planning are essential. A focus and place in the globalization of the world's economy are top priorities. A solid, committed executive management team and board of directors are fundamental to the company's success.

At the end of 2013, the stocks of slightly more than 45,000 public companies traded throughout the world. Since 1997, the number of companies whose stock trades on a U.S. exchange has been declining. The total number stood at 5,008 at the end of 2013, a far cry from the 8,884 that traded on U.S. exchanges at the end of 1997. There was a modest bump up in 2013 (92 companies), the first annual increase since 1997.[12]

Public companies have been dramatically impacted by the growth of institutional investors: mutual funds, state pension funds, hedge funds, labor union pension funds, corporate pension funds, and the like. From 1900 to 1945, the percentage of public company stocks owned by institutional investors always hovered in the 5 percent range. After World War II, institutional ownership ballooned. By 1980, institutions held $473 billion, 34 percent of the total market value of U.S. common stocks. By 2010, institutional ownership had grown to $11.5 trillion, 67 percent of all U.S. stocks.[13]

A further complicating factor is that an estimated 70 to 80 percent of the outstanding stock of public corporations is held in "street name" through custodians, such as banks and brokerage firms.[14] The custodians, in turn, hold the shares through accounts at Depository Trust Company (DTC), a depository institution and the record owner registered on the books of the company. The result is that it is difficult, often impossible, for a public company to ascertain the identity of the beneficial owners of its outstanding stock at any given time.

Public companies have always been classified by the size of their market capitalization ("market cap"), which is determined by multiplying the number of the company's total shares outstanding by the market share price for the company's stock. The historical three categories of large-cap, mid-cap, and small-cap have generally been expanded as follows:

---

12. World Federation of Exchanges Statistics Report for December 2013.

13. Working paper of Wharton Professors Marshall E. Blume and Donald B. Keim entitled "Institutional Investors and Stock Market Liquidity: Trends and Relationships."

14. See, generally, M. Kahan & E. Rock, *The Hanging Chads of Corporate Voting,* 96 The Georgetown L. J. 1227 (2008).

- Mega-cap (over 200 billion market cap)

- Large-cap (from 10 billion to 200 billion market cap)

- Mid-cap (two billion to 10 billion market cap)

- Small cap (250 million to two billion market cap)

- Micro-cap (below 250 million market cap)

- Nano-cap (below 50 million market cap)

Public companies also are slotted into sectors based on the nature and scope of their respective products and services. These sectors are further divided into industry groups, industries, and sub industries. The performance standards of the companies included in a particular category become the yardstick for measuring the performance for a specific company in the category and for sizing up the relative strengths of various sectors and industries in the overall economy. Key sectors include:

- Materials (everything from chemicals to steel)

- Consumer discretionary (example industry groups include apparel, auto, leisure, media)

- Consumer stables (example industry groups include food and stables, household and personal products, and beverage and tobacco)

- Healthcare (example industry groups include healthcare equipment and services and pharmaceuticals)

- Energy (all types)

- Utilities

- Technology (example industry groups include computers, software, office equipment, semiconductors)

- Financials (example industry groups include banks, real estate, insurance, diversified financials)

- Industrials (example industry groups include capital goods, transportation, commercial and professional services)

- Information technology (example industry groups include software, hardware, semiconductors);

- Telecommunication service

C. ENTITY DIFFERENCES

Businesses operate through different entity forms. A lawyer must understand the basics of these various forms. The last two chapters focus on important core details regarding these various entity forms, including tax differences and factors that should be considered in selecting the best entity form for a particular business. Following are brief descriptive recaps of the most common forms.

1. SOLE PROPRIETORSHIP

Sole proprietorships are for single owners who operate simple businesses and do not want the hassles of dealing with a separate entity, such as a corporation or a limited liability company. Tax-wise, everything is reflected through the individual owner's tax return. This form's greatest virtue is its simplicity, but it offers few other benefits. For this reason, it generally is confined to small businesses that create no significant liability concerns for their owners.

2. C CORPORATION

The C corporation is a regular corporation that pays its own taxes. It is a creature of state law and is recognized as a separate legal and taxable entity. Public companies and many closely held businesses are C corporations. The earnings and losses of a C corporation are taxed at the entity level, not passed through to the shareholders. The result is that C status often triggers a double tax burden - one at the entity level and another at the shareholder level when dividends or liquidating distributions are paid. The tax basics of C corporations are reviewed in Chapter 9.

A C Corporation may have different classes of stock and any number of shareholders. It offers its shareholders personal protection from the debts and liabilities of the business and a host of tax benefits. It is a popular choice for many service organizations, emerging public companies, operating companies that need to retain modest earnings each year, and owners who do not want to endure the administrative and tax hassles of a pass-through entity. Any corporation that does not qualify and elect to be taxed as an S corporation will be taxed as a C corporation.

3. S CORPORATION

The S corporation is the preferred choice for many. It is organized as a corporation under state law and offers the same corporate limited liability protections as a C corporation. But unlike a C corporation, it is taxed as a pass-through entity under the provisions of Subchapter S of the Internal Revenue Code. The taxable income and losses of the entity are passed through and taxed to the shareholders, eliminating the double tax consequences of a C corporation. These S tax provisions are similar, but not identical, to the partnership provisions of Subchapter K. The tax basics of S corporations are reviewed in Chapter 9.

The S corporation is particularly attractive to shareholders of a corporate entity that makes regular earnings distributions or that may be sold for a substantial profit in a taxable exchange. And usually conversion to S status is the only viable option for a C corporation that wants to eliminate future double-tax bites by converting to a structure that offers pass-through tax benefits.

There are certain limitations and restrictions with an S corporation that often pose problems. Not every corporation is eligible to elect S status. If a corporation has a shareholder that is a corporation, a partnership, a non-resident alien or an ineligible trust, S status is not available.[15]   Banks and insurance companies cannot elect S status.[16]   Also, the election cannot be made if the corporation has more than 100 shareholders or has more than one class of stock.[17] For purposes of the 100-shareholder limitation, a husband and wife are counted as one shareholder and all the members of a family (six generations deep) may elect to be treated as one shareholder.[18]   The one-class-of-stock requirement is not violated if the corporation has both voting and nonvoting common stock and the only difference is voting rights.[19]

In defining S status eligibility, trusts have received serious Congressional attention over the years. There has been a constant expansion of the trust eligibility rules, but many commonly used trusts still cannot qualify as S corporation shareholders.[20]

Electing in and out of S status requires attention to important details.   An election to S status requires the consent of all shareholders.[21] A single dissenter can hold up the show.   For this reason, often it is advisable to include in an organizational agreement among all the owners (typically a shareholder agreement) a provision that requires all owners to consent to an S election if a designated number of the owners at any time approve the making of the election. The election, once made, is effective for the current tax year if made during the preceding year or within the first two and one-half months of the current year.[22] If made during the first two and one-half months of the year, all shareholders who have owned stock at any time during the year, even those who no longer own stock at election time, must consent in order for the election to be valid for the current year.[23]

Exiting out of S status is easier than electing into it; a revocation is valid if

---

15. I.R.C. § 1361(b).

16. I.R.C. § 1361(b)(2).

17. I.R.C. § 1361(b)(1)(A) & (D).

18. I.R.C. § 1361(c)(1).

19. I.R.C. § 1361(c)(4). Also, there is an important straight debt safe harbor provision that easily can be satisfied to protect against the threat of an S election being jeopardized by a debt obligation being characterized as a second class of stock. I.R.C. § 1361(c)(5). To fit within the safe harbor, there must be a written unconditional promise to pay on demand or on a specified date a sum certain and (1) the interest rate and payment dates cannot be contingent on profits, the borrower's discretion, or similar factors; (2) there can be no stock convertibility feature; and (3) the creditor must be an individual, an estate, a trust eligible to be a shareholder, or a person regularly and actively engaged in the business of lending money.   For planning purposes, it is an easy fit in most situations.

20. Trusts that are now eligible to qualify as S corporation shareholders include: voting trusts; grantor trusts; testamentary trusts that receive S corporation stock via a will (but only for a two-year period following the transfer); testamentary trusts that receive S corporation stock via a former grantor trust (but only for a two-year period following the transfer); "qualified subchapter S" trusts (QSSTs), which generally are trusts with only one current income beneficiary who is a U.S. resident or citizen to whom all income is distributed annually and that elect to be treated as the owner of the S corporation stock for tax purposes; and "electing small business" trusts (ESBTs), which are trusts that elect to be treated as an S corporation shareholder and whose beneficiaries are qualifying S corporation shareholders who acquired their interests in the trust by gift or inheritance, not purchase, and who are willing to pay the highest individual marginal income tax rates on all S corporation income allocated to them. I.R.C. §§ 1361 (e)(1)(A), 1361(c)(2)(b)(v).

21. I.R.C. § 1362(a). See generally Reg. § 1.1362-6.

22. I.R.C. § 1362(b)(1).

23. I.R.C. § 1362(b)(2). For potential relief on a late election where there is reasonable cause for the tardiness, see I.R.C. § 1362(b)(5) and Rev. Proc. 2004-48, 2004-2 C.B. 172.

approved by shareholders holding more than half of the outstanding voting and nonvoting shares.[24] For the organization that wants to require something more than a simple majority to trigger such a revocation, the answer is a separate agreement among the shareholders that provides that no shareholder will consent to a revocation absent the approval of a designated supermajority. The revocation may designate a future effective date. Absent such a designation, the election is effective on the first day of the following year, unless it is made on or before the fifteenth day of the third month of the current year, in which case it is retroactively effective for the current year.[25]

4. PARTNERSHIP OPTIONS

A partnership form often is used for a venture that holds appreciating assets, such as real estate or oil and gas interests. Historically, partnerships also have been effective family planning tools to shift income to family members, freeze estate values, and facilitate gifting of minority interests at heavily discounted values. Often partnerships are used in conjunction with one or more other business entities. Their use with operating businesses has diminished in recent decades as the limited liability company has taken center stage.

Generally, there are four types of partnerships: general partnerships, limited liability partnerships, limited partnerships, and limited liability limited partnerships.

In a general partnership, each partner is personally liable for the debts and liabilities of the entity and has a say in the management of the business. No formal documentation is required to form a general partnership. All that is required is for two or more persons to manifest an intention to carry on a business for a profit. Thus, parties can inadvertently form a general partnership without knowing they have done so.

A limited liability partnership ("LLP") is a partnership that, pursuant to applicable state law, has filed a statement of qualification (sometimes called an "application") with the state's secretary of state to eliminate the personal liability exposure of the partners. The name of an LLP must end with the words "Registered Limited Liability Partnership," "limited liability partnership," or the abbreviation "R.L.L.P," "RLLP," "L.L.P.," or LLP."

A limited partnership is an entity that has one or more general partners ("GPs") and one or more limited partners ("LPs") and is formed under a state's limited partnership act. GPs have the authority to manage and conduct the business of the partnership and are personally liable for the debts and obligations of the partnership. LPs typically are investors who have no or minimal control over business decisions of the partnership and have no personal liability for the obligations of the partnership beyond their capital contributions to the partnership.

The limited liability limited partnership ("LLLP") is to a limited partnership

---

24. I.R.C. § 1362(d)(1).
25. I.R.C. § 1362(d)(1)(C) & (D).

what an LLP is to a general partnership. Its role is to eliminate the personal liability exposure that general partners have for the obligations of a limited partnership. It's a relatively new entity form that has been adopted in roughly half the states. An LLLP must elect LLLP status in the limited partnership's filed certificate and use a name that includes the phrase "limited liability limited partnership," "LLLP," or "L.L.L.P." With LLLP status, a general partner is not personally liable for an obligation of the limited partnership incurred while the partnership is an LLLP, whether arising in contract, tort, or otherwise. This limited liability protection exists even if the partnership agreement contained inconsistent provisions before making the election to become an LLLP.

Although partnerships file separate returns, they are not taxpaying entities. The profits and losses of the partnership are passed through and taxed to the partners under the provisions of Subchapter K of the Internal Revenue Code. The tax basics of partnership-taxed entities are reviewed in Chapter 9.

5. *LIMITED LIABILITY COMPANY*

The limited liability company ("LLC") is a relatively new candidate. All states now have statutes authorizing LLCs, most of which were adopted during the 1980s. Many advisors claim that the LLC is the ultimate entity, arguing that it offers the best advantages of both corporations and partnerships and few of the disadvantages. It's an overstatement, but not by much in some situations.

As discussed in Chapter 10, there is no question that the arrival of the LLC has made the choice-of-entity challenge easier in many cases. Like a corporation, the LLC is an entity organized under state law. It offers liability protection to all owners, making it possible for its owners to fully participate in the management of the business without subjecting themselves to personal exposure for the liabilities of the business. LLCs are classified as either "member-managed" (managed by all members) or "manager-managed" (managed by designated managers).

Although similar to a corporation for state law purposes, a limited liability company is taxed as a partnership for federal income tax purposes unless it elects otherwise. As such, it offers better pass-through benefits than an S corporation and completely avoids all the S corporation eligibility and election hassles. It can have more than 100 owners, and partnerships, corporations, nonresident aliens, and any kind of trust can be included as owners. For these reasons, many wrongfully conclude that the LLC eliminates the need to consider S corporations and partnerships as viable pass-through entity candidates. As we will see in Chapter 10, there are still many situations where an S corporation or a partnership will be the best entity choice.

The professional limited liability company ("PLLC") is a state-chartered entity that allows licensed professionals (e.g., doctors and lawyers) to enjoy the benefits of a limited liability company. A PLLC does nothing to reduce a professional's personal liability for his or her own mistakes or malpractice, but it eliminates a professional's liability for the errors, omissions, negligence, incompetence or malfeasance of other professionals who are not under his or her supervision and control. It also eliminates personal exposure for contract liabilities that the professional has not personally guaranteed. States often require that a PLLC register with the applicable state licensing board before filing its organizational documents with the state.

D. CHARACTERISTIC DIFFERENCES

Every business has specific characteristics that define the nature and role of the business and reveal its uniqueness, strengths, weaknesses, market position, vulnerabilities, and a host of other important factors. These characteristics are key indicators of the business' growth potential, most significant risk factors, and long-term survival prospects. The following fifteen factors illustrate some of the common ways businesses are characterized and contrasted. In no sense is it an all-inclusive list.

1. PRODUCT VS. SERVICE

Whether a business is product-based or service-based is a core defining factor. Generally, a product-based operation is more complicated, poses greater downside risks, and offers the potential of higher yields for the owners of the business. The initial challenges of designing the product, developing manufacturing processes and relationships, and assessing and creating demand for the product set the stage for success or failure. Key operational challenges include managing inventory levels, developing supply chains to efficiently get the product to end-users, monitoring competitive conditions and other product life-cycle factors, and making smart pricing decisions that reflect market realities and preserve profit margins. It usually takes substantial capital and a talented management team. And, of course, the challenges are magnified many times when there is a group of products, as is so often the case.

Getting the product to end-users is a threshold, strategic consideration. Often the only viable option is traditional brick-and-mortar retail that requires a supply chain of regional and national distributors, local wholesalers, and a wide variety of retail outlets. Smart management is required to ensure product availability without ballooning inventories to risky levels, to protect and police the incentives and profit margins of all players in the chain, and to maintain the image of the product and the manufacturer. For example, wholesalers typically are prohibited from cutting out retailers by selling directly to end-users, and often there are manufacturer-imposed prohibitions on selling to businesses outside the approved chain of players or unreasonably discounting the product.

Every manufacturer must assess the role of the Internet in getting product to consumers. For many, it is a powerful tool to enhance product demand, educate potential consumers, and drive end-users into approved retail outlets. For others, the Internet is the sole and ultimate answer to their product delivery challenge, enabling direct communication and shipping to end-users while ignoring or eliminating the hassles and costs of traditional middleman players. The technological advances of e-commerce and ballooning popularity of online shopping have opened opportunities for many manufactures that could not otherwise effectively complete for retail shelf space or reach distant markets.

The profit potential for a product-based business often trumps by many times those of a service business. The driving factors are demand for the product, volume, and profit margins. The traditional service-constraints of time spent and hourly yields do not apply.

A service-based business is a very different and often a simpler enterprise. The focus is on defining the service, identifying and reaching a market, and generating a profit. In some situations, owner-investors can generate a yield by imposing price points that exceed the costs of running the business, including amounts paid to those who actually provide the services. In many others, the business is used to generate an income for employee-owners. Take, for example, the typical law firm that collects fees (usually based on hourly rates) for professional services rendered by members of the firm. Key challenges include professional training and recruiting, developing and exploiting a smart marketing plan and firm reputation, and implementing efficient office (or multiple office) procedures. Such challenges are very different from those required for a successful product-based company.

2. *ASSET-BASED VS. OPERATIONAL-BASED*

Some businesses are asset-based. The business exists because of an asset or group of assets. It may be a tract of real estate, a group of oil wells, a movie script, a valuable intellectual property right, a proprietary manufacturing process, or some other valuable, unique asset. Without the asset, there is no business or, at the minimum, a much different business. The useful life of the asset often defines the life cycle of the business.

The defining asset for some businesses is their brand. Often a brand has been developed over decades and has a perceived unshakeable stability, although there are brands that develop and fade quickly. The strength of a brand often is the supreme factor that enables the business to secure a strong market share and generate substantial profit margins by avoiding the competitive pressures of less profitable players. Such a brand can work for a multinational product-based company, a local service business, and everything in between. That's why the development of a strong brand is an overriding goal of many businesses, although very few succeed in enjoying the profitable benefits of a strong brand over the long-term. In 2013, the top five on Forbes' list of the world's most valuable brands (brand value only) were Apple (104.3 billion), Microsoft (56.7 billion), Coca-Cola (54.9 billion), IBM (50.7 billion), and Google (47.3 billion).[26]

However, a unique, valuable asset or strong brand often is not a prerequisite for success. Many successful businesses have neither. They succeed long-term by delivering services or moving products through operations that profitably exploit a defined niche in a market. Their value is measured by the strength, growth potential, and stability of their earnings. Their asset base often is not substantial and has little or nothing to do with their goodwill and going concern values. They often have a reputation for quality, but not the kind of brand

---

26. Kurt Badenhausen, "Apple Dominates List Of The World's Most Valuable Brands," Forbes (November 6, 2013).

identity that drives demand or transcends competitive pressures.

3. STAND-ALONE VS. AFFILIATED

Most businesses are stand-alone enterprises that are able to operate free from any direct controls by another system or company. They usually have important strategic relationships, but the business itself is not controlled by another entity or dependant on an affiliated system that the business does not control.

Other businesses are part of a broader affiliated group or system. Their success is tied directly to key decisions of the broader group and factors that impact the broader group. The most common examples are holding companies that have layers of subsidiaries, the control and ownership of which can be traced to a common parent holding company. The business of some of the subsidiaries often serves a niche function or market of a product line or service operation that reaches across the whole or a major segment of the affiliated group. Other subsidiaries may operate self-contained businesses that simply diversify the operations of the holding company and add to its consolidated earnings. One of the biggest examples of such a holding company is General Electric, whose multinational affiliated group includes hundreds of companies throughout the world, purchases dozens of companies each year, and maintains huge integrated operations in power and water, oil and gas, aviation, healthcare, transportation, home and business solutions, and capital formation. It is believed that GE files the largest tax return in the U.S.; its return for 2010, for example, totaled more than 57,000 pages.[27]

Franchising is an affiliated business expansion strategy that has spawned thousands of new companies since the 1950s. Although independently owned, each of these companies is tied to and dependant on a franchisor. Fast food outlets are the best example, but there are many other large franchise operations. The franchisor develops a specific business strategy, usually supported by a distinctive trade name and trademark, a broad-based consumer marketing and advertising campaign, detailed operating procedures, approved vendor sources, site approval procedures, and various other support systems. Expansion is funded by franchisees putting up money to establish their own franchise outlet businesses that are governed by a detailed franchise agreement. The agreement mandates operating requirements and imposes royalty obligations, usually a percent of gross revenues. The strength of the franchisor's control varies among different franchise operations, but it is always a crucial factor that limits flexibility and creates conflict potentials. For these reasons and the fact that franchisees usually must spec investment capital against the promises of a business plan developed and sold by the franchisor, the Federal Trade Commission has rules and many states have statutes that specify disclosure requirements, sometimes require advance registration, and often mandate the inclusion of specific franchisee-protection provisions in the franchise agreement.

---

27. John McCormack, "*GE Filed 57,000-Page Tax Return, Paid No Taxes on $14 Billion in Profits,*" The Weekly Standard (November 14, 2011).

Multilevel marketing is another form of affiliated business expansion that has resulted in the creation of thousands of small businesses over the past five decades. Sometimes it is referred to as network marketing or referral marketing, and legally defective programs are often referred to as pyramid schemes. The typical multilevel marketing program recruits salespeople, each of whom receives commissions through the direct sale of products and direct sales generated by others in the "downline" that he or she recruits. Each salesperson operates as an independently owned business. Such marketing programs have often been criticized for their high entry costs, tendency to promote unrealistic profit expectations, price fixing risks, aggressive sales practices, and more. But the fact remains that highly successful multilevel marketing programs operate in all 50 states and have done so for decades. Examples of large, successful programs include Amway and Shaklee. Products that meet a consumer demand independent of any business opportunity factors are the key to long-term success and legality. If product sales predominately occur only as an incidental part of the salesperson recruitment process, the FTC and state regulators will likely deem the program an illegal pyramid scheme that is doomed to fail. Plus, many states have adopted business opportunity statutes that impose disclosure requirements on those who seek to sell business opportunities to others.

4. *MARKET POWER OR NOT?*

Some businesses have real market power, which is the power to control or influence the price or availability of a product or service in a given market. The best example is a monopolist, defined as the exclusive seller of a product or service for which there is no close substitute. Being a monopolist is not illegal per se, and even a very small business can enjoy the benefits of a monopolist if that business is the only provider of a product or service that has a demand in the relevant market. The sole plumber or newspaper in a small town may each have strong market power.

Market power is not limited to monopolists. Some markets have a few key sellers, each of whom may easily cue off the actions of the others so that the collective group, without any agreement or understanding, maintains prices and output levels that maximize profits. It's called an "oligopoly," and the expected behavior is called "oligopolistic interdependence."

At the opposite end of the spectrum are atomism markets that have many sellers, none of whom are large enough to influence the market price. The withdrawal of a given seller's entire supply from the market will not affect the market price. Often this is referred to as pure competition. Each seller accepts that it will sell its share of the market at the price established by the market, and that any attempt to exceed the market price will quickly halt sales.

5. *GEOGRAPHIC EXPANSION POTENTIAL OR NOT?*

The geographic reach of a business is always an important factor. A multinational business is defined as a business that maintains offices or assets in at least one country other than its own. Although some multinationals have budgets that exceed those of many small countries, a relatively small business that maintains inventories and sales personnel in a foreign land may meet the definition of a multinational business. Technological advances and world market conditions are pushing many businesses of all sizes to seriously explore the benefits of international expansion.

A PwC family business survey in 2013 found that nearly half (47 percent) of U.S. family businesses were selling goods and services outside the country and even more (54 percent) anticipate they will be selling internationally by 2017. This represented a major increase from two years earlier when only 30 percent of surveyed family businesses were intending to develop markets abroad and a huge jump from 2007 when only 21 percent planned on exploring international markets. As for the most likely targeted markets, 30 percent of the surveyed companies are eyeing the Americas (primarily Brazil, Canada, and Mexico), 25 percent have their sights on the Asia Pacific region (China alone garnered 14 percent), and 14 percent are focused on Europe.[28]

Any geographic expansion increases complexities and costs. In addition to new employee and management challenges, there are a host of planning issues, including increased risk-management assessments, enhanced regulatory burdens, cultural differences, and the need for an expanded multi-entity business structure. Often a separate subsidiary company needs to be formed to conduct operations in a different state and certainly a different country. It usually makes no sense to expose the main business entity to the regulatory, tax, and liability risks of a new jurisdiction.

6. HIGH VS. LOW LEVERAGE

Leverage refers to the use of debt in financing a business. The yield realized on the capital invested by the owners of a business can be increased by leveraging the borrowed dollar to finance a portion of the business. For example, if the business can grow its earnings by borrowing funds at a 6 percent interest cost and generating a return of 12 percent on the borrowed funds, the spread between the cost and the yield directly boosts the return to the owners. It's Business 101. In nearly all businesses, smart leveraging makes sense. It's not a question of whether. It's a question of how much.

The risks of too much leverage are real. When leverage is overused, a significant drop in asset values or earnings may wipe out the equity capital in the business, leaving the company with liabilities that exceed its asset base and the inability to service its ever-ballooning debt load. The company will be headed for bankruptcy absent one or more of three remedies. The first is a quick reversal of values and earnings, which often becomes progressively less likely as others in and out of the company react to the company's deteriorating condition. The second is an infusion of new equity capital, which usually becomes much tougher when debt takes over. The third is a government bailout, the "too large to fail" answer for the grossly over-leveraged financial institutions that found themselves upside down with debt when their asset values crumbled in the fiscal crisis of 2008.

---

28. PwC Family Business Survey 2012/2013 (US Findings). PwC is a network of firms in 158 countries with more than 180,000 employees that provide assurance, tax, and advisory services.

The risks of no or too little leverage are just as real, but not as severe. Owners of successful businesses eventually face a basic decision regarding the profits generated by the business. Are the profits going to accumulate in the company or be distributed to the owners of the company? The easy answer for many is to stockpile. Keep the profits in the company. Let them ride as the business expands and matures.

During the building period of most businesses, stockpiling usually is the only viable alternative. The earnings are needed to finance inventories, receivables, facilities, better technology, and new personnel. More debt isn't possible or prudent. As the business begins to mature, the retained profits are used to retire debt and the pressure to accumulate begins to fade and often disappears completely. But in many cases, this accumulation pattern has been set. The owners enjoy watching the net worth of the business expand every year with a corresponding increase in the value of their equity. Their success is measured and quantified by the accumulations. As time goes on, the balance sheet of the business becomes rock solid – lots of equity, little or no debt – while the balance sheets of the owners become lopsided – a large net worth and a big taxable estate, the bulk of which is represented by a single business equity interest. Concentrating wealth in the business can be risky, imprudent, and damaging in the long run. Beyond diluting the owner's yield, it can hike risk management pressures (too much of the owners' wealth is exposed to business risks), make it harder to transition the business, and reduce the benefits of income and estate tax planning.

There is no stock answer to the "How much leverage?" question. As explained in Chapter 3, a debt-to-equity ratio is often used as a measure of a business' leverage. Generally speaking (and I do mean "generally"), a ratio of under 5-to-1 is considered reasonable for a profitable, mature business while a ratio in excess of 10-to-1 is usually suspect. The gap between five and 10 often is a grey area. This ratio may be a measure, but often is not a sole determining factor. For example, two businesses may each reasonably use a bank line equal to 90 percent of their current collectible accounts receivable and 50 percent of the cost of their current salable inventories. Because of differences in the asset mixes of the two businesses, the bank line produces a 6-to-1 ratio in one business and a 4-to-1 ratio in the other. For many businesses, various factors must be considered in setting a smart leverage level, including industry standards, the asset base of the business, the stability of earnings, current banking practices, and more.

7. SCALABLE OR NOT?

Scalability is an important factor in assessing the growth potential of a business. A scalable business is one that can maintain or increase its profit margins as the volume of the business expands to higher levels. The operations, asset requirements, and market conditions easily accommodate a growth in volume without a hit to profit margins. Many non-manufacturing businesses are scalable. A service business often can continually increase its profitability by adding more personnel to service a growing demand. So too, a product-based company that continually distributes a higher volume of finished goods that it sources from others may preserve or enhance its margins and thereby increase its profitability as it continues to grow.

A non-scalable business is one that cannot handle a higher volume without making investments or other changes that currently reduce margins. Higher volumes may require significant infrastructure improvements, expensive expansion into new markets, and more. Assume, for example, that a company has the capacity to produce 100,000 units. A production level of 50,000 units results in a cost per unit of $7.00. As volumes increase and production moves upwards towards 100,000 units, positive economies of scale kick in, high equipment fixed costs are spread over more units, and the cost per unit eventually drops to $5.00. Production beyond 100,000 units requires a significant new investment in equipment and systems that drives up the cost per unit to $8.00, resulting in a corresponding decrease in profit margins.

8. SMALL VS. LARGE EMPLOYEE BASE

Few businesses can survive without the loyal support of dedicated employees. But nearly all business owners appreciate (or certainly should appreciate) that the challenge goes beyond motivation and management. Laws have continually evolved to give employees more rights; and these rights pose risks for the uninformed business owner who is determined to run the show just as he or she did 20 years ago.

The role of a company's employment base often is a defining factor for a business. In many businesses, it's everything. The existence, profitability, and growth potential of the business is dependent on an ever-evolving base of rank-and-file and management employees. Every expansion requires, at a minimum, a proportional increase in the employee base.

Other businesses are able to grow with disproportionately small increases in their employment ranks. Technology and management innovations and personal incentives are designed to enhance the productivity of each employee. The focus is higher productivity, not just more employees. Often this is coupled with strategic outsourcing relationships that enable the company to shift specific operations and functions to outside independent contractors.

There are reasons why a company may want to explore options for reducing its dependence on an ever-growing employee base. Recruiting, retaining and motivating a work force usually get progressively more difficult as the base grows. Required cutbacks are painful and expensive. The uncertainties and ballooning costs of employee benefits often put pressure on the bottom line and create ongoing expectation challenges and cost sharing conflicts.

Employee terminations are always a challenge. While most employers believe they operate under the "at will" doctrine as regards their employees, the company takes a risk every time it terminates an employee. Wrongful discharge suits have popped up with increasing frequency throughout the country. Many employee victories have been publicized. New laws have been made in the courts and the legislatures, chipping away at the old "at will" standard. Each victory and law change has provided incentives to aggrieved, discharged employees and lawyers who are willing to fight their cases. Many companies have had to endure the pain of paying big legal fees to defend the termination, only to pay more when the employee prevails. The operative word is "caution" when terminating an employee.

Employees pose potential liability risks that should be mitigated with smart planning. In general, a company is responsible and liable for those acts of its employees that are carried out within the scope of their employment. This is a true vicarious liability. It is one of the broadest forms of vicarious, third-party liability in the law. The company may be fully liable, even though it had no direct involvement with, or knowledge of, the event creating the problem. In most instances, the liability pops up because an employee has committed one of four wrongs: (1) the employee exceeds his or her authority in making a deal on behalf of the company; (2) the employee, in the process of carrying out his or her duties, negligently or recklessly injures another party; (3) the employee ignores or violates a black letter law that has been established for the good of all; or (4) the employee engages in intentional misconduct that, in some cases, may rise to the level of criminal conduct. Businesses usually need to take specific steps to reduce or mitigate the scope of the liability that may be created by employees

9. *UNION VS. NON-UNION*

A relatively small percentage of employees in the private (as opposed to government) sector are represented and protected by union relationships. The percentage of private sector union employment has consistently fallen for decades. In 2013, for example, the private sector percentage was 6.7 percent, about one-fifth of the percentage for public sector employees. In the private sector, industries with high unionization rates included utilities (25.6 percent), transportation and warehousing (19.6 percent), telecommunications (14.4 percent), and construction (14.1 percent).[29]

Union employees usually are subject to contracts that offer various protections. Examples: employee discipline and discharge often are subject to grievance procedures and binding arbitration; wages, benefits and working conditions are subject to negotiation; hiring and promotion decisions may be governed by contractual provisions that impose seniority and other requirements; labor and management are contractually obligated to listen and negotiate and pursue reasonable compromises; contractual changes require the consent of both labor and management.

10. *HEAVY REGULATION OR NOT?*

Increasing government regulation is a fact of life for business. According to the Congressional Research Service, over 13,000 final rules were published in the Federal Register from 2009 to 2012. Small businesses are hit the hardest by increased regulation. Small businesses now bear a regulatory cost of $10,585 per employee, estimated to be 36 percent higher than the regulatory per-employee compliance cost for large businesses. Small business environmental compliance

---

29. News Release, Department of Labor Statistics, U.S. Department of Labor (January 24, 2014).

costs exceed by more than four times the corresponding costs for large firms.[30]

The highest three regulated sectors are financial, healthcare, and energy. Any business in these industries must continually be tuned in to government regulators. But since nearly all businesses need energy, want healthcare benefits for their employees, and require financing, the positive benefits and associated increased costs and burdens of ever-growing regulation in these and other industries are ultimately felt across the economy.

11. INTERNET-DEPENDENT OR NOT?

The Internet is the most powerful communication tool that has ever been available to business enterprises. For business purposes, it has shrunk the world and created countless entrepreneurial opportunities that couldn't possibly exist without it.

Many businesses are not inherently dependent on the Internet. They use the Internet to promote their businesses and educate their customers, but their core operations are not directly tied to their use of the Internet. Generally, they need not fear that a new or expanding company from anywhere in the world may threaten their market share with an Internet-based strategy.

Other businesses exist because of the Internet. These include those that provide Internet support services, such as website design, optimization, and app development services. It also includes businesses that must use the Internet to conduct their businesses. Take Dena, for example, a stay-at-home mom of three young children who imports her custom designed infant parasols from a China manufacturer, takes orders principally from European and African buyers who want quality parasols that bear the names of their children or grandchildren, and customizes and ships the parasols from a garage in a small Northwest town. A tiny business of this type that reaches from China to Africa would be impossible without the Internet, the tool that attracts customers in a foreign land at an insignificant cost. Dena is able to compete heads-up with her competition, but understands that anyone from anywhere could use the same tool she uses to challenge her market share.

12. LOW–TECH VS. HIGH–TECH

A low-tech business is one that does not rely heavily on new technology to sustain its market position. It does not have to keep coming up with new technology concepts to support the viability of its product mix. It offers a group of products that are readily recognized as non-technical. In contrast, a high-tech business is dependent on its ability to create new ideas and new products. Often the success of the high-tech business is tied directly to the talent of individuals who work in the business. The overriding, ongoing challenge is to secure and recruit new talent.

From a profit perspective, seldom will a low-tech business be able to match the upside potential of a successful high-tech operation. High-tech usually poses

---

30. Small Business Fact Sheet, U.S. House of Representatives Committee on Small Business (May 21, 2013).

greater risks, and offers the potential of larger and faster rewards. A successful high-tech start-up can quickly secure the financial future of its founders. As we have seen many times, the age and business acumen of the innovators often are not limiting factors.

Regarding risk and stability, often a low-tech business will be in a much stronger position than a struggling high-tech business. Today's high-tech business can quickly end up being tomorrow's defunct no-tech business if it cannot keep pace by producing new products that play well in the marketplace. The competition in high-tech businesses progressively grows at a rapid pace as players from around the world continue to surface and expand. The past 30 years suggests that no one can comfortably predict who will be the dominant high-tech players in the following decades.

13. STRATEGICALLY–BASED VS. RELATIONSHIP–BASED

The strength of some businesses is primarily attributable to key personal relationships that have been developed over many years. The relationships may be with suppliers, customers, key employees or all three. These relationships give the business its advantage and make it possible for the business to succeed. In contrast, there are other businesses that are strategically-based. They have identified and filled a market niche that is not dependent or tied to personal relationships. The business succeeds because it is strategically situated to competitively deliver goods or services in its identified market niche.

Obviously, a strategically-based business has a better chance of surviving long-term than a relationship-based business. Relationships are often difficult, if not impossible, to transfer. A child, for example, may develop a friendly interface with a crucial vendor, but that interface may never match the strength of the personal relationship that the child's father had with the vendor. The challenge becomes even more difficult when the vendor's successor takes charge. The reality is that, over time, the strength of personal relationships often breaks down and fizzles out as attempts are made to transition relationships. As this occurs, there is a substantial risk that the business activity between the parties will diminish unless both parties identify a strategic business advantage for maintaining the relationship.

Often it is assumed that a business is strategically-based, when, in fact, the basis of its success is personal relationships that have been developed over many years. Similarly, there are some businesses that appear to be propped up by relationships, but that could be strategically strengthened with some careful analysis, restructuring and public relations. The ongoing challenge is to identify key personal relationships, assess the importance of those relationships to the overall success of the business, and evaluate the capacity of the business to enhance its strategic base.

14. INSTITUTIONALIZATION OR NOT?

A central challenge for many businesses is to begin the process of institutionalization. In this context, an institutionalized business is one that is bigger than any one individual. Its operations and growth do not primarily depend on the person who started it all. It has developed systems, personnel, management structures, and expertise to allow it to function like an institution. Usually, this condition is easily recognized by the employees of the company and outsiders who deal with the company on a regular basis. The contrast is the business that is operationally dependent on one individual. That individual is the key to all that happens. Without the daily presence of that individual, the business lacks direction and suffers. The systems, support personnel, and expertise are absent.

Often founders of a business do not want to invest the time or capital required to build systems and personnel that will allow the business to effectively function on its own. In some cases, it takes a financial commitment that the owners are unwilling to make. In others, it's an issue of control or ego. The owner enjoys the importance of his or her invaluable presence. The challenge is to fairly assess whether appropriate steps are being taken to institutionalize the business. Usually these steps are critical if the business is going to survive long term.

15. HIGH VS. LOW MARGIN TOLERANCE

Does the business have the capacity to survive and prosper if it is faced with some tough price competition? A helpful question: What would be the impact if the business was forced to cut its gross margin by 3 or 4 percent to remain competitive? If the response is a roll of the eyes and a "No way" exclamation, this may suggest that the long-term survival prospects for the business are weak.

In most businesses, price competition is intensifying. Others have found better ways of producing the same products or delivering comparable services at lower prices. New manufacturing techniques and operating systems are being developed to allow businesses to operate more efficiently. Businesses are "right sizing" to cut out the fat and to have the capacity to operate on lean, tough margins. New players are not tied to old systems and old investments.

Often a business finds itself at an extreme competitive disadvantage as bigger and stronger players, sometimes from foreign lands, enter the market. It does not have the capital or the sales volume to justify the development of the economies of scale and operating systems that would allow it to remain tough on price. This condition prompts may to consider selling while the company's market share is still intact. If the opportunity is missed, the owners may be forced to sacrifice or eliminate profitability by cutting margins to preserve the business. This has been the fate of many businesses that have been unable to survive a second generation.

E. BUSINESS PLANS

A business plan is a written document created and used by entrepreneurs and others who desire to develop or expand a business. It's much more than just a marketing plan. It explains in detail all the key aspects (sometimes called the "DNA") of the business. A well-conceived and written business plan takes time, research, analysis, and an intellectual honesty that continually questions base assumptions and core underpinnings of the proposed business. Plus, the writing must reflect quality – a style that is clear, concise, and convincing and avoids overstated adjectives, convoluted sentences, and sloppy grammar. The role of legal advisors usually never goes beyond select technical aspects of the plan, such as entity choice, tax, and securities law considerations. Although lawyers do not write business plans for their clients, it often helps to have a basic understanding of the purposes and elements of a plan and what separates the good from the bad.

1. PURPOSE AND ROLE

Is a business plan always necessary? There are countless blogs and articles that try hard to make the case that detailed written business plans often are a waste of time and effort and that business schools should scrap their business plan courses and competitions. Although there are examples of successful company launches without a business plan and virtually no guarantees that a business plan itself will turn an idea into a successful business, the value of a business plan to two vital groups is hard to deny in the real world.

The first group is the organizers of the enterprise, those who must create the plan. The process of creating a plan and reducing it to writing often pushes everything and everybody to a higher level: better critical thinking, deeper market knowledge, smarter risk factor strategies, better understanding of funding needs and expectations, and more. The result is that the key players are more capable and confident to tackle the new enterprise. If done right, the plan becomes a living, evolving document that is continually used as a tool to define and measure performance and success.

The second group that benefits from and needs the document is the potential investors who often are essential to funding and jumpstarting the enterprise. While a few ideas may be sufficiently attractive on their face to attract investor interest without a written business plan, the great bulk of ideas will go nowhere unless the details are fleshed out and the case for success is made in a smartly crafted business plan.

2. PLAN ELEMENTS

A business plan typically includes the following elements:

• **Executive Summary** – Brief review of plan that sparks interest by recapping mission statement, product or service, relevant markets, key customers, financial requirements, management's background and expertise, and potential yield to investors.

• **Product or Service** – Detailed description, potential of different versions, why needed and valued by customers, status of development and readiness for market, intellectual property elements, any licensing and royalty requirements, future enhancement potentials, and challenges to volume growth.

• **Market and Competition** – Definition of relevant market(s), size of market, market growth potential, market profitability potential, technology and regulatory impacts on market, customer descriptions and customer segmentation criteria, competitor strengths and weaknesses, positioning opportunities against existing competitors, future competitor risks, anticipated competitor and market reactions.

- **Sales and Marketing** – Pricing considerations and challenges, volume expectations, consumer education needs and risks, selling process, strategies for reaching customers and getting product or service to customers, advertising strategies and risks, reliance on third parties in supply chain, Internet role and options, launch and ongoing budget needs.

- **Business Organization** – Form of entity, organizational chart, lines of authority, key outside company relationships, needed technical expertise and sources, quality assurance challenges, risk management measures, location of business.

- **Management Team** – Description of key players and their backgrounds, common vision of group, complementary attributes and strengths, staying power and individual commitments to enterprise, prior history working together.

- **Plan Implementation** – Implementation schedule, investment timing and variables, human resources planning, key milestones, bottleneck risks.

- **Financial Elements** – Detailed financial projections (three to five years) under three alternative scenarios, key assumptions and their reasonableness, breakeven timing and key factors, cash flow analysis and risks, setback impacts and alternatives, investor return potentials.

- **Risks** – Description of key market and delivery risks, technology challenges, interest rate risks, key human resources risks, strategies and options for mitigating risks.

- **Appendix** – Management resumes, organization chart, supplemental market and competitor information, key articles, other relevant outside sources.

3. APPEALING TO INVESTORS

Many business plans contain all the requisite elements, read like a novel, and completely fail to capture the interest of investors. Often they resemble a canned "paint-by-numbers" project that was approached and executed as a chore. They look complete on their face, but lack genuineness, a demonstrated expertise, and smart, thoughtful analysis. A superficial review by an experienced investor will quickly trigger concerns about management's vision, passion, and understanding of what lies ahead.

In order to appeal to experienced investors, a plan usually must persuasively explain why and how the proposed company will profitably meet a definable need and be relevant. It must demonstrate that the proponents, through tough analysis and research and their development of market expertise, know their customers, the competition, industry trends, and how specific competitors will be impacted or eliminated. The plan must convincingly describe how a quality team has come together to develop a vision, priorities, and processes that will convert a smart idea into an efficient, well-managed, profitable business.

STUDENT PROBLEM 1-1

Jennifer, a lawyer who works with many businesses, is having lunch with Jeff, a client who owns and operates a successful trucking company. Jeff explains that his brother-in-law Sam has given him the opportunity to invest in a company ("Twilight") that operates retirement homes in two states. Sam, Twilight's chief financial officer, has explained to Jeff that Twilight is owned by five individuals (including Sam), has become very profitable, plans on expanding into six more states, and is seeking expansion capital from a small group (no more than 10) of new investor-owners. Sam characterized the investment opportunity as "a no-brainer windfall." Jeff has set up a meeting with Sam and other key Twilight officers.

After explaining this background, Jeff states to Jennifer, "I know trucking, but retirement homes and this type of an investment are completely foreign to me. I would like to be able to ask some smart questions at this upcoming meeting in order to assess the opportunity and, perhaps most importantly, to dispel any notion held by my brother-in-law that I am a soft-touch fool who happens to have some money. If you were in my shoes, what are the key questions you would ask?"

Assume that you are Jennifer. Based on what you have read in the prior 24 pages and your general instincts, list the top 10 questions that you would recommend to Jeff.

CHAPTER 2

Financial Statement Basics

———

A. THE LANGUAGE OF BUSINESS

Accounting is the language of business. It's the primary source of quantitative information in every enterprise. A quality accounting system is a prerequisite to long-term success. It produces internal reports that management must have to effectively manage the enterprises and external reports designed to meet the needs and demands of owners, government agencies, and other third parties. A substandard or defective accounting system often results in poor strategic decisions, the inability to effectively plan, and inaccurate and misleading documents. In many situations, such a system can lead to broken careers and serious legal problems that threaten the survival of the enterprise.

The primary external outputs of a company's accounting system are its financial statements. These are the scorecards of every business. They are the ultimate measures of success and failure, important trends, and management quality.

A lawyer should have a basic understanding of financial statements and the ability to read them. They routinely surface in all types of legal disputes and challenges. A lawyer who must rely on others for the basics usually will be at a significant disadvantage. There is no need to master the art of debits and credits or to know the detailed requirements for a quality accounting system. But there is a need to understand core concepts that underlie financial statements, the components of each of the key financial statements, how the statements relate to one another, how key transactions impact financial statements, and the role and limits of standard safeguards.

B. UNDERLYING CONCEPTS

1. OBJECTIVITY – GAPP AND IFRS

Objectivity is a threshold goal of the accounting process. It requires freedom from bias and adherence to principles, standards, and procedures that are designed to promote conformity and produce reasonable, objectively determined results. In the United States, these standards are known as generally accepted accounting principles (GAAP), which are a flexible set of principles and rules that, in large part, define the outer limits of reasonableness for reporting specific transactions. US public companies must comply with GAAP requirements in reporting their results of operations, and generally (although not always) GAAP requirements are followed in the preparation of financial statements for closely held enterprises.

GAAP standards are primarily determined by the Financial Accounting Standards Board (FASB), a seven-member board created with the support of the premier accounting organization in the Unites States (the American Institute of Certified Public Accountants (AICPA)) and the Securities and Exchange Commission. The AICPA and the SEC also have the authority to promulgate GAAP standards. FASB board members serve fulltime for five-year terms, and a member may serve no more than two terms. To promote objectivity and independence, members are required to sever connections with any firms or institutions they worked with prior to becoming a board member. The members have diverse backgrounds in accounting, finance, business, accounting education, and research, and each must have a demonstrated concern for users of financial statements and the public interest in matters of accounting and financial reporting.

GAAP standards are not the controlling authority outside the United States. The International Financial Reporting Standards (IFRS) are the primary international standards. Designed to meet the demands of expanding international trade and shareholder ownership, the IFRS requirements have become a common global language for business affairs, promoting accounting uniformity across international boundaries and progressively replacing national accounting standards. They are important to any company that has significant dealings in several countries. IFRS reporting requirements have been adopted by many countries, including Australia, Canada, European Union, India, Japan, Russia, Taiwan, and more.

Although efforts are continually being made to unify ("converge" is the term often used) GAAP and IFRS reporting requirements, significant differences remain. These differences are important to U.S. companies that engage in cross-border mergers and acquisitions, report to major non-US shareholders and institutions that demand IFRS compliant information, and own and manage non-U.S. subsidiaries that must comply with IFRS requirements. The differences are also important to the growing number of U.S. investors who invest in non-U.S. public companies that comply only with IFRS standards.

2. *ENTITY FOCUS*

An accounting system is designed to record the transactions of a specific entity and report the results of operates for that entity. The nature of the entity defines the scope of the accounting system. It may be a large conglomerate of multiple companies, a component company of such a conglomerate, a division of a company, a small stand-alone business, or any other definable economic unit. Transactions that are part of the specific entity fall within the scope of the accounting system. Outside transactions do not. For example, the sale of a company's truck would be a recordable accounting transaction for the company while the purchase of a new truck for personal use by the company's owner would not be a recordable transaction for the company.

3. GOING CONCERN

The accounting process assumes that an entity is a going concern that will continue to operate and carry on its business indefinitely. The process makes no attempt to measure the impacts of a shutdown in the near term that would result in a liquidation of the company's assets. This going concern assumption necessarily is based on the premise that assets and resources will be consumed and replenished during the ongoing operation of the business and that liabilities and debts will be paid and incurred in due course.

4. MONETARY MEASURE

The dollar is the measuring unit for recording transactions in an accounting system. But except in very limited circumstances, no attempt is made to account for changes in the value of the dollar. Inflation is ignored. Thus, for example, a $30,000 equipment purchase in 1999 is recorded the same as a $30,000 equipment purchase in 2014 even though a 1999-dollar was worth considerably more than a 2014-dollar. As Henry Sweeney stated decades ago in his book *Stabilized Accounting* (Harper & Bros 1936), "The truthfulness of accounting depends largely on the truthfulness of the dollar, and the dollar is a liar."

Constant dollar accounting is an accounting method that is used in select situations to provide supplemental information. It adjusts financial statements for changes in the value of the dollar, using a price index such as the consumer price index (CPI). The premise is that such information may facilitate better comparisons of companies that had significant asset transactions in different years. But a fundamental weakness is that the index used (CPI for example) often will not reflect actual price changes in the underlying assets.

5. HISTORICAL DOLLAR COST

The accounting process generally records and carries assets at their historical dollar cost, adjusted for depreciation and amortization as appropriate. Thus, if an asset purchased in 2005 for $100,000 is now worth $150,000, the $50,000 appreciation will not be reflected in the accounting system until the asset is sold and the gain is recognized. There are exceptions for liquid investment assets that have readily ascertainable market values and are capable of being sold into established markets. These assets are "marked-to-market" to reflect their current values.

Many claim that a major cause of the subprime mortgage and banking crisis of 2008 was aggressive, irresponsible mark-to-market accounting by financial institutions. These institutions supported extreme borrowing levels by marking up mortgage-backed securities and other assets to levels that many in hindsight characterized as unsustainable and not reflective of true market conditions. When the markets for these securities crashed in the face of rapidly declining real estate prices, values plummeted and many institutions were buried in debt with no equity. They were forced to fire sell assets at distressed prices. The fire sales accelerated the rapid descent of values and the ongoing deterioration of balance sheets. The federal government ultimately stepped in with favorable loans to bailout many, including those deemed "too big to fail."

6. REALIZATION

Realization is the concept that defines when revenue is realized and recorded by an accounting system. For every sale of a product or service, there are various key events in the transaction process: when the order is received; when the inventory is produced or acquired; when the order is processed; when the goods or services are delivered; and when the revenue is collected in the form of cash. Under the realization concept, the event that triggers the realization of revenue is the delivery of the goods and services. In most businesses, a completed legal right to be paid for the goods and services is created at that time. Except in very limited situations, such as long-term construction contracts, no attempt is made to allocate the realization of revenue to various events that occur during the process of completing an order or project.

7. ACCRUAL

Closely related to the realization concept is the accrual concept. A cash method of accounting recognizes income when cash is collected and recognizes expenses when they are paid in the form of cash. For example, under such a system a lawyer would recognize income when fees are actually collected and recognize rental expense when the rent is paid. An accrual method recognizes income when it is realized (the delivery of the product or service) and recognizes an expense when a liability is created for costs incurred. Thus, under this system a lawyer would recognize income when services are completed and billed and would recognize rental expense when the applicable rental period expires. Financial statements nearly always reflect the accrual method, although there are limited exceptions.

Depreciation and amortization are expenses that receive like treatment under cash and accrual methods of accounting. For example, the cash method would not currently expense $100,000 paid to acquire a piece of equipment that has a useful life of 10 years. As under the accrual method, the cost of the equipment would be expensed (depreciated) in allocable shares over its useful life.

The accrual method of accounting is more complicated and demanding than the cash method. Special entries (often called adjusting journal entries) must be made to reflect accrual elements that are not picked up by transaction journals maintained daily. Examples include accrued wages, prepaid income, accrued interest, prepaid expenses (e.g. insurance), and the like.

8. CONSERVATISM

Conservatism is a fundamental accounting concept. In the broadest sense, it means that the accounting process prefers to run the risk of erring on the side of understating, rather than overstating, results and values. When in doubt, yield to the downside. The concept often surfaces in determining balance sheet asset values. Three common examples:

- **Accounts Receivable.** These are the amounts that a company is legally entitled to collect for services and goods previously delivered. The total of the amounts due must be reduced for estimated bad debt amounts that won't be collected (usually called an "Allowance for Doubtful Accounts), discounts, returns and price allowances. The bad debt allowance is based on the company's prior history. For example, if the company generally has failed to collect five percent of its accounts receivable, conservatism requires that the balance sheet accounts receivable balance be reduced by a 5-percent bad debt contra-asset account.

- **Inventories.** Inventories are goods that are being processed and held for future sale to customers. The cost of the inventories is carried as an asset on the balance sheet. Since goods with varying cost levels are continually being added to and pulled from the inventories, the accounting system must have a method for determining, at any given time, the cost of goods actually sold and the cost of the remaining inventory. There are various costing methods: (1) a moving average method, which continually combines new and old inventory costs to arrive at a moving average that is used to value sold and unsold goods; (2) a first-in, first-out (FIFO) method, which assumes the first items acquired are the first items sold at their cost; and (3) a last-in, first-out (LIFO) method, which assumes the last items acquired are the first items sold at their costs. Whichever costing method is used, conservatism requires that the inventory value on the balance sheet does not exceed the lower of the cost determined under the applicable costing method or the market value of the inventory. This lower-of-cost-or-market requirement is designed to protect against inflated inventory values. On the flip side, there is no capacity to write up the inventory if the market value exceeds the cost determination. For purposes of the requirement, market value usually is defined as current replacement cost, but it may not exceed what the company expects to realize from the inventory (net of selling costs) and may not be less than such net realized amount reduced by a normal profit margin.

- **Depreciable and Amortizable Assets.** The cost of tangible and intangible fixed assets that have a useful life beyond one year generally must be incrementally written off and expensed over the useful life of the asset. Conservatism requires this even if the underlying value of the asset remains constant or appreciates.

9. CONSISTENCY

The consistency concept recognizes that companies have discretion and flexibility in selecting alternative accounting methods, all of which may comply with generally accepted accounting principles. Examples include alternative inventory costing and depreciation methods. The consistency concept encourages use of the same methods from year to year in the financial statements of the company. Year-to-year comparisons are an important element of financial statements. That is why key statements typically set forth, side-by-side, results for the last three years. Absent this consistency concept, year-to-year comparisons may be difficult or impossible, and the potential for year-to-year manipulation and abuse would escalate. Departures from this consistency concept have to be carefully considered and often require special disclosure in the footnotes to the financial statements.

10. *DISCLOSURE*

The disclosure concept establishes a simple working rule: when in doubt disclose. Basic financial statements generally won't do the job of adequately disclosing the results of a company's operations. Footnotes are the answer. Often the footnotes are long and carefully crafted. They provide vitally important, clarifying details that enable the user of the financial statements to understand important elements of the statements and the financial condition of the company. Any critical analysis of a company's financial statement should include a thorough review of the accompanying footnotes.

In addition to the footnotes, a document entitled "Management's Discussion and Analysis of Financial Condition and Results of Operations" (MD&A) will accompany the financial statements of a public company. In this document, the top executives of the company express their views of the company's financial performance and condition; discuss important trends, events or uncertainties known to management; and provide management perspectives and information to investors.

C. READING FINANCIAL STATEMENTS

SEC Guide to Financial Statements[1]

The Basics

If you can read a nutrition label or a baseball box score, you can learn to read basic financial statements. If you can follow a recipe or apply for a loan, you can learn basic accounting. The basics aren't difficult and they aren't rocket science.

This is designed to help you gain a basic understanding of how to read financial statements. Just as a CPR class teaches you how to perform the basics of cardiac pulmonary resuscitation, this will explain how to read the basic parts of a financial statement. It will not train you to be an accountant (just as a CPR course will not make you a cardiac doctor), but it should give you the confidence to be able to look at a set of financial statements and make sense of them.

Let's begin by looking at what financial statements do.

"Show me the money!"

We all remember Cuba Gooding Jr.'s immortal line from the movie *Jerry Maguire*, "Show me the money!" Well, that's what financial statements do. They show you the money. They show you where a company's money came from, where it went, and where it is now.

There are four main financial statements. They are: (1) balance sheets; (2) income statements; (3) cash flow statements; and (4) statements of shareholders' equity. Balance sheets show what a company owns and what it owes at a fixed point in time. Income statements show how much money a

---

1. U.S. Securities and Exchange Commission, Beginners' Guide to Financial Statements (February 5, 2007).

company made and spent over a period of time. Cash flow statements show the exchange of money between a company and the outside world also over a period of time. The fourth financial statement, called a "statement of shareholders' equity," shows changes in the interests of the company's shareholders over time.

Let's look at each of the first three financial statements in more detail.

Balance Sheets

A balance sheet provides detailed information about a company's assets, liabilities and shareholders' equity.

Assets are things that a company owns that have value. This typically means they can either be sold or used by the company to make products or provide services that can be sold. Assets include physical property, such as plants, trucks, equipment and inventory. It also includes things that can't be touched but nevertheless exist and have value, such as trademarks and patents. And cash itself is an asset. So are investments a company makes.

Liabilities are amounts of money that a company owes to others. This can include all kinds of obligations, like money borrowed from a bank to launch a new product, rent for use of a building, money owed to suppliers for materials, payroll a company owes to its employees, environmental cleanup costs, or taxes owed to the government. Liabilities also include obligations to provide goods or services to customers in the future.

Shareholders' equity is sometimes called capital or net worth. It's the money that would be left if a company sold all of its assets and paid off all of its liabilities. This leftover money belongs to the shareholders, or the owners, of the company.

> The following formula summarizes what a balance sheet shows:
>
> ASSETS = LIABILITIES + SHAREHOLDERS' EQUITY
>
> A company's assets have to equal, or "balance," the sum of its liabilities and shareholders' equity.

A company's balance sheet is set up like the basic accounting equation shown above. On the left side of the balance sheet, companies list their assets. On the right side, they list their liabilities and shareholders' equity. Sometimes balance sheets show assets at the top, followed by liabilities, with shareholders' equity at the bottom.

Assets are generally listed based on how quickly they will be converted into cash. Current assets are things a company expects to convert to cash within one year. A good example is inventory. Most companies expect to sell their inventory for cash within one year. Noncurrent assets are things a company does not expect to convert to cash within one year or that would take longer than one year to sell. Noncurrent assets include fixed assets. Fixed assets are those assets used to operate the business but that are not available for sale, such as trucks, office furniture and other property.

Liabilities are generally listed based on their due dates. Liabilities are said to be either current or long-term. Current liabilities are obligations a company expects to pay off within the year. Long-term liabilities are obligations due more than one year away.

Shareholders' equity is the amount owners invested in the company's stock plus or minus the company's earnings or losses since inception. Sometimes companies distribute earnings, instead of retaining them. These distributions are called dividends.

A balance sheet shows a snapshot of a company's assets, liabilities and shareholders' equity at the end of the reporting period. It does not show the flows into and out of the accounts during the period.

Income Statements

An income statement is a report that shows how much revenue a company earned over a specific time period (usually for a year or some portion of a year). An income statement also shows the costs and expenses associated with earning that revenue. The literal "bottom line" of the statement usually shows the company's net earnings or losses. This tells you how much the company earned or lost over the period.

Income statements also report earnings per share (or "EPS"). This calculation tells you how much money shareholders would receive if the company decided to distribute all of the net earnings for the period. (Companies almost never distribute all of their earnings. Usually they reinvest them in the business.)

To understand how income statements are set up, think of them as a set of stairs. You start at the top with the total amount of sales made during the accounting period. Then you go down, one step at a time. At each step, you make a deduction for certain costs or other operating expenses associated with earning the revenue. At the bottom of the stairs, after deducting all of the expenses, you learn how much the company actually earned or lost during the accounting period. People often call this "the bottom line."

At the top of the income statement is the total amount of money brought in from sales of products or services. This top line is often referred to as gross revenues or sales. It's called "gross" because expenses have not been deducted from it yet. So the number is "gross" or unrefined.

The next line is money the company doesn't expect to collect on certain sales. This could be due, for example, to sales discounts or merchandise returns.

When you subtract the returns and allowances from the gross revenues, you arrive at the company's net revenues. It's called "net" because, if you can imagine a net, these revenues are left in the net after the deductions for returns and allowances have come out.

Moving down the stairs from the net revenue line, there are several lines that represent various kinds of operating expenses. Although these lines can be reported in various orders, the next line after net revenues typically shows the costs of the sales. This number tells you the amount of money the company spent to produce the goods or services it sold during the accounting period.

The next line subtracts the costs of sales from the net revenues to arrive at a subtotal called "gross profit" or sometimes "gross margin." It's considered "gross" because there are certain expenses that haven't been deducted from it yet.

The next section deals with operating expenses. These are expenses that go toward supporting a company's operations for a given period – for example, salaries of administrative personnel and costs of researching new products. Marketing expenses are another example. Operating expenses are different from "costs of sales," which were deducted above, because operating expenses cannot be linked directly to the production of the products or services being sold.

Depreciation is also deducted from gross profit. Depreciation takes into account the wear and tear on some assets, such as machinery, tools and furniture, which are used over the long term. Companies spread the cost of these assets over the periods they are used. This process of spreading these costs is called depreciation or amortization. The "charge" for using these assets during the period is a fraction of the original cost of the assets.

After all operating expenses are deducted from gross profit, you arrive at operating profit before interest and income tax expenses. This is often called "income from operations."

Next companies must account for interest income and interest expense. Interest income is the money companies make from keeping their cash in interest-bearing savings accounts, money market funds and the like. On the other hand, interest expense is the money companies paid in interest for money they borrow. Some income statements show interest income and interest expense separately. Some income statements combine the two numbers. The interest income and expense are then added or subtracted from the operating profits to arrive at operating profit before income tax.

Finally, income tax is deducted and you arrive at the bottom line: net profit or net losses. (Net profit is also called net income or net earnings.) This tells you how much the company actually earned or lost during the accounting period. Did the company make a profit or did it lose money?

Earnings Per Share or EPS

Most income statements include a calculation of earnings per share or EPS. This calculation tells you how much money shareholders would receive for each share of stock they own if the company distributed all of its net income for the period.

To calculate EPS, you take the total net income and divide it by the number of outstanding shares of the company.

Cash Flow Statements

Cash flow statements report a company's inflows and outflows of cash. This is important because a company needs to have enough cash on hand to pay its expenses and purchase assets. While an income statement can tell you whether a company made a profit, a cash flow statement can tell you whether the company generated cash.

A cash flow statement shows changes over time rather than absolute dollar amounts at a point in time. It uses and reorders the information from a company's balance sheet and income statement.

The bottom line of the cash flow statement shows the net increase or decrease in cash for the period. Generally, cash flow statements are divided into three main parts. Each part reviews the cash flow from one of three types of activities: (1) operating activities; (2) investing activities; and (3) financing activities.

Operating Activities

The first part of a cash flow statement analyzes a company's cash flow from net income or losses. For most companies, this section of the cash flow statement reconciles the net income (as shown on the income statement) to the actual cash the company received from or used in its operating activities. To do this, it adjusts net income for any non-cash items (such as adding back depreciation expenses) and adjusts for any cash that was used or provided by other operating assets and liabilities.

Investing Activities

The second part of a cash flow statement shows the cash flow from all investing activities, which generally include purchases or sales of long-term assets, such as property, plant and equipment, as well as investment securities. If a company buys a piece of machinery, the cash flow statement would reflect this activity as a cash outflow from investing activities because it used cash. If the company decided to sell off some investments from an investment portfolio, the proceeds from the sales would show up as a cash inflow from investing activities because it provided cash.

Financing Activities

The third part of a cash flow statement shows the cash flow from all financing activities. Typical sources of cash flow include cash raised by selling stocks and bonds or borrowing from banks. Likewise, paying back a bank loan would show up as a use of cash flow.

Read the Footnotes

A horse called "Read The Footnotes" ran in the 2004 Kentucky Derby. He finished seventh, but if he had won, it would have been a victory for financial literacy proponents everywhere. It's so important to *read the footnotes*. The footnotes to financial statements are packed with information. Here are some of the highlights:

- Significant accounting policies and practices – Companies are required to disclose the accounting policies that are most important to the portrayal of the company's financial condition and results. These often require management's most difficult, subjective or complex judgments.

- Income taxes – The footnotes provide detailed information about the company's current and deferred income taxes. The information is broken down by level – federal, state, local and/or foreign, and the main items that affect the company's effective tax rate are described.

- Pension plans and other retirement programs – The footnotes discuss the company's pension plans and other retirement or post-employment benefit programs. The notes contain specific information about the assets and costs of these programs, and indicate whether and by how much the plans are over- or under-funded.

- Stock options – The notes also contain information about stock options granted to officers and employees, including the method of accounting for stock-based compensation and the effect of the method on reported results.

Read the MD&A

You can find a narrative explanation of a company's financial performance in a section of the quarterly or annual report entitled, "Management's Discussion and Analysis of Financial Condition and Results of Operations." MD&A is *management's* opportunity to provide investors with its view of the financial performance and condition of the company. It's management's opportunity to tell investors what the financial statements show and do not show, as well as important trends and risks that have shaped the past or are reasonably likely to shape the company's future.

The SEC's rules governing MD&A require disclosure about trends, events or uncertainties known to management that would have a material impact on reported financial information. The purpose of MD&A is to provide investors with information that the company's management believes to be necessary to an understanding of its financial condition, changes in financial condition and results of operations. It is intended to help investors to see the company through the eyes of management. It is also intended to provide context for the financial statements and information about the company's earnings and cash flows.

Financial Statement Ratios and Calculations

You've probably heard people banter around phrases like "P/E ratio," "current ratio" and "operating margin." But what do these terms mean and why don't they show up on financial statements? Listed below are just some of the many ratios that investors calculate from information on financial statements and then use to evaluate a company. As a general rule, desirable ratios vary by industry.

- *Debt-to-equity ratio* compares a company's total debt to shareholders' equity. Both of these numbers can be found on a company's balance sheet. To calculate debt-to-equity ratio, you divide a company's total liabilities by its shareholder equity, or

Debt-to-Equity Ratio = Total Liabilities / Shareholders' Equity

If a company has a debt-to-equity ratio of 2 to 1, it means that the company has two dollars of debt to every one dollar shareholders invest in the company. In other words, the company is taking on debt at twice the rate that its owners are investing in the company.

- *Inventory turnover ratio* compares a company's cost of sales on its income statement with its average inventory balance for the period. To calculate the average inventory balance for the period, look at the inventory numbers listed on the balance sheet. Take the balance listed for the period of the report and add it to the balance listed for the previous comparable period, and then divide by two. (Remember that balance sheets are snapshots in time. So the inventory balance for the previous period is the beginning balance for the current period, and the inventory balance for the current period is the ending balance.) To calculate the inventory turnover ratio, you divide a company's cost of sales (just below the net revenues on the income statement) by the average inventory for the period, or

Inventory Turnover Ratio = Cost of Sales / Average Inventory for the Period

If a company has an inventory turnover ratio of 2 to 1, it means that the company's inventory turned over twice in the reporting period.

- *Operating margin* compares a company's operating income to net revenues. Both of these numbers can be found on a company's income statement. To calculate operating margin, you divide a company's income from operations (before interest and income tax expenses) by its net revenues, or

Operating Margin = Income from Operations / Net Revenues

Operating margin is usually expressed as a percentage. It shows, for each dollar of sales, what percentage was profit.

- *P/E ratio* compares a company's common stock price with its earnings per share. To calculate a company's P/E ratio, you divide a company's stock price by its earnings per share, or

P/E Ratio = Price per share / Earnings per share

If a company's stock is selling at $20 per share and the company is earning $2 per share, then the company's P/E Ratio is 10 to 1. The company's stock is selling at 10 times its earnings.

- *Working capital* is the money leftover if a company paid its current liabilities (that is, its debts due within one-year of the date of the balance sheet) from its current assets.

Working Capital = Current Assets – Current Liabilities

Bringing It All Together

Although this discusses each financial statement separately, keep in mind that they are all related. The changes in assets and liabilities that you see on the balance sheet are also reflected in the revenues and expenses that you see on the income statement, which result in the company's gains or losses. Cash flows provide more information about cash assets listed on a balance sheet and are related, but not equivalent, to net income shown on the income statement. And so on. No one financial statement tells the complete story. But combined, they provide very powerful information for investors. And information is the investor's best tool when it comes to investing wisely.

D. SAMPLE FINANCIAL STATEMENTS

Following are the primary financial statements (without accompanying notes) of Caterpillar Inc. for the year ending December 31, 2012. These statements were filed with the SEC on February 19, 2013. They are offered as examples of financials of a successful public company. Caterpillar was selected solely because your author is a big fan of CAT products. The notes to these financial statements (not included here) are long and very detailed. The following clarifying points (a tiny fraction of what are in the official notes) are offered solely to help a reader understand a few basics of these statements.

- These consolidated statements include the accounts of Caterpillar Inc. and all subsidiaries in which Caterpillar has a controlling financial interest.

- Inventories are stated at the lower of cost or market, and cost is primarily determined using the last-in, first-out (LIFO) method. If the first-in, first-out (FIFO) method had been used, inventories would have been $2.75 billion higher at the end of 2012.

- The balance for property, plant and equipment at the end of 2012 ($16.461 billion) reflects the difference between the historical cost of $29.932 billion and the accumulated depreciation of $13.471 billion.

- The balances for receivables are net of allowances for bad debts and impaired loans and financial leases. A bad debt allowance for a Machinery and Power System receivable is established when it becomes probable that a receivable will not be collected. The allowance for such bad debts is not significant.

- Intangible assets consist principally of purchased customer relationships (with a weighted amortizable life of 15 years) and intellectual property (with a weighted amortizable life of 12 years).

- Goodwill represents the excess of the cost paid to acquire businesses over the fair value of the assets acquired in the acquisitions.

- Long-term debt consists principally of medium-term notes in the financial products segment of the business and notes and debentures (with maturities stretching from 2014 to 2097) in the machinery and power systems segment of the business.

- The $11 billion liability for postemployment benefits at the end of 2012 includes $4.9 billion for US pensions, $1.4 billion for non-US pensions, and $4.7 billion for benefits other than pensions.

- Note that the amounts paid by Caterpillar over time to acquire its own treasury stock ($10.074 billion) exceed by more than two-to-one the amounts received by Caterpillar from the sale of its stock ($4.481 billion).

- Note the substantial increase in stockholders' equity from 2011 ($12.929 billion) to 2012 ($17.582 billion) and cumulative retained earnings at the end of 2012 ($29.558 billion).

- The accumulated other comprehensive loss in the stockholders' equity section reflects cumulative losses from currency gains and losses resulting from translating the financial statements of foreign subsidiaries, unrealized gains and losses on securities available for sale, gains and losses on derivatives held as cash flow hedges, and actuarial gains and losses on defined benefit retirement plans. In 1997, FASB issued Statement on Financial Accounting Standards No. 130 that required that the cumulative balance of such items, which impact the value of stockholders' equity but are not treated as normal income statement items that are closed to retained earnings each period, be reflected in the stockholders' equity section of the balance sheet. Effective January 1, 2012, FASB permitted companies to show such items in a statement (typically called a "consolidated comprehensive income" statement) that is separate from and supplemental to the income statement. Like many public companies, Caterpillar opted to use this separate statement. Note that the items reflected on this statement, which directly follows the income statement, are also listed in the stockholders' equity statement.

- The provision for income taxes on the income statement ($2.528 billion) for 2012 equals 30.7 percent of consolidated pretax net income. The difference between this percentage and the 35 percent US corporate tax rate is principally attributable to non-US subsidiaries that are taxed at a lower rate, nondeductible goodwill, and prior year interest and tax adjustments.

- Note the cash dividends per share ($2.02) in 2012 as compared to the earnings per share ($8.71). The difference represents the addition to the retained earnings for 2012 that is reflected in the changes in the stockholders' equity statement.

- Note that depreciation expenses for the current year are reflected in the consolidated cash flow statement, as are goodwill charges, annual changes in non-cash asset amounts, and investing and financial activity cash impacts.

- Note how the consolidated profit on the income statement ($5.722 billion for 2012) becomes the starting point for the cash flow statement and the first reconciling item on the changes to stockholders' equity statement.

- Note how the accrued dividends shown on the 2011 balance sheet as a liability ($298 million) exactly equals the difference between the total dividends paid in 2012 ($1.617 billion) as reflected in the cash flow statement and the dividends declared in 2012 ($1.319 billion) as reflected in the changes to stockholders' equity statement.

Caterpillar Inc. – Sample Balance Sheet

Consolidated Financial Position at December 31
(Dollars in millions)

Assets	2012	2011	2010
Current assets:			
Cash and short-term investments	$ 5,490	$ 3,057	$ 3,592
Receivables - trade and other	10,092	10,285	8,494
Receivables - finance	8,860	7,668	8,298
Deferred and refundable income taxes	1,547	1,580	931
Prepaid expenses and other current assets	988	994	908
Inventories	15,547	14,544	9,587
Total current assets	42,524	38,128	31,810
Property, plant and equipment - net	16,461	14,395	12,539
Long-term receivables - trade and other	1,316	1,130	793
Long-term receivables - finance	14,029	11,948	11,264
Investments in unconsolidated affiliated companies	272	133	164
Noncurrent deferred and refundable income taxes	2,011	2,157	2,493
Intangible assets	4,016	4,368	805
Goodwill	6,942	7,080	2,614
Other assets	1,785	2,107	1,538
Total assets	**$ 89,356**	**$ 81,446**	**$ 64,020**
Liabilities			
Current liabilities:			
Short-term borrowings:			
Machinery and Power Systems	$ 636	$ 93	$ 204
Financial Products	4,651	3,895	3,852
Accounts payable	6,753	8,161	5,856
Accrued expenses	3,667	3,386	2,880
Accrued wages, salaries and employee benefits	1,911	2,410	1,670
Customer advances	2,978	2,691	1,831
Dividends payable	—	298	281
Other current liabilities	2,055	1,967	1,521
Long-term debt due within one year:			
Machinery and Power Systems	1,113	558	495
Financial Products	5,991	5,102	3,430
Total current liabilities	29,755	28,561	22,020
Long-term debt due after one year:			
Machinery and Power Systems	8,666	8,415	4,505
Financial Products	19,086	16,529	15,932
Liability for postemployment benefits	11,085	10,956	7,584
Other liabilities	3,182	3,583	2,654
Total liabilities	**71,774**	**68,044**	**52,695**
Commitments and contingencies (Notes 20 and 21)			
Redeemable noncontrolling interest (Note 24)	—	473	461
Stockholders' equity			
Common stock of $1.00 par:			
Authorized shares: 2,000,000,000			
amount	4,481	4,273	3,888
shares			
and 2010 - 176,071, 910 shares) at cost	(10,074)	(10,281)	(10,397)
Profit employed in the business	29,558	25,219	21,384
Accumulated other comprehensive income (loss)	(6,433)	(6,328)	(4,051)
Noncontrolling interests	50	46	40
Total stockholders' equity	**17,582**	**12,929**	**10,864**
Total liabilities, redeemable noncontrolling interest and stockholders' equity	**$ 89,356**	**$ 81,446**	**$ 64,020**

Caterpillar Inc. – Sample Income Statement

Consolidated Results of Operations for the Years
Ended December 31
(Dollars in millions except per share data)

	2012	2011	2010
Sales and revenues:			
Sales of Machinery and Power Systems	$ **63,068**	$ 57,392	$ 39,867
Revenues of Financial Products	**2,807**	2,746	2,721
Total sales and revenues	**65,875**	60,138	42,588
Operating costs:			
Cost of goods sold	**47,055**	43,578	30,367
Selling, general and administrative expenses	**5,919**	5,203	4,248
Research and development expenses	**2,466**	2,297	1,905
Interest expense of Financial Products	**797**	826	914
Goodwill impairment charge	**580**	—	—
Other operating (income) expenses	**485**	1,081	1,191
Total operating costs	**57,302**	52,985	38,625
Operating profit	**8,573**	7,153	3,963
Interest expense excluding Financial Products	**467**	396	343
Other income (expense)	**130**	(32)	130
Consolidated profit before taxes	**8,236**	6,725	3,750
Provision (benefit) for income taxes	**2,528**	1,720	968
Profit of consolidated companies	**5,708**	5,005	2,782
Equity in profit (loss) of unconsolidated affiliated companies	**14**	(24)	(24)
Profit of consolidated and affiliated companies	**5,722**	4,981	2,758
Less: Profit (loss) attributable to noncontrolling interests	**41**	53	58
Profit 1	$ **5,681**	$ 4,928	$ 2,700
Profit per common share	$ **8.71**	$ 7.64	$ 4.28
Profit per common share — diluted 2	$ **8.48**	$ 7.4	$ 4.15
Weighted-average common shares outstanding (millions)			
- **Basic**	**652.6**	645	631.5
- **Diluted 2**	**669.6**	666.1	650.4
Cash dividends declared per common share	$ **2.02**	$ 1.82	$ 1.74

Caterpillar Inc. – Sample Statement of Consolidated Comprehensive Income

Consolidated Comprehensive Income for the Years Ended December 31
(Millions of dollars)

	2012	2011	2010
Profit of consolidated and affiliated companies	$ 5,722	$ 4,981	$ 2,758
Other comprehensive income (loss), net of tax:			
Foreign currency translation, net of tax (expense)/benefit of: 2012 - $9; 2011 - $3; 2010 - ($73)	60	(312)	(34)
Pension and other postretirement benefits:			
Current year actuarial gain (loss), net of tax (expense)/benefit of: 2012 - $372; 2011 - $1,276; 2010 - $214	(731)	(2,364)	(540)
Amortization of actuarial (gain) loss, net of tax (expense)/benefit of: 2012 - ($243); 2011 - ($221); 2010 - ($173)	458	412	310
Current year prior service credit (cost), net of tax (expense)/benefit of: 2012 - ($12); 2011 - ($51); 2010 - $3	23	95	(8)
Amortization of prior service (credit) cost, net of tax (expense)/benefit of: 2012 - $17; 2011 - $11; 2010 - $12	(31)	(21)	(17)
Amortization of transition (asset) obligation, net of tax (expense)/benefit of: 2012 - ($1); 2011 - ($1); 2010 - ($1)	1	1	1
Derivative financial instruments:			
Gains (losses) deferred, net of tax (expense)/benefit of: 2012 - $29; 2011 - $12; 2010 - $29	(48)	(21)	(50)
(Gains) losses reclassified to earnings, net of tax (expense)/benefit of: 2012 - ($10); 2011 - $21; 2010 - ($18)	16	(34)	35
Available-for-sale securities:			
Gains (losses) deferred, net of tax (expense)/benefit of: 2012 - ($13); 2011 - $2; 2010 - ($25)	26	(5)	37
(Gains) losses reclassified to earnings, net of tax (expense)/benefit of: 2012 - $1; 2011 - ($1); 2010 - $2	(3)	1	(4)
Total other comprehensive income (loss), net of tax	(229)	(2,248)	(270)
Comprehensive income	5,493	2,733	2,488
Less: comprehensive income attributable to the noncontrolling interests	(24)	(82)	(78)
Comprehensive income attributable to stockholders	$ 5,469	$ 2,651	$ 2,410

Caterpillar Inc. – Sample Cash Flow Statement

Consolidated Statement of Cash Flow for the Years Ended December 31
(Millions of dollars)

	2012	2011	2010
Cash flow from operating activities:			
Profit of consolidated and affiliated companies	$ 5,722	$ 4,981	$ 2,758
Adjustments for non-cash items:			
Depreciation and amortization	2,813	2,527	2,296
Net gain from sale of businesses and investments	(630)	(128)	—
Goodwill impairment charge	580	—	—
Other	439	585	469
Changes in assets and liabilities, net of acquisitions and divestitures:			
Receivables - trade and other	(173)	(1,345)	(2,320)
Inventories	(1,149)	(2,927)	(2,667)
Accounts payable	(1,868)	1,555	2,570
Accrued expenses	183	308	117
Accrued wages, salaries and employee benefits	(490)	619	847
Customer advances	241	173	604
Other assets - net	252	(91)	358
Other liabilities - net	(679)	753	(23)
Net cash provided by (used for) operating activities	5,241	7,010	5,009
Cash flow from investing activities:			
Capital expenditures - excluding equipment leased to others	(3,350)	(2,515)	(1,575)
Expenditures for equipment leased to others	(1,726)	(1,409)	(1,011)
Proceeds from disposals of leased assets and property, plant and equipment	1,117	1,354	1,469
Additions to finance receivables	(12,010)	(10,001)	(8,498)
Collections of finance receivables	8,995	8,874	8,987
Proceeds from sale of finance receivables	132	207	16
Investments and acquisitions (net of cash acquired)	(618)	(8,184)	(1,126)
Proceeds from sale of businesses and investments (net of cash sold)	1,199	376	—
Proceeds from sale of available-for-sale securities	306	247	228
Investments in available-for-sale securities	(402)	(336)	(217)
Other - net	167	(40)	132
Net cash provided by (used for) investing activities	(6,190)	(11,427)	(1,595)
Cash flow from financing activities:			
Dividends paid	(1,617)	(1,159)	(1,084)
Distribution to noncontrolling interests	(6)	(3)	—
Common stock issued, including treasury shares reissued	52	123	296
Excess tax benefit from stock-based compensation	192	189	153
Acquisitions of redeemable noncontrolling interests	(444)	—	—
Acquisitions of noncontrolling interests	(5)	(8)	(132)
months):			
- Machinery and Power Systems	2,209	4,587	216
- Financial Products	13,806	10,873	8,108
Payments on debt (original maturities greater than three months):			
- Machinery and Power Systems	(1,107)	(2,269)	(1,298)
- Financial Products	(9,992)	(8,324)	(11,163)
Short-term borrowings - net (original maturities three months or less)	461	(43)	291
Net cash provided by (used for) financing activities	3,549	3,966	(4,613)
Effect of exchange rate changes on cash	(167)	(84)	(76)
Increase (decrease) in cash and short-term investments	2,433	(535)	(1,275)
Cash and short-term investments at beginning of period	3,057	3,592	4,867
Cash and short-term investments at end of period	$ 5,490	$ 3,057	$ 3,592

Caterpillar Inc. – Sample Changes in Stockholders' Equity Statement (2011 to 2012)

Changes in Consolidated Stockholders' Equity for the Years Ended December 31
(Dollars in millions)

	Common stock	Treasury stock	Profit employed in the business	Accumulated other comprehensi income (loss)	Noncontrol interests	Total
Balance at December 31, 2011	$ 4,273	$ (10,281)	$ 25,219	$ (6,328)	$ 46	$ 12,929
Profit of consolidated and affiliated companies	—	—	5,681	—	41	5,722
Foreign currency translation, net of tax	—	—	—	83	(23)	60
Pension and other postretirement benefits, net of tax	—	—	—	(285)	5	(280)
Derivative financial instruments, net of tax	—	—	—	(32)	—	(32)
Available-for-sale securities, net of tax	—	—	—	22	1	23
Change in ownership from noncontrolling interests	—	—	—	—	(4)	(4)
Dividends declared	—	—	(1,319)	—	—	(1,319)
Distribution to noncontrolling interests	—	—	—	—	(6)	(6)
Common shares issued from treasury stock for stock-based compensation: 7,515,149	(155)	207	—	—	—	52
Stock-based compensation expense	245	—	—	—	—	245
Net excess tax benefits from stock-based compensation	192	—	—	—	—	192
Cat Japan share redemption 2	(74)	—	(23)	107	(10)	—
Balance at December 31, 2012	$ 4,481	$ (10,074)	$ 29,558	$ (6,433)	$ 50	$ 17,582

E. SAFEGUARDS

1. *THE AUDIT PROCESS*

False and misleading financial statements are dangerous. They can lead to bad management actions, poor investment decisions, deceptive business practices, and a lack of confidence in the accounting process. When a serious problem surfaces, the root cause usually is some combination of incompetence, a reckless disregard of protocol, cronyism fueled by mutual greed, pressures to meet expectations, or willful misconduct. And, of course, we have witnessed time and again the power of using bad statements as a tool to fuel outright fraud.

The audit process has always been the primary safeguard against false and misleading statements. An accounting firm that stands independent of the company spends many hours applying established auditing standards to test the transactions and internal controls of the company and verify account balances. The desired end product is a document from the firm (sample below) that opines that the company's financial statements "present fairly, in all material respects" the financial condition and operating results of the company in accordance with generally accepted accounting principles and that the company has "maintained, in all material respects, effective internal controls over financial reporting."

Any company whose stock is publicly traded is required to annually file audited financial statements with the SEC. Closely held businesses generally are not required to have audited financial statements, and most don't. However, there are many situations where a private company will need to have audited statements in order to meet the demands of investors, lenders, key customers, or other important players or to prepare for the potential of going public in the future.

Audits are detailed, time consuming, and expensive. According to the 2013 audit survey of Financial Executives International, the average audit fee paid by public companies in 2012 was $4.5 million, a four percent increase over the previous year. In 2012, it took an average of 16,737 audit hours to complete a public company audit.[2] The corresponding averages for private company audits were a fraction of these public company averages, but still significant and beyond the reach of most small businesses. Audit fees of private companies in 2012 averaged $147,800, a three percent increase over the prior year, and the number of audit hours expended averaged 1,769.

In the audit of a public company, the auditing firm must comply with standards established by the Public Company Accounting Oversight Board (PCAOB), a private-sector, non-profit corporation created by the Sarbanes-Oxley Act of 2002 (SOX). This board oversees the audits of public companies and public company auditors through registration, inspection, standard-setting, and enforcement processes. The creation of the PCAOB put an end to the accounting profession's self-regulation of its public company auditing activities. Headquartered in Washington, D.C., the PCAOB has five board members, no more than two of whom may be certified public accountants. The members are

---

2. Financial Executives International (FEI) Audit Survey 2013 (July 30, 2013).

appointed by the SEC, after consultation with the Chairman of the Board of Governors of the Federal Reserve System and the Secretary of the Treasury.

An audit of a non-public company must be in accordance with the Statements on Auditing Standards promulgated by the Auditing Standards Board of the American Institute of Certified Public Accountants. These statements provide guidance to auditors on generally accepted auditing standards.

The internal control element of the audit process is usually based on criteria established by the Committee of Sponsoring Organizations of the Treadway Commission (COSO) through its Internal Control - Integrated Framework. First released in 1992 and continually refined, this framework has gained broad acceptance throughout the world and is recognized as a leading framework for designing, implementing, and conducting internal control and for assessing the effectiveness of an internal control system. An effective internal system includes policies and procedures that provide reasonable assurance that (1) records are maintained to accurately and fairly reflect transactions and permit preparation of financial statements in accordance with generally accepted accounting principles, (2) receipts and expenditures are made in accordance with authorizations of management and directors, and (3) protections are in place to prevent or timely detect the unauthorized acquisition, use, or disposition of assets.

The audit of a public company requires a firm with substantial expertise and personnel. The result is that 87 percent of public companies use one of the "Big Four" for their auditing needs.[3] The Big Four include Deloitte, PwC, Ernst & Young, and KPMG. Each is a group of multinational companies that employ in excess of 150,000 people and generate annual revenues ranging from $23 billion to $32 billion. Only one of the Big Four (Deloitte) is headquartered in the United States, but each maintains substantial offices throughout the country.

The audit process must necessarily depend on materiality concepts and conclusions drawn from examinations that occur on a test basis. No matter the magnitude and massive expense of the process or the pedigree of those orchestrating the process, there is no guarantee that the process will accomplish the ultimate goal of preventing false and misleading statements. That is why every lawyer should know something about the Enron debacle and its aftermath.

2. *ENRON AND SARBANES-OXLEY*

The Enron scandal is one of the darkest stories in American corporate history. The root cause of the tragedy was not a function of bad market conditions. It was greed and the power to manipulate financial statements and reports, facilitated by a host of players who benefited by assuming the best and never demanding answers to tough, obvious questions. The collapse of giant Enron was triggered in 2001 when Lynn Brewer, an Enron executive, notified members of the U.S. government of her witness to corrupt dealing including bank fraud, espionage, unlawful price manipulation, and gross overstatements to the press and public. It eventually led to the bankruptcy of the Enron Corporation and the *de facto* dissolution of Arthur Andersen, one of the largest accounting

---

3. Id.

firms in the world. Enron was the largest bankruptcy reorganization in American history at that time.

Enron was organized in 1985, when it started operations as an interstate pipeline company. It was the product of a merger of Houston Natural Gas and Omaha-based InterNorth. Kenneth Lay, the former chief executive officer of Houston Natural Gas, became the CEO and chairman of Enron. A sign in Enron's Houston headquarters announced that Enron was to become "the World's Greatest Company." Lay was widely hailed as a visionary, a man with strong political connections, and a friend of President George W. Bush, who referred to Lay as "Kenny boy."

In 1999, Enron launched EnronOnline, an Internet-based trading system for electricity, natural gas, crude oil, and a wide range of other products. It soon became the largest business site in the world, with 90 percent of Enron's income coming from trades over EnronOnline. It was a perfect fit for the dot.com-driven stock market boom of the '90s. As Enron mushroomed on the Internet, Wall Street propelled its stock upward. At its peak, Enron was worth about $70 billion, with its shares trading in the $90 range.

Enron enjoyed spectacular growth with its revenues tripling from 1998 to 2000, reaching $100 billion in 2000. Enron had become the seventh-largest Fortune 500 company and the sixth-largest energy company in the world.

When things began to unravel, it was revealed that Enron had formed a dozen "partnerships" with companies it had created to hide huge debts and heavy trading losses. Chief Financial Officer Andrew Fastow and others were successful in misleading Arthur Anderson and Enron's board of directors and audit committee on high-risk accounting practices. Everything crashed when Enron admitted that it had misstated its income and that its equity value had been significantly overstated. Enron's natural gas trading desk, which dominated its business, was shut down. Soon credit rating agencies downgraded Enron to "junk bond" level, Enron stopped paying its bills, and others halted all business with Enron. Enron's stock plunged from a high of $90 a share to less than 61 cents in less than a year. Thousands of Enron employees were thrown out of work and, together with thousands of investors, lost billions as Enron's shares shrank to penny-stock levels.

Enron's collapse pulled down the stocks of Citigroup Inc. and J.P. Morgan Chase & Co., who had granted Enron several hundred million dollars of unsecured loans within weeks of the collapse. The hit to Citigroup and J.P. Morgan Chase, both Dow Jones companies, knocked more than 30 points off the Dow. The collapse also triggered widespread selling on Wall Street, with both the Standard & Poor's 500 and the Nasdaq composite index experiencing significant Enron-related declines.

Enron executives were indicted on a variety of charges and were later sentenced to prison. Arthur Andersen, Enron's auditor, was found guilty in a United States District Court, but the ruling was eventually overturned by the U.S. Supreme Court. Nevertheless, the firm lost the bulk of its clients during the scandal and was forced to close its doors. Enron employees and shareholders received limited returns in lawsuits, nothing close to the billions that had been lost in pensions and stock prices.

Enron wasn't the only corporate scandal during the dot.com bust period. Other corporate accounting scandals surfaced at Tyco International, WorldCom, and other companies, none quite as sensationally sinister as Enron, but all bad. These failures eventually led to new regulations and legislation designed to improve the quality of financial reporting for public companies, including the Sarbanes-Oxley Act of 2002 ("SOX"). SOX had huge bipartisan support, with 423 approving votes in the House and 99 in the Senate. When signing the bill, President George W. Bush heralded it as "the most far-reaching reforms of American business practices since the time of Franklin D. Roosevelt." Bush claimed, "The era of low standards and false profits is over; no boardroom in America is above or beyond the law."[4]

SOX ushered in a number of important changes, all designed to improve confidence in the capital markets of the U.S. and the veracity of corporate financial statements. Key provisions of SOX include the following:

• The Public Company Accounting Oversight Board was established to provide independent oversight of public accounting firms providing audit services. It also was tasked with registering auditors, defining the specific processes and procedures for compliance audits, inspecting and policing conduct and quality control, and enforcing compliance with specific SOX mandates.

• SOX enhanced reporting requirements for financial transactions, including off-balance-sheet transactions, pro-forma figures, and stock transactions of corporate officers. It required internal controls for assuring the accuracy of financial reports and disclosures, and mandated both audits and reports on those controls. It also required timely reporting of material changes in financial condition and enhanced reviews by the SEC or its agents of corporate reports.

• Standards were established for external auditor independence, to limit conflicts of interest, to address requirements for new auditor approval, audit partner rotations, and auditor reporting, and to restrict auditing companies from providing non-audit services (e.g., consulting) for the same clients.

• SOX mandated that senior executives take individual responsibility for the accuracy and completeness of corporate financial reports. It defined the interaction of external auditors and corporate audit committees, and specified the responsibility of corporate officers for the accuracy and validity of corporate financial reports. It enumerated specific limits on the behaviors of corporate officers and mandated forfeitures of benefits and civil penalties for non-compliance.

• SOX included measures designed to help restore investor confidence in reporting by securities analysts by defining a code of conduct for securities analysts and requiring disclosure of knowable conflicts of interest.

---

4. Bumiller, *"Bush Signs Bill Aimed at Fraud in Corporations,"* The New York Times (July 31, 2002).

• SOX defined the SEC's authority to censure or bar securities professionals from practice and defined conditions under which a person can be barred from practicing as a broker, advisor, or dealer.

• SOX required the Comptroller General and the SEC to perform various studies and report their findings.

• SOX included sections called the "Corporate and Criminal Fraud Accountability Act of 2002" that mandated specific criminal penalties for manipulation, destruction or alteration of financial records or other interference with investigations and provided certain protections for whistle-blowers.

• SOX's sections called "White Collar Crime Penalty Enhancement Act of 2002" increased criminal penalties associated with white-collar crimes and conspiracies, recommended stronger sentencing guidelines, and specified that the failure to certify corporate financial reports is a criminal offense.

• SOX required a company's Chief Executive Officer to sign the company's tax return.

• SOX's sections called "Corporate Fraud Accountability Act of 2002" identified corporate fraud and records tampering as criminal offenses, revised sentencing guidelines, strengthened penalties, and enabled the SEC to temporarily freeze transactions for payments deemed "large" or "unusual."

In looking back at the Enron tragedy, it's hard to comprehend how a company could grow so fast and promise so much to so many and then completely collapse even faster. A useful insight as to how it happened was provided by Lynn Brewer, the Enron executive who blew the whistle, in the following passage from her foreword to a book written in 2003:[5]

> I know crisis. I've felt it breed through an organization one office, one individual at a time. I've seen how the presence of opportunity with supporting pressures and available validation creates an environment ripe for self-serving acts with unfathomable consequences.

> I know crisis. I've watched leaders so preoccupied with short-term appearances and the security of their current power base that they lose all capacity to distinguish what is right from what they believe may be justifiable. I've experienced the inertia of a large institution hurling itself into destruction as the fight to make right dies with determined avoidance of any conflict or murmur of transgression.

> I know lies. I've witnessed the posturing and manipulation of numbers, reports and financial records to defensibly mislead uninformed masses. I've observed first-hand how the need for money and capital can force subordination of intellectual honesty to practical pressures of delivering on expectations of empty promises. I've worked alongside good intentioned people who lose all capacity to acknowledge past blunders and wrongdoings for fear of what they know is inevitable.

---

5. Dwight Drake, "*Gutless Neglect: America's Biggest Money Crisis*" (Enterprise Actions 2003), p. i.

I know these things. In fact, I have lived them. It was my abhorrence of these realities that prompted me to do what I did at Enron. It is the continued presence of these realities that has driven me to devote my career to improving the position and practice of integrity in our corporate world and capital markets.

3. RESPONSIBLE PARTIES

There are many who play a role in the audit process. Each bears some responsibility for the quality of the process and the ultimate outcomes.

a. Shareholders

Although not required, most public companies give their shareholders the right to ratify the board's selection of the outside auditor. It's generally considered a best practice of corporate governance. Although the dynamics of the proxy process nearly always result in a near unanimous ratification, many claim that the process of seeking ratification promotes the all-important independence perception and establishes a stronger accountability link between investors and the company's auditor.

b. Board Members

The board of directors is the ultimate management authority in a corporation and is charged with playing a key oversight role in the audit process. This is done through an audit committee of the board, which consists of board members (usually no more than six) who are independent outside directors. At least one audit committee member must qualify as a financial expert. The responsibilities of the audit committee typically include overseeing and monitoring of various audit-related challenges, including:

- The financial reporting and disclosure process

- The selection of accounting policies and principles

- Outside auditor issues (hiring, performance, and independence)

- Regulatory compliance

- Internal control issues and challenges

- Internal audit practices, procedures and personnel

- Risk management practices and procedures

- Ethics and whistleblower issues

While the oversight duties assigned to an audit committee are impressive on their face, the tough question in nearly every situation is: How much can realistically be expected from a group of independent outsiders who are engaged fulltime in unrelated activities? Robert Jaedicke, chairman of Enron's audit committee, provided a sobering, insightful answer to this question in his Congressional testimony before the Subcommittee on Oversight and Investigations on February 7, 2002. Jandicke stated:

I am the Chairman of the Audit Committee of the Board of Directors of Enron Corporation. I have held that position since the mid-1980s.

Let me tell you about my background. I joined the faculty of the Stanford Graduate School of Business in 1961. I served as Dean of the Business School from 1983 until 1990. At that time, I returned to the faculty of the Business School, and retired in 1992.

What happened at Enron has been described as a systemic failure. As it pertains to the Board, I see it instead as a cautionary reminder of the limits of a director's role. We served as directors of what was then the seventh largest corporation in America. Our job as directors was necessarily limited by the nature of Enron's enterprise—which was worldwide in scope, employed more than 20,000 people, and engaged in a vast array of trading and development activities. By force of necessity, we could not know personally all of the employees. As we now know, key employees whom we thought we knew proved to be dishonest or disloyal.

The very magnitude of the enterprise requires directors to confine their control to the broad policy decisions. That we did this is clear from the record. At the meetings of the Board and its committees, in which all of us participated, these questions were considered and decided on the basis of summaries, reports and corporate records. These we were entitled to rely upon. Directors are also, as the Report recognizes, entitled to rely on the honesty and integrity of their subordinates and advisers until something occurs to put them on suspicion that something is wrong.

We did all of this, and more. Sadly, despite all that we tried to do, in the face of all the assurances we received, we had no cause for suspicion until it was too late.

Each Enron director was paid approximately $350,000 in annual compensation benefits for services as a director. Many questioned the plausibility of the directors' "see-no-evil, hear-no-evil" defense. The directors were charged with ignoring many red flags, including multiple warnings from Enron's outside auditors that Enron's accounting practices were "high-risk," "pushing the limits," and "at the edge" of acceptable practice. Ultimately, the directors settled the shareholders' legal claims by contributing $13 million to a $168 million settlement. It was widely reported that the Enron directors' $13 million personal contribution to the settlement represented about 10 percent of the profits realized by the directors from trading in Enron stock in the months leading up to the energy giant's collapse.

c. Officers

The officers of the company are in a much stronger position than the audit committee of the board to influence, for good or bad, the effectiveness of a company's accounting system and internal controls. As stated above, SOX recognized this by expanding the responsibilities and personal liabilities of company officers, principally the chief executive officer (CEO) and chief financial officer (CFO).

SOX section 302 requires such officers to submit a statement that accompanies the audit report and certifies that "based on such officer's knowledge, the financial statements, and other financial information included in the report, fairly present in all material respects the financial condition and results of operations of the issuer as of, and for, the period presented in the report." Certification of false or inaccurate statements can result in harsh personal consequences for such officers, including substantial fines, penalties, criminal sanctions (including jail time), costly civil and criminal litigation, and potentially being barred by the SEC from ever serving as an officer or director of a public company. The rationale for such SOX provisions is that enhanced responsibilities and personal risks for the top executives will create strong top-down pressure on officers, managers, operating personnel, and internal auditors to maintain quality accounting systems and internal controls.

d. Auditors

An auditing firm that issues a clean opinion in connection with false or misleading statements often has legal exposure to others who suffer losses in the course of trading the company's stock. In the case of Enron, such exposure ended up toppling Arthur Andersen, one of the premier firms of its time. The primary source of liability is the securities laws. Since the auditors often had no prior knowledge of the defects in the statements, the threshold question in many cases is: What level of culpability must a plaintiff prove to establish auditor liability when the auditor is duped or unknowingly fails to detect a material defect in the statements?

In *Ernst & Ernst v. Hockfelder*,[6] the Supreme Court held that something more than ordinary negligence was required in an action by investors under SEC Rule 10b-5[7] who alleged that they were injured as a result of trading in the company's stock in reliance on false statements. The case did not involve a proxy or registration statement. In that case, the victims of a fraudulent Ponzi scheme alleged that Ernst & Ernst had aided and abetted the perpetrator of the fraud by negligently conducting audits over many years. In rejecting the SEC's argument for a negligence standard, the Court stated:

> The argument simply ignores the use of the words "manipulate," "device," and "contrivance," terms that make unmistakable a congressional intent to proscribe a type of conduct quite different from negligence. Use of the word "manipulate" is especially significant. It

---

6. 425 U.S. 185 (1976)

7. Chief Justice Rehnquist once described Rule 10b-5 as "a judicial oak which has grown from little more than a legislative acorn." Blue Chip Stamps v. Manor Drug Stores, 421 U.S. 723, 737 (1975). The Rule makes it "unlawful for any person, directly or indirectly, by the use of any means or instrumentality of interstate commerce, or of the mails or of any facility of any national securities exchange, (a) To employ any device, scheme, or artifice to defraud, (b) To make any untrue statement of a material fact or to omit to state a material fact necessary in order to make the statements made, in the light of the circumstances under which they were made, not misleading, or (c) To engage in any act, practice, or course of business which operates or would operate as a fraud or deceit upon any person, in connection with the purchase or sale of any security."

is and was virtually a term of art when used in connection with securities markets. It connotes intentional or willful conduct designed to deceive or defraud investors by controlling or artificially affecting the price of securities. 425 U.S. at 193.

Although the Court in *Ernst & Ernst* left open the issue of whether recklessness would support a 10b-5 claim, the federal circuit courts have answered the question by uniformly holding that reckless behavior by an auditing firm is actionable under 10b-5.[8]

A negligence standard will apply when the defective financial statements are part of a registration statement for a securities offering. Rule 10b-5 is not the governing source of liability when a registration statement is involved. Section 11 of the Securities Act establishes negligence as the applicable test in such a situation.

The question is open on whether the 10b-5 scienter requirement disappears – that is, will ordinary negligence work? – when a claim is made under section 14(a) of the Securities Exchange Act based on a false or misleading proxy statement. In footnote 5 of its decision in *Virginia Bankshares, Inc. v. Sandberg,*[9] the Supreme Court stated that it was reserving the question of "whether scienter was necessary for liability generally under § 14(a)." Lower courts are split on the issue. In *Gould v. American-Hawaiian S. S. Co.,*[10] the Third Circuit held that ordinary negligence was the requisite standard by comparing a section 14(a) violation to a false or misleading registration statement claim under section 11 and concluding that the "parallel between the two sections would strongly support adoption of negligence as the standard." In contrast, the Sixth Circuit has held that 10b-5 scienter was the appropriate standard for an accountant who aided in the preparation of misleading financial statements in a proxy statement.[11] After observing that an "accountant's potential liability for relatively minor mistakes would be enormous under the negligence standard," the Sixth Circuit said that it saw "no reason for a different standard of liability for accountants under the proxy provisions than under 10b-5."[12]

4. *EXAMPLE AUDIT AND INTERNAL CONTROLS OPINION*

Following is the opinion that PricewaterhouseCoopers LLP issued in connection with Caterpillar Inc.'s financial statements for the year ending 2012. Note how it describes the scope of the opinion and references generally accepted accounting principles, the materiality concept, inherent internal control limitations, test basis examinations, the standards of the Public Company Accounting Oversight Board, and the internal control criteria of the *Internal Control - Integrated Framework* issued by the Committee of Sponsoring Organizations of the Treadway Commission.

---

8. See *Hollinger v. Titan Capital Corp.*, 914 F.2d 1564 (9th Cir. 1990), and various circuit cases cited in footnote 6 of that opinion.
9. 501 U.S. 1083 (1991).
10. 535 F.2d 761 (3rd Cir. 1976).
11. Adams v. Standard Knitting Mills, 623 F.2d 422 (6th Cir. 1980).
12. 623 F.2d at 429.

REPORT OF INDEPENDENT REGISTERED PUBLIC ACCOUNTING FIRM

To the Board of Directors and Stockholders of Caterpillar Inc.:

In our opinion, the accompanying consolidated statement of financial position and the related consolidated statements of results of operations, comprehensive income, changes in stockholders' equity, and of cash flow, including pages A-5 through A-97, present fairly, in all material respects, the financial position of Caterpillar Inc. and its subsidiaries at December 31, 2012, 2011 and 2010, and the results of their operations and their cash flows for each of the three years in the period ended December 31, 2012 in conformity with accounting principles generally accepted in the United States of America. Also in our opinion, the Company maintained, in all material respects, effective internal control over financial reporting as of December 31, 2012, based on criteria established in *Internal Control - Integrated Framework* issued by the Committee of Sponsoring Organizations of the Treadway Commission (COSO). The Company's management is responsible for these financial statements, for maintaining effective internal control over financial reporting and for its assessment of the effectiveness of internal control over financial reporting, included in Management's Report on Internal Control Over Financial Reporting appearing on page A-3. Our responsibility is to express opinions on these financial statements and on the Company's internal control over financial reporting based on our integrated audits. We conducted our audits in accordance with the standards of the Public Company Accounting Oversight Board (United States). Those standards require that we plan and perform the audits to obtain reasonable assurance about whether the financial statements are free of material misstatement and whether effective internal control over financial reporting was maintained in all material respects. Our audits of the financial statements included examining, on a test basis, evidence supporting the amounts and disclosures in the financial statements, assessing the accounting principles used and significant estimates made by management, and evaluating the overall financial statement presentation. Our audit of internal control over financial reporting included obtaining an understanding of internal control over financial reporting, assessing the risk that a material weakness exists, and testing and evaluating the design and operating effectiveness of internal control based on the assessed risk. Our audits also included performing such other procedures as we considered necessary in the circumstances. We believe that our audits provide a reasonable basis for our opinions.

A company's internal control over financial reporting is a process designed to provide reasonable assurance regarding the reliability of financial reporting and the preparation of financial statements for external purposes in accordance with generally accepted accounting principles. A company's internal control over financial reporting includes those policies and procedures that (i) pertain to the maintenance of records that, in reasonable detail, accurately and fairly reflect the transactions and dispositions of the assets of the company; (ii) provide reasonable assurance that transactions are recorded as necessary to permit preparation of financial statements in accordance with generally accepted accounting principles, and that receipts and expenditures of the company are being made only in accordance with authorizations of management and directors of the company; and (iii) provide reasonable assurance regarding prevention or timely detection of unauthorized acquisition, use, or disposition of the company's assets that could have a material effect on the financial statements.

Because of its inherent limitations, internal control over financial reporting may not prevent or detect misstatements. Also, projections of any evaluation of effectiveness to future periods are subject to the risk that controls may become inadequate because of changes in conditions, or that the degree of compliance with the policies or procedures may deteriorate.

As described in Management's Report on Internal Control Over Financial Reporting, management has excluded ERA Mining Machinery Limited, including its wholly-owned subsidiary Zhengzhou Siwei Mechanical Manufacturing Co., Ltd., commonly known as Siwei, from its assessment of internal control over financial reporting as of December 31, 2012 because Siwei was acquired by the Company in May 2012. We have also excluded Siwei from our audit of internal control over financial reporting. Siwei is a wholly owned subsidiary of Caterpillar Inc. whose total assets and total sales and revenues represent approximately 1 percent and less than 1 percent, respectively, of the related consolidated financial statement amounts as of and for the year ended December 31, 2012.

/s/PricewaterhouseCoopers LLP

Peoria, Illinois

February 19, 2013

STUDENT PROBLEM 2-1

As the financial statements of Caterpillar Inc. (set forth above) indicate, the book value of the stockholders' equity of Caterpillar Inc. increased from $10.864 billion on December 31, 2010 to $17.582 billion on December 31, 2012, a 62 percent growth in value. Based solely on your review of the statements, what factors contributed most to this impressive (extraordinary?) growth in value over a 24-month period?

STUDENT PROBLEM 2-2

Refer to the financial statements of Caterpillar Inc. set forth above. Assume that Caterpillar Inc. determines that these statements need to be changed to account for the four hypothetical unrecorded transactions or adjustments described below. How would the recording of each transaction change specific line items in each of the financial statements? Treat each transaction separately, assume each transaction is material, and ignore tax considerations.

1. The board of Caterpillar Inc. declared an additional shareholder cash dividend of $1.2 billion in December 2012 that is payable on January 15, 2013.

2. Caterpillar Inc. overstated the amount of its inventories on December 31, 2012 by $3.2 billion and understated its cost of goods sold by a like amount. It must adjust its statements for such error.

3. Caterpillar Inc. failed to record a bonus of $2.5 million earned by its CEO in 2012 and payable in March 2013.

4. Caterpillar Inc. failed to record an equipment cash sale of $1.2 million that occurred in November 2012. The cost of the equipment sold was $900,000. Such cost was included in the inventory balance on December 31, 2012.

CHAPTER 3

Core Business Performance Factors

A. FUNDAMENTAL BUSINESS CONCEPTS

A lawyer should understand basic business concepts. These concepts help explain and illustrate how well a business is performing. Without an understanding of these concepts, a lawyer will struggle to comprehend business objectives and participate in intelligent business-focused conversations. Knowledge of sophisticated accounting or financial principles is not necessary. What is required is a working knowledge of those basic concepts that drive all businesses: income, cash flow, leverage, opportunity costs, expense structures, economies of scale, depreciation, return on equity, etc. The following simple description of a tiny company's first three years of operation is designed to illustrate the most important business concepts.

Party Time Inc.

Jane knows food and is a party animal. After much thought and analysis, she quit her job at the end of 2008 to start her own catering business in early 2009. She formed a corporation named Party Time, Inc., contributed $60,000 for the stock, and started business on January 1. Initially, Party Time's targeted clients were high-income couples who wanted the very best when they threw a party.

During the first year of operation, Jane was Party Time's sole employee and handled every detail of every event. When she needed assistance, Party Time hired temporary help for a flat hourly rate of $13. Party Time rented a small commercial kitchen and used $50,000 of its capital to buy a van and essential equipment items.

In 2009, Party Time's gross client billings totaled $100,000, of which $80,000 was collected during the year. The uncollected $20,000 represented billings from the busy year-end holiday season that were collected during the first two months of 2010. Party Time's expenses in 2009 totaled $81,700, of which $11,000 remained unpaid at year-end. Key expenses included rent, food, advertising, temporary help, and gas. Jane took no compensation from the company during 2009.

B. TEN KEY FACTORS

1. INCOME

What was Party Time's income in 2009? Income is an essential concept of business, but it has different meanings based on what it is measuring. The starting point for most business owners is operating income, which is the earnings from the business before any reductions for interest, income taxes, depreciation, and amortization. It is commonly referred to as "EBITDA." EBITDA measures the profitability of the company's operations. Party Time's EBITDA in 2009 was $18,300, the excess of its total billings of $100,000 over its operating expenses of $81,700.

Exhibit 1
Party Time Inc. Income Statements

	2009	2010	2011 No-Debt	2011 Debt
Revenues	$ 100,000	$ 180,000	$ 640,000	$ 640,000
Expenses				
Rent	$ 18,000	$ 18,000	$ 18,000	$ 18,000
Food	25,000	39,600	137,300	137,300
Advertising	22,000	22,000	22,000	22,000
Salaries	-	50,000	275,000	275,000
Payroll Taxes	-	4,500	24,750	24,750
Gas	1,100	1,900	7,500	7,500
Help	14,000	22,000	4,800	4,800
Misc. Expenses	1,600	2,900	3,400	3,400
Total	$ 81,700	$ 160,900	$ 492,750	$ 492,750
Operating Income	$ 18,300	$ 19,100	$ 147,250	$ 147,250
Depreciation	10,000	10,000	42,000	42,000
Interest Expense	-	-	-	13,500
Income Before Taxes	$ 8,300	$ 9,100	$ 105,250	$ 91,750
Income Taxes	1,245	1,365	24,297	19,445
Net Income	$ 7,055	$ 7,735	$ 80,953	$ 72,305

The next income definition is net income before taxes. This definition factors in all expenses except the income taxes that the company must pay on its earnings. It is calculated by reducing the EBITDA by expenses for interest, depreciation, and amortization. Party Time had no interest expense in 2009 because it had no debt, nor did it have any amortizable assets. But it did own a van and equipment that will wear out over time and will need to be replaced. This wearing out cost is referred to as depreciation. It is not an expense that is based on a cash outlay; it reflects the diminution in value of assets owned by the business. Since the equipment purchased by Party Time for $50,000 at the beginning of 2009 was expected to wear out over a useful life of five years, Party Time's annual depreciation expense for that equipment was $10,000. Thus, Party Time's net income before taxes in 2009 was $8,300, its EBITDA of $18,300 less its depreciation expense of $10,000.

The third income component is net income after taxes. This component factors in the income taxes that need to be paid on the company's income. At a federal corporate tax rate of 15 percent on the first $50,000 of earnings, Party Time's income tax liability on its $8,300 of earnings in 2009 was $1,245. Thus, its net income after taxes equaled $7,055. All three of the income concepts described above are reflected in Party Time's income statement for 2009 (Exhibit 1, 2009 column).

2. CASH FLOW

Cash flow is a concept different than income, although it is heavily influenced by the income of the business. Cash flow is just what its name implies; it measures the cash that goes in and out of the business. The starting point for the cash flow analysis is the net income after taxes of the business, which was $7,055 in 2009.

Exhibit 2
Party Time Inc. Cash Flow Summary

Beginning Cash	$ 60,000
Plus:	
Net Income	$ 7,055
Accounts Payable Increase	11,000
Income Tax Payable Increase	1,245
Depreciation	10,000
Total Additions	$ 29,300
Less:	
Equipment Purchases	$ 50,000
Accounts Receivable Increase	20,000
Total Reductions	$ 70,000
Net Change	(40,700)
Ending Cash	$ 19,300

To arrive at the cash flow, this income number must be increased for expenses that did not require any cash outlay during 2009, which for Party Time included the depreciation expense of $10,000, the $11,000 of operating expenses that remained unpaid at the end of the year (typically referred to as accounts payable increase), and the income tax liability of $1,245 that was not paid until the following year.

For cash flow purposes, the net income must be decreased by the $20,000 of gross billings that were not actually collected during the year (the accounts receivable increase) and the $50,000 that was used to purchase the van and equipment. Exhibit 2 is Party Time's Cash Flow Summary for 2009.

As Exhibit 2 indicates, even though Party Time showed a net after-tax income of $7,055 in 2009, its cash resources plummeted from $60,000 at the beginning of the year to $19,300 at year-end. This is why many say "cash is king" in start-up operations and why undercapitalization is the reason so many promising businesses fail. The income statement and cash flow summary show the activity of the company over a given period, here calendar year 2009. This activity is reflected in the balance sheets of Party Time at the beginning and end of the year (Exhibit 3), each of which provides a snapshot of the assets and liabilities of the company at a specific time.

Exhibit 3
Party Time Inc. Balance Sheet

	As of 1/1/2009	As of 12/31/2009
Assets		
Cash	$ 60,000	$ 19,300
Accounts Receivable		20,000
Total Current Assets		$ 39,300
Equipment		50,000
Less: Accum. Depreciation		(10,000)
Total Assets	$ 60,000	$ 79,300
Liabilities		
Accounts Payable		$ 11,000
Taxes Payable		1,245
Total Current Liabilities		$ 12,245
Owner Equity		
Contributed Capital	$ 60,000	$ 60,000
Retained Earnings		7,055
Total Owner Equity		$ 67,055
Total Liabilities and Equity	$ 60,000	$ 79,300

3. *CURRENT AND QUICK ASSET RATIOS*

A business needs to be able to meet its obligations as they become due. A popular technique for measuring a business' capacity to timely fund its obligations is to compare the company's current assets with its current liabilities. Current assets are those assets that will be converted to cash within one year, and current liabilities are those debts that must be paid within a year. The number obtained by dividing the current assets by the current liabilities is known as the "current ratio." Party Time's current ratio at the end of 2009 was 3.2, strong by any standard.

Another ratio that is often used is known as a "quick ratio" or "acid test" ratio. It is the same as the current ratio, except that inventories are excluded from current assets in making the calculation. Since Party Time had no inventories, its quick ratio would be the same as its current ratio. A company that carries substantial inventories typically will have a quick ratio that is much smaller than its current ratio. Depending how quickly such a company sells and replenishes ("turns" is the verb often used) its inventories, the quick ratio may be the best indicator of the company's capacity to timely discharge its cash flow obligations.

4. OPPORTUNITY COSTS

Beyond the costs actually incurred in operating the business, business owners must always consider the opportunity costs of any decision they make. Opportunity costs are the benefits that are lost because a particular course is pursued.

In this case, Jane chose to form a new business that generated a bottom line profit of $7,055 in 2009 and consumed a large portion of the $60,000 that she contributed to the business. She worked hard in 2009, but drew no salary or income from the business. This course of action triggered at least three opportunity costs. First, if she had left the $60,000 that she invested in the company in a bank certificate of deposit that earns five percent annually, she would have earned $3,000 of interest in 2009, and she would have had all of her cash at year end. Second, if she had stayed at her old job, she would have earned a salary and other benefits valued at $75,000 in 2009. Third, if she had remained at her old job, she would have racked up another year of experience and seniority. These are significant opportunity costs that she incurred in starting the business.

Smart business decisions are made by factoring in all costs, both real and opportunity. Standard financial statements do not reflect or account for opportunity costs. And often it isn't advisable to approach an opportunity cost analysis based solely on specific numbers. For example, when Jane decided to make her move in 2009, she knew that she would risk $60,000 of capital, would work hard in 2009 for no pay, and would give up her secure job and all the benefits that it promised. Any short-term quantitative analysis of those opportunity costs likely would have encouraged Jane to sit tight and count her blessings. Many business plans never come to fruition because the short-term pain of making the move and taking the risks (the opportunity costs) is perceived as being too great. But in this case, Jane weighed these known opportunity costs against the opportunity benefits of doing something she loved and potentially building a valuable going concern that she would own. Although her numbers in 2009 were nothing to write home about, she knew momentum was building and the numbers would improve going forward. And they did.

5. FIXED vs. VARIABLE EXPENSES

Through word of mouth, the demand for Party Time's custom catering services grew rapidly in 2010. By mid-year, Jane was regularly turning away more business than she accepted. As her revenue (her top line) number grew, she noticed that her bottom line income number grew at a faster rate. This was because certain key expenses – rent and advertising – were fixed in amount and did not increase with the growth in revenues. Other expenses, such as food and temporary labor, were variable with the revenues.

The ability to leverage fixed expenses is very important in the growth cycle of any business. Proportionately high fixed costs permit a greater leveraging as the costs are spread over a greater number of units with volume increases and the fixed cost per unit drops. In 2010, Jane grew Party Time's total revenues to $180,000, but profitability grew fast enough to allow Jane to draw personal compensation benefits of $50,000 from the business and still drop $7,735 to the bottom line as income. Party Time's income statement for 2010 is in Exhibit 1, 2010 column.

6. ECONOMIES OF SCALE

Although Jane was pleased with the activity in 2010, she was frustrated with the work she was being forced to turn away. Many of her clients owned or ran businesses or professional practices, and she was constantly being offered lucrative opportunities to cater business events. She was forced to turn down all but the smallest of these jobs because of her limited personnel and her one-truck operation. She soon discovered that the economy of scale of her business was not large enough to accommodate the kind of growth she wanted.

Every business must be geared to operate at a given level of activity. Its resources and planning are based on a defined level of activity, commonly referred to as its economy of scale. Some businesses are very "scalable," which means they can easily adjust their economy of scale to accommodate more volume. On the other end of the scalability spectrum are those businesses that must make significant additional investments and take on much greater risks to build an expanded economy of scale.

Jane quickly determined that she needed to build a new economy of scale to meet the expanded demand for her services. After careful analysis, she decided to purchase and outfit three large trucks and to hire three full-time "event lieutenants," each of whom would be paid compensation and benefits equal to $50,000 a year. Jane easily identified the best candidates from a talented pool of temporary assistants. She knew that each of the three candidates adored the business, would work hard, and would jump at the opportunity to have a full-time job that paid well. Jane's new economy of scale required an additional investment of $180,000 to cover the costs of the trucks and equipment and the necessary working capital to fund the expansion. Jane dipped deeper into her savings and made the additional investment.

Jane's expanded economy of scale was in full swing by the start of 2011. It all worked. Jane was able to effectively use her lieutenants to leverage her personal touch across all major events. As Party Time began catering larger corporate events, its reputation ballooned in all markets. Its gross revenues grew to $640,000 in 2011.

7. LEVERAGE AND RETURN ON EQUITY

Jane's expansion plan required an additional investment of $180,000, bringing her total investment in Party Time to $240,000. And it all paid off. In 2011, she was able to pay herself $75,000 from the business and still generate a bottom line net profit of $80,953, as indicated by Party Time's 2011 income statement (See Exhibit 1, 2011 No-Debt column). This net profit represented a 33.73 percent annual return on her total equity investment of $240,000.

Suppose that Jane did not fund her expansion plan with more private investment capital. Assume instead that she went to her local bank, presented her operating history and future plans, and secured a bank line of credit for $180,000 at an annual interest cost of 7.5 percent. Jane would be spared the burden of having to come up with more personal capital, but Party Time would have a new annual interest expense of $13,500.

This interest expense, net of income tax impacts, would reduce Party Time's net income in 2011 to $72,305, as illustrated in Party Time's revised income statement for 2011 (see Exhibit 1, 2011 Debt column). Although the net income would be reduced by the net after-tax cost of the interest expense, the yield on Jane's equity investment would skyrocket. With this debt leverage, her original equity investment of $60,000 would generate an annual yield in 2011 of $72,305, more than 120 percent. This is known as positive leverage. The business operations created the opportunity to leverage the existing equity by generating a yield off borrowed funds that far exceeded the cost of the funds. This leverage often is the key to maximizing business equity. It's business 101.

8. DEBT-TO-EQUITY RATIO

The potential of debt leverage encourages some to overdo it. The ratio of the debt to the equity of the business must be reasonable for business and tax purposes. Reasonableness is measured by a debt-to-equity ratio, which is determined by dividing the company's debt by the equity of the business. Sometimes the ratio is based on all the debt of the business; other times it includes only the long-term debt.

There is no mandated acceptable ratio. Debt-to-equity ratios vary widely among industries and particular businesses. Generally (and I really mean generally), a ratio of less than 5-to-1 is considered reasonable, and any ratio in excess of 10-to-1 is usually suspect. If Jane had used the bank line to finance her expansion plan, the book value of the owner's equity on the company's balance sheet at the end of 2011 would equal $147,095. This is calculated by increasing the owner's equity balance at the end of 2009 (Exhibit 3) by the net retained income in 2010 and 2011 (Exhibit 1, Debt Column). Thus, even with a bank line of $180,000, her debt-to-equity ratio would have been less than 2-to-1, reasonable by any standard.

9. GROSS MULTIPLIERS AND CAPITALIZATION RATES

By the end of 2011, many were aware of Jane's success. Party Time had a superb reputation, and Jane was known as the inspiration behind its success. A profitable high-end regional restaurant chain (Chain) had been planning a move into the corporate catering business. Chain was faced with a choice. It could endure the start-up expense and hassle of trying to compete with Party Time's reputation and Jane's golden touch, or it could try to buy Party Time and make Jane part of its team.

Chain's management decided that a purchase would make sense if the purchased operation would generate a pre-tax operating yield of 13 percent on the price paid for the business. This is known as the capitalization rate, the rate used to determine the purchase price based on a known EBITDA.

Party Time's EBITDA in 2011 was $147,250 (Exhibit 1, 2011 Debt column). Dividing this amount by the desired capitalization rate of 13 percent produced a purchase price of $1,132,692. If Jane accepted Chain's offer of this amount for the business, she would pay off the $180,000 bank line, pay her tax hit, put the rest in her pocket, and negotiate a lucrative employment contract with Chain. Sometimes the capitalization rate is expressed as an equivalent income multiple. They are two sides of the same coin. In this case, an EBITDA income of $147,250 was the basis of a purchase price of $1,132,692 based on a 13 percent capitalization rate. This represents an income multiple of 7.69 (147,250/1,132,692). Thus, specifying an EBITDA income multiple of 7.69 is the equivalent of specifying a capitalization rate of 13 percent.

10. GOODWILL AND GOING CONCERN VALUE

Under the foregoing analysis, the corporate equity owned by Jane at the time of sale had a value of approximately $953,000, after the purchase price of $1,132,692 was reduced by the $180,000 bank line of credit balance. But, as indicated above, the book value of Jane's equity on the company's balance sheet at the end of 2011 was only $147,095. Valuing the business' equity on the basis of the earnings power of the operation produced a value that was many times greater than the equity book value derived from the assets and liabilities of the company. This excess value, which is huge for many companies, is known as goodwill and going concern value. It recognizes that Jane has built an ongoing, profitable operation that has valued customers and employees and a coveted market reputation. A large, ever-growing goodwill and going concern value is the ultimate goal of all operating businesses.

STUDENT PROBLEM 3-1

Refer to the financial statements of Caterpillar Inc. in Section D of Chapter 2 and the related clarifying points included in that section.

1. Based on such financial statements, what was Caterpillar Inc.'s:

- Current ratio at the end of 2012?

- Quick ratio at the end of 2012?

- Increases or decreases in its cash position in 2010, 2011 and 2012.

- Total debt-to-equity ratio at the end of 2012?

2. What was Caterpillar's EBITDA for 2011 and 2012? Refer to its Income Statements and Cash Flow Statements for these periods and assume that Goodwill Impairment Charges are a relevant factor in computing its EBITDA.

3. Assume Caterpillar Inc. could be sold for a price determined by applying a 12.5 percent capitalization rate to the average of its EBITDA for 2011 and 2012. What would be the purchase price?

CHAPTER 4

Leveraging Debt

A. BUSINESS DEBT BASICS

As we saw with Jane's catering business in Chapter 3, bank debt enabled Jane to expand her business to a new level without any additional capital out of her pocket. Although the interest cost of the debt reduced the bottom line net income of her enterprise, the debt catapulted the yield on the capital that she had invested in the business and freed her other capital to be diversified into other investments or businesses. Ongoing debt leverage is the norm for nearly all successful businesses. Creditor-debtor relationships are created regularly to fund the enterprise, finance specific transactions, and generate a yield on investable assets.

Each such relationship triggers an interest cost. Interest is the cost that is paid for the temporary use of another party's money. The amount of the interest cost depends on the interest rate charged and the length of time the money is used. Although advertisements often tout interest-free financing, it's usually just a signal that the interest burden of the financing has been buried in the cost of the product. In business, something for nothing doesn't work. The use of money is no exception.

A lawyer should understand the basic concepts and vocabulary of common creditor-debtor business transactions. Following are descriptions of five transactions that illustrate many such concepts and the related vocabulary. Bonds, a powerful debt tool for major corporations and government entities, are discussed separately in the following section.

B. FIVE ILLUSTRATIVE DEBT TRANSACTIONS

1. CARLA'S CERTIFICATE OF DEPOSIT

Carla's business has generated $100,000 of cash that she wants to safely invest for the next twelve months. She plans to use the cash in the following year to finance an expansion of her office and the hiring of an additional salesperson. She purchases a one-year, $100,000 certificate of deposit from her bank that will pay interest at an annual rate of 3 percent. In this transaction, Carla is the creditor and her bank is the debtor.

Certificate of Deposit (CD). This is a time deposit that is payable at the end of a specific length of time ("term"). Terms can range from seven days to ten years. A CD typically pays a fixed rate of interest that usually is higher than rates paid on other types of deposit accounts. The CD requires Carla to pay a penalty to withdraw funds from the CD before the end of the designated term.

Simple Interest. This is the interest paid only on the principal amount deposited by Carla. It does not reflect any interest that is earned on any interest accumulated in the account. A straight 3 percent on Carla's $100,000 deposit would generate $3,000 of simple interest over the twelve month term.

Compound Interest. This is interest paid on both the principal deposited by Carla and interest accumulated in the account. For example, if Carla's CD specified that interest would be compounded semiannually, Carla's CD would earn $1,500 of interest ($100,000 at 3 percent annual rate for half a year) during the first six months and would earn $1,522.50 of interest (($101,500 at 3 percent annual rate for half a year) during the second six months of the CD. The amount of the compound interest is a function of the designated compounding period and the length of the deposit. A two-year deposit that compounds interest quarterly will generate more interest than one that compounds semiannually.

Nominal or Quoted Rate. This is the rate quoted by the bank on the deposit, irrespective of any compounding impacts. This would be 3 percent in Carla's situation.

Effective or Annual Percentage Rate (APR). This is the rate at which interest is earned over the term, inclusive of all compounding impacts. With semiannual compounding, Carla would earn a total of $3,022.50 of interest, an effective rate of 3.023 percent.

Accumulated Interest vs. Accumulated Balance. The accumulated interest is the total interest earned on the deposit over a given time. The accumulated balance is the total of the principal deposit and accumulated interest at a point in time. At the end of six months, Carla's CD would have $1,500 of accumulated interest and an accumulated balance of $101,500. Determining the accumulated balance via a formula[1] can be challenging when there are multiple compounding periods. The easiest approach is to ignore the formula and just use a compound interest table (they are all over the Internet) or an Internet compound interest calculator (e.g., www.calculator.net).

Maturity Value. This is the accumulated balance at the end of the designated term of the CD, the time at which the CD matures and is paid. The maturity value in Carla's CD at the end of the one-year term would be $103,022.50.

Federal Deposit Insurance Corporation (FDIC). This is an independent agency of the United States government that protects depositors against the loss of their insured deposits (checking, savings and money market accounts and CDs) if an FDIC-insured bank fails. Protection is available for each depositor up to $250,000 (per bank). This protection is backed by the full faith and credit of

---

1. The common formula is P x $(1-i)^t$ where P is the principal, i is the interest rate, and t is the number of time periods.

the United States.

2. NED'S EQUIPMENT NOTE

Ned needs to buy a $200,000 piece of equipment to expand his business. He has secured from his bank a loan for $200,000, payable in equal payments of principal and interest over a sixty-month term. The loan is secured by a perfected security interest on the equipment and Ned's personal guarantee.

Promissory Note. This is a written, signed, unconditional promise to pay a stated sum of money in accordance with the terms specified in the note. The note signed by Ned would set forth the terms that govern the loan he has secured from the bank.

Principal Balance. This is the amount that Ned borrows from the bank - $200,000.

Unpaid Principal Balance. This is the portion of the loan's principal balance that remains unpaid at a specified time. For example, at the end of twenty months, the unpaid balance on Ned's note would be $144,046. At the end of forty months, the unpaid balance would be $74,565.

Fixed Rate. This means that the rate on the loan is fixed (7 percent in Ned's case) for the life of the loan.

Installment Payment or Periodic Payment. This is the fixed amount that Ned will have to pay each month for sixty months to fully repay the principal balance of the loan and the monthly interest that is charged each month on the unpaid balance at the fixed rate during the term of the loan. In Ned's case, the required monthly payment will be $3,960. This payment can be easily calculated with a financial or online calculator (just input the principal balance, interest rate, and number of monthly payments). A portion of each $3,960 monthly payment will represent the repayment of the principal balance, and the remaining portion will represent the interest charge for the last month on the unpaid balance. Since the unpaid principal balance declines each month, the interest element will decline each month, and there will be a corresponding increase in the principal repayment element each month. For example, in month one, $1,167 of Ned's $3,960 payment will be interest and $2,793 will be principal; in month 30, $653 will be interest and $3,307 will be principal; and in month 50, $246 will be interest and $3,714 will be principal.

Amortization Schedule. This is a schedule that shows the interest and principal component of each payment over the term of the loan and the unpaid principal balance after each payment has been made. Ned will have sixty rows (one for each monthly payment) on his amortization schedule. An amortization schedule can easily be prepared on an Excel worksheet or through an online calculator, such as www.calculator.net. Ned's amortization schedule is set forth at the end of this chapter.

Fully Amortizing Loan. This term means that the payments on the loan have been structured to pay off the entire principal balance and all interest charges over the term of the loan. Ned has such a loan.

Balloon Payment Loan. This term means that the payments on the loan have been structured to not pay off the entire principal balance and all interest charges over the term of the loan. At the end of the loan term, a portion of the principal balance will remain unpaid and will need to be paid in full at that time (hence, a balloon payment). Suppose in Ned's case that the bank would not agree to a loan in excess of 36 months, but agreed that Ned could make monthly payments based on an amortization schedule of sixty months. Ned's payment would still be $3,960 and this would help his current case flow situation. But Ned's amortization schedule confirms that he must plan for a balloon payment of $88,462 at the end of 36 months.

Debt-to-Value Ratio. This ratio measures the principal balance of the loan against the value of the collateral (in this case, the $200,000 equipment). A loan of $200,000 in Ned's situation would produce a ratio of 100 percent. A loan of $120,000 would yield a ratio of 60 percent, which would be considered safer from the bank's perspective and might provide a basis for a lower interest rate, a longer term, or no need for a personal guarantee (see below). The value of an equipment item generally will decline over time, but, so too, the principal balance of the loan will be declining in accordance with the amortization schedule as payments are made. The sharpness of these comparative descents often is a factor in setting the term of the loan

Default Events. These are designated events in the promissory note that constitute a default by the borrower. In Ned's case, these events likely would include failure to make any required payment, any bankruptcy or assignment for the benefit of creditors, and any sale or impairment of the equipment. Often the note specifies a cure or grace period, a limited period for the borrower to remedy the default. A penalty or extra interest charge is typical for any late payment.

Acceleration. This term refers to the creditor's right to accelerate the debt and demand that the unpaid principal balance and all accrued interest be paid immediately in the event of a default that is not timely cured. The debtor loses the right to pay the loan in installments.

Perfected Security Interest. Ned would grant to the bank a security interest in the equipment to secure his obligations under the promissory note. This would give the bank preferential rights to the equipment, including the right to seize and sell the equipment in the event of Ned's default. The bank's security interest would "attach" when the bank has given value (made the loan), Ned has acquired the equipment or the right to transfer the equipment as collateral for the loan, and the security interest has been "authenticated" by Ned signing a security agreement that grants the security interest (with all associated details) and defines the collateral. In order to protect its priorities to the collateral against third parties or in the event of Ned's bankruptcy, the bank would "perfect" its security interest in the equipment by filing a U.C.C. financing statement (which names the debtor and the secured party and defines the collateral) with the appropriate public office, usually a department in the Secretary of State's office.

Personal Guarantee. Suppose Ned operates his business through a corporation or a limited liability company (LLC). In such event, the corporation or LLC would be the party that buys the equipment, secures the loan, and grants the security interest, with no personal exposure for Ned. In order to more fully protect itself, the bank might require that Ned personally guarantee the entity's obligations under the promissory note. This guarantee would expose Ned's personal assets to the bank's rights under the loan and, as to the loan, would effectively override any liability protection provided by the corporation or LLC. Whether such a personal guarantee will be required in a given situation is a function of negotiation, which often is influenced by the financial strength of the entity, the debt-to-value ratio, and the relative bargaining power (based on competitive market conditions) of the parties.

3. MARTHA'S MORTGAGE

Martha owns an LLC that is going to buy a building to house its growing business at a cost of $1.6 million. The LLC will put up $400,000 (25 percent) of the purchase price. The balance will be funded by a $1.2 million loan from a mortgage lender. The loan carries a fixed rate of 6 percent, requires monthly payments based on a 240-month (20 year) amortization schedule, and balloons (the balance comes due) at the end of ten years. Most of the concepts and terms described above in Ned's situation are directly applicable to this loan. But mention of a few additional concepts and terms is warranted because Martha's loan involves real estate.

Mortgage vs. Deed of Trust. Mortgages or deeds of trust, while technically different, share a common purpose: to grant the lender an interest in the real estate to secure the loan. If Martha defaults, the lender has the right to foreclose on the property – secure and sell the property and apply the sales proceeds to fully pay off its loan and recover any costs associated with the default. The balance of the sales proceeds (if any) would be paid to the debtor, Martha's LLC. Because of this common purpose, the term "mortgage" is often used to refer to both mortgages and deeds of trust. Technically, a mortgage is a document between two parties, where the owner of the real estate transfers an interest in the real estate to a lender to secure the performance of a debt. The document spells out the terms and conditions of the interest and the lender's rights with respect to the real estate. In contrast, a deed of trust is a document that involves three parties, the real estate owner who transfers an interest in the property to a neutral third-party trustee (e.g., a title company), who in turn exercises the rights under the deed of trust for the benefit of the designated beneficiary, the lender. The trustee is the legal owner of the property while the loan is outstanding, but the debtor remains the equitable owner. The mortgage or deed of trust must be recorded as a real estate document in the county in which the property is located in order to protect the interests of the lender against third parties. In comparing the two forms (mortgage vs. deed of trust), the deed of trust is the most common (only a handful of states remain mortgage-only states), a deed of trust often makes foreclosure possible without judicial involvement (a mortgage typically requires judicial foreclosure), and a deed of trust often grants broader rights for a debtor to pay all amounts due and "redeem" the property for a limited period following the foreclosure sale.

Recourse vs. Nonrecourse. Unlike Ned's equipment, Martha's real estate may go up in value over time. Although there are countless exceptions, historically real estate has been viewed as a growth asset, an effective hedge against inflation. In recognition of this reality, sometimes a nonrecourse real estate loan can be obtained. With such a loan, the lender looks solely to the real estate for protection in the event of default. If the proceeds from a foreclosure sale are insufficient to pay the amount due under the loan, the shortfall (often called a "deficiency") is not recoverable from the debtor on the loan. With a recourse loan, the debtor (Martha's LLC in this case) would remain liable for any deficiency, along with Martha if she has provided a personal guarantee. Obtaining nonrecourse financing typically requires some combination of a low loan-to-value ratio, a quality piece of real estate, a strong ownership team, and favorable market conditions.

Adjustable Rate. Some real estate loans are structured for the interest rate to change at a given time. In Martha's situation, the rate may remain fixed for the first five years and then adjust annually for the next five years based on changes in the twelve-month Treasury Average Index (MTA). There are various indexes that are commonly used. An adjustable rate loan often provides an opportunity for a lower rate during the initial term because the lender's long-term rate risk is reduced. Thus, if Martha anticipates that she may sell or refinance the building within the first five years or shortly after the five-year mark, an adjustable rate loan with a lower initial rate may be the preferred choice.

Closing Costs. The costs to close a real estate loan typically are much higher than other loans. Such costs usually include, among others, a title insurance premium (to insure the lender's interest in the real estate), appraisal fees, escrow fees, loan origination fees, upfront points to the lender, document preparation fees, and recording fees.

Refinance. As a real estate property appreciates in value, often the owners will have the capacity to refinance the property for higher amounts. The refinancing proceeds are first used to pay off the unpaid balance on the old loan, and the remaining proceeds are distributed to the owners, usually tax free.

Construction Financing. Often a construction real estate loan is used to finance the construction of a new building. This loan permits the owner of the property to "draw" against the loan as needed to fund construction costs as they are incurred. Typically interest is charged monthly at a variable rate based on the amount of the loan drawn to date. This construction period interest is usually treated as a cost of the project that is rolled into the loan. When the building is completed, a "permanent" loan is obtained to pay off the construction loan. In some situations, the construction loan is designed to convert to a permanent loan.

4. LUCY'S LINE OF CREDIT

In order to finance the growth of its business, Lucy's corporation obtains a line of credit from its bank that allows it to borrow at any time up to 90 percent of its current outstanding accounts receivable. If sales are strong and accounts receivable escalate to $3 million, the available line would grow to $2.7 million. If sales drop and outstanding accounts receivable contract to $2 million, the available line would drop to $1.8 million. The credit line is available for one year, with the parties anticipating that the line will be renewed ("rolled") annually if the business remains strong. Interest charges adjust monthly based on changes in the bank's prime lending rate. Payments of interest only are required each month. The bank's interest in the accounts receivable is protected by a security agreement and a properly filed U.C.C. financing statement (see Ned's note above).

Room on Line. This refers to the difference in the amount that may be drawn on the line and the amount that has actually been drawn at any point in time. This is the amount (the room) that remains to finance working capital needs of the business.

Lockbox. This refers to a service where the customers of a business send their payments to a post office box that is under the direction of the lending bank. It is sometimes called a "Remittance Service" or a "Remittance Process." Through this process the bank is assured that all accounts receivable collections will be applied to reduce the line of credit balance, thereby freeing up more room on the line or making certain that the outstanding balance on the line is reduced in accordance with any decline in receivable balances. The company manages its cash flow needs through fluctuations in the room on the line.

Covenants. Covenants are used in commercial loan agreements to require that the borrower take certain actions and perform at designated levels. Breach of a covenant can result in a termination of the line and a demand that the outstanding line balance be paid. Covenants can cover a host of items, including repayment terms, collateral protection obligations, reporting requirements, officer salary and owner distribution (or dividend) limitations, working capital requirements (current ratio or quick-asset ratio standards), debt limitations (debt-to-equity ratio standards), and more. Covenants are a function of negotiation, which is impacted by the strength of the business, the relative leverage of the parties, market conditions, and the policies of the lender.

Debt Service Coverage (DSC) Covenant. This covenant focuses on how the cash flow of the business for a given time frame compares to the business' total debt service obligations during the same time frame. For example, the covenant may require that the DSC ratio (cash flow divided by debt service) not be less than 1.15-to-1.

Prime Rate. The prime rate is the interest rate that a bank charges its most creditworthy customers. Often, a line of credit will charge a variable rate that is a few percentage points higher than its prime rate at a given time. Lucy's line, for example, mandated a rate equal to the bank's prime rate plus 2 percent. There is a general perception that the prime rate of most banks is about 3 percent (300 basis points) above the Federal Funds Rate (see below), which is the interest rate banks charge each other for overnight loans needed to meet reserve funding requirements.

Wall Street Journal Prime Rate. This is the base rate on corporate loans charged by at least 70 percent of the ten largest banks in the United States. Many lenders set their prime rates according to the Wall Street Journal prime rate. Interest rates on credit cards, auto loans and other consumer debt often fluctuate based on changes in this rate because so much consumer debt is tied to this rate. Changes in this rate are a function of decisions made by the largest banks and, thus, occur at regular intervals.

LIBOR. The is the London Interbank Offered Rate, which is the average interest rate that leading banks in London estimate they would be charged for borrowing from other banks. LIBOR is calculated for ten currencies and fifteen borrowing periods ranging from overnight to one year. It is published daily at 11:30 am (London time). Many financial institutions, mortgage lenders and credit card agencies set their rates based on LIBOR. Most believe that LIBOR is the primary benchmark for short-term interest rates throughout the world.

Federal Funds Rate. Federal funds transactions refer to short-term transactions in immediately available funds (balances at the Federal Reserve) between depository institutions (banks and others who maintain funds primarily from deposits by investors) and other institutions that maintain accounts at the Federal Reserve. The Federal Funds rate is the interest rate charged on such transactions, which can vary among depository institutions from day to day.

5. DUKE'S LETTER OF CREDIT

Duke's corporation (D Corp) has decided to buy its raw materials from a foreign supplier. Each shipment will be large, but the price per unit will be far better than any alternative available to D Corp. The foreign seller is unwilling to ship goods overseas on D Corp's promise that it will pay for the goods when they arrive. So too, D Corp is not willing to pay the price of a shipment until it has received confirmation that the goods have been properly finished and shipped. A bank letter of credit is the answer in this situation and countless others like it.

A letter of credit (LC) is a written promise from D Corp's bank to pay the foreign seller the price due on a shipment when the seller satisfies the conditions of the LC by presenting the documentation specified in the LC. D Corp initiates the process by a having its bank (often called the "opening" or "issuing" bank) approve the issuance of the LC based on D Corp's creditworthiness and willingness to pay the bank's fees for the LLC. When the issuing bank selected by the buyer (D Corp in this case) is unknown to the seller, a confirmed LLC is often required. This is an LLC where a second bank (often called the "prime bank") approved by the seller guarantees the obligations of the issuing bank under the LC.

Conditions. LC payment conditions typically specify delivery dates, product specifications, and the timely delivery of specific documents, such as bills of lading, inspection certificates, commercial invoices, and packing lists. A bill of lading is a written document of title issued by a carrier or transport company and confirming its receipt of merchandise in transit and its contractual obligation to deliver the merchandise to a specified party at a specified location. A negotiable bill of lading (one that is "to the order of a specified party") permits the title of the property to be transferred by the issuing party.

Payment of LC. The documents presented to the paying bank include a draft, which resembles a check and is sometimes called a "bill of exchange." The draft is the seller's formal demand for payment. A sight draft requires the bank issuing the LC to pay the amount indicated on the draft when it has received the proper documentation (usually within no more than seven days). A time draft requires payment within the time specified in the LC (e.g., 60 days after receipt of proper documentation). Payment of a sight draft or accepting a time draft is often called "honoring the draft."

Revocable vs. Irrevocable. An irrevocable LC accepted by a seller cannot be altered or cancelled without the consent of the seller. Any change requires the consent of all parties, including the issuing and any confirming banks. With a revocable LC, the issuing bank (the buyer's bank) may alter or cancel its obligations at any time before payment of a sight draft or acceptance of a time draft. Revocation is permitted even if goods have been shipped in reliance on the LC.

Stand-By LC. This is a letter of credit that is not expected to be the primary source of payment from the buyer to the seller. It "stands by" to pay amounts due the seller if the buyer fails to make the payments contemplated by the parties.

If Duke's company becomes an exporter of goods to buyers in foreign countries and wants payment protection, it should instruct the foreign buyers to open irrevocable letters of credit, payable 100 percent at sight, fully negotiable, and confirmed by a bank in the United States acceptable to Duke.

STUDENT PROBLEM 4-1

Refer to the financial statements of Caterpillar Inc. in Section D of Chapter 2. Assume that the management of Caterpillar Inc. has decided to raise an additional $4 billion to finance its growth plans. It has identified three options for securing the needed capital:

1. A term loan for $4 billion, with the principal and interest at a fixed annual rate of 5.5 percent on the unpaid balance being paid and fully amortized in equal monthly installments over a ten-year period.

2. A $4 billion line of credit, requiring interest-only payments each month calculated on the average line balance during the month at the Wall Street Prime Rate (currently 3.25 percent) as of the last business day of the preceding month. The line would be available on such terms for two years, and thereafter could be renegotiated and renewed for successive two-year terms.

3. The issuance of $4 billion of additional common stock.

What factors would Caterpillar Inc.'s management likely consider important in evaluating and comparing these three options?

If the management would consider issuing more stock only on a basis that values the company's existing outstanding common stock at a capitalization rate of 8 percent on its 2012 after-tax profit of consolidated and affiliated companies, what percentage of the total outstanding stock of Caterpillar Inc. would be issued for the $4 billion of new equity capital?

C. BONDS

A bond is a debt security that allows institutions to borrow money directly from investors. The issuer of the bond promises to pay a fixed rate of interest over the life of the bond and to repay the principal amount on the designated maturity date. The description of a corporate bond generally includes the corporation's name, the coupon rate, and the maturity date. For example: "General Motors (GM) 5.25% due 12/31/2015" would mean the bond was issued by General Motors, pays an annual interest rate of 5.25 percent, and matures on December 31, 2015.

According to the Securities Industry and Financial Markets Association (SIFMA), the United States bond market as of September 2013 totaled $39.519 trillion. Of this total, $3.685 trillion represented debt of municipalities, $11.590 trillion represented debt of the federal treasury, and $9.561 trillion represented corporate debt.

Corporate bonds offer investors a consistent fixed-income yield, long-term capital preservation, and liquidity – the capacity to sell the bond at any time. Bonds are often used by investors to hedge against the higher risks of stock investments. Some corporate bonds have a call option that allows the issuing corporation to redeem the bond before its maturity date. Other bonds offer a conversion feature that allows an investor to convert the bond into equity stock of the company.

A bond's interest rate, as compared to current interest rate levels, is usually the most important factor that influences a bond's market price and total return. Changes in the overall level of interest rates will cause the price of a bond owned by an investor to move in the opposite direction. If interest rates fall, an existing bond's value will move up, all other factors being equal. If interest rates rise, a bond's value will drop.

Creditworthiness is always a factor in valuing bonds. Rating agencies, such as Moody's and Standard & Poor's, rate bonds based on their credit strength. The value of the bond moves in the same direction of any rating change. Corporate bonds often are listed on major exchanges, although the bulk of the trading volume in corporate bonds is done through decentralized, dealer-based, over-the-counter markets.

Bonds have their own language. Following are the definitions of some of the key bond terms:[2]

Ask Price (or Offer Price): The price at which a seller offers to sell a security.

Basis Point: Smallest measure used in quoting yields on bonds and notes. One basis point is 0.01 percent of yield. For example, a bond's yield that changed from 6.52 percent to 7.19 percent would be said to have moved 67 basis points.

Bid: Price at which a buyer is willing to purchase a security.

---

2. See Sifma, Investing in Bonds.com/Glossary

Bond year: An element in calculating average life of an issue and in calculating net interest cost and net interest rate on an issue. A bond year is the number of twelve-month intervals between the date of the bond and its maturity date, measured in $1,000 increments. For example, the "bond years" allocable to a $5,000 bond dated April 1, 2014, and maturing June 1, 2014, is 5.830 [1.166 (14 months divided by 12 months) x 5 (number of $1,000 increments in $5,000 bond)]. Usual computations include "bond years" per maturity or per an interest rate, and total "bond years" for the issue.

Call: Actions taken to pay the principal amount prior to the stated maturity date, in accordance with the provisions for "call" stated in the bond. Another term for call provisions is redemption provisions.

Call Premium: A dollar amount, usually stated as a percentage of the principal amount called, paid as a "penalty" or a "premium" for the exercise of a call provision.

Call Price: The specified price at which a bond will be redeemed or called prior to maturity, typically either at a premium (above par value) or at par.

Coupon: The rate of interest payable annually.

Covenant: The issuer's pledge, in the financing documents, to do or to avoid certain practices and actions.

Current Yield: The ratio of interest to the actual market price of the bond, stated as a percentage. For example, a $1,000 bond with a current market price of $900 that pays $60 per year in interest would have a current yield of 6.67 percent.

Junk Bond: A debt obligation with a rating of Ba or BB or lower, generally paying interest above the return on more highly rated bonds, sometimes known as high-yield bonds.

Premium or Discount Price: When the dollar price of a bond is above its face value, it is said to be selling at a premium. When the dollar price is below face value, it is said to be selling at a discount.

Treasury Bond: A long-term debt instrument issued by the U.S. Treasury, having a maturity of 10 years or more, issued in denominations of $1,000 or more, and paying interest semiannually. In contrast, a Treasury note has a maturity of one year to 10 years, is issued in $1,000 denominations, and pays interest semiannually. A Treasury bill is a short-term debt that has a maturity of less than a year and is sold at a discount (the yield is the difference between the price paid and the amount paid at maturity).

Yield to Maturity: A yield on a security calculated by assuming that interest payments will be made until the final maturity date, at which point the principal will be repaid by the issuer. Yield to maturity is essentially the discount rate at which the present value of future payments (investment income and return of principal) equals the price of the security.

Zero-Coupon Bond: A bond for which no periodic interest payments are made. The investor receives one payment at maturity equal to the principal invested plus interest (compounded semiannually) earned through the date of maturity.

STUDENT PROBLEM 4-2

Julie has $100,000 that she wants to invest in a safe fixed-income investment that will pay her interest on a regular basis for ten years and repay her the $100,000 upon maturity at the end of year 10. She is trying to decide between two options: (1) ten-year municipal bonds issued by the City of Denver that offer a tax-free annual coupon rate of 4.15 percent and (2) corporate bonds issued by Caterpillar Inc. that offer a coupon rate of 6.65 percent.

What factors should Julie consider in making her decision between these two options? Assume Julie's marginal federal income tax rate is 33 percent and that the state of her residence does not have an income tax.

D. LEVERAGED REAL ESTATE – AN EXAMPLE

A drive through any significant town in America will reveal warehouses, apartments, storefronts, office buildings, strip malls, and other commercial properties that are an income source for someone. Typically these buildings perpetually generate income with favorable tax breaks.

Some powerful positives come with real estate. Everyone needs it, and there's only so much of it. High quality real estate often goes up in value as it ages. It can be a wonderful hedge against inflation, that force that constantly devalues our dollars. And the escalating value prospects of good real estate encourage lenders to provide money to help make an income real estate play happen. Positive leverage is the name of the game in real estate.

Then add to this leverage potential the tax breaks of real estate. The interest payments on the debt are currently tax deductible. More importantly, for income tax purposes, depreciation deductions are available all along the way based on the premise that the building's cost must be written off over time, even though everyone knows that the building's value is likely inching upward. It's the best real estate fiction in the Internal Revenue Code. As time goes on, the gap between the building's true value and its undepreciated cost (the cost that has not yet been written off) is forever widening. When the building is sold, that gap, which is the profit on the sale, is usually taxed at favorable capital gain rates. And if the building's owner can pull out tax-free cash through re-financings predicated on ever-growing values and thereby hold onto the building until death, the taxable income hit on the gap disappears at death.[3]

Let's illustrate how it can work with a simple example.

Linda's Triumph

Linda, a 30-year old who likes numbers, went to work as an assistant in a mortgage brokerage firm. In her job of reviewing mortgage deals for commercial

---

3. Under I.R.C. § 1014, a decedent's basis in property (that portion that can be recovered tax free on a sale) is increased to the property's fair market value at death.

properties, she learned how the lending world of real estate works. Plus she learned all about appraisals, capitalization rates, lease rates and terms, and other information that makes for a good real estate play. She learned her market, the hot spots and where the action in town was trending. She learned the identity of the best contractors in town and how real pros work with contractors to get the best deals. With this information, Linda started snooping around for valuable pieces of raw land, dreaming that one day she might go for it.

Shortly thereafter, Linda attended a holiday party with friends and relatives. She overheard her Uncle Pete, the owner of a solid, fast growing manufacturing business, tell her husband Frank that he would need more space in the upcoming year, about 30,000 square feet of warehouse and 10,000 square feet of office space. Linda got excited because she spotted the opportunity.

Within seven days, Linda presented Uncle Pete with a proposal. She would provide his company with a new building, finished to his specifications, on a choice parcel that she had already tied up for sixty-days on a feasibility contingency. Pete's monthly rent would be 50 cents a square foot for warehouse and $1.00 per square foot for office space, triple net. These prices were slightly less than existing market rental prices. Triple net (very standard) means that the tenant, Uncle Pete's company, would pay all taxes, insurance and upkeep on the building (which, in this case, were estimated to collectively equal 2.23 percent of the value of the building).

As an incentive kicker to get the deal done and secure a long-term lease from Pete, Linda offered Pete a 10 percent equity interest in any sale or refinancing proceeds realized from the building.

When Pete agreed to the deal, Linda knew that she had the two most valuable ingredients to a smart deal – a lease with a solid, long-term tenant and a quality parcel of land. Based on the lease that would initially pay a monthly rental of $25,000 ($300,000 a year) and her plans for the building, she secured an appraisal on the to-be-built building, which came in at $3,340,000. With the strength of the lease and this appraisal, Linda was able to secure a commitment for a 6.5 percent mortgage loan for $2,666,000, roughly 80 percent of the appraised value. The monthly payment, based on a twenty-year amortization period, would be $19,900.

Linda then went to work on the contractors in town. Working hard to eliminate soft costs and negotiate the best deals, she ended up with a total project cost of $2,900,000. The result was that she needed a cash infusion of $234,000 to cover the difference between the total cost and her loan amount. She went to her dad, Pete's brother, who had an investment nest egg that was bouncing up and down in the markets. She showed her dad her projections and then made her offer: If he'd put up the $234,000, she'd pay him an annual 8 percent yield until his capital was returned, would repay the loan in full at the end of year 10, and would give him a 20 percent interest in all sale and refinancing proceeds for as long as she owned the building. Her dad looked at her numbers and asked: "You can do this?" Her response: "Just watch".

Linda formed a limited liability company (LLC) and went to work to implement her plan. The building was built, and Pete's company moved in and started paying a triple net rent of $25,000 a month. Out of this amount, Linda's LLC made the mortgage payment of $19,900 and paid Linda's dad $1,560 a month, the 8 percent yield on his investment. That left $3,540 for Linda each month. Her husband, Frank, shook his head and exclaimed, "Not bad?" Linda's pat response: "Just watch."

At the end of year 3, the rents on the building jumped to 60 cents a month for warehouse space and $1.10 a month for office space under the lease. This netted Linda a monthly cash flow of over $7,540. Now husband Frank was very excited.

At the end of year 6, the monthly rents went to 70 cents a foot warehouse and $1.25 office under the lease. A new appraisal valued the building at $5,025,000. The principal balance on the loan had been paid down to $2,190,000. Linda showed Frank the numbers, an owner equity value of over $2,800,000. Frank screamed "Sell, Sell." Linda smiled and responded, "And what, pay a big sales commission and a bunch of closing costs and income taxes and kill the golden goose for the future? Just watch."

Linda's LLC refinanced the building – a new loan for $3,750,000 (75 percent of the new appraised value). Based on a twenty-year amortization period, the monthly loan payment increased to $27,900. The monthly cash flow from the building dropped back to $5,600. But the LLC generated $1,560,500 cash, the excess of the new loan over the balance due on the old loan. Uncle Pete got a check for $156,000. Linda's dad got back his initial $234,000, which to this point had been yielding 8 percent like clockwork, plus a kicker for $312,000. Both Uncle Pete and Dad were ecstatic with their yield and the realization that a new round was just beginning. Frank fell off his chair when he saw Linda's share of the tax-free refinancing proceeds ($780,000), learned that $5,600 a month would keep coming from the building, and discovered that bigger numbers would be realized in the future as the rents and values continued to slowly move upward.

Experiences like these make real estate an attractive investment for many. Note that a key element of Linda's success was that she had a strong tenant under a long-term lease. This is the reason so many successful business owners invest in the real estate their business needs. The business is the golden tenant, the most precious ingredient to success. Beyond the benefits of the real estate itself, the business owner doesn't have to worry about a third-party landlord terminating an important lease to favor a more valued client or to unreasonably hike renewal rates. Plus, reasons the owner, why give my precious lease to some third party? Keep it in the family and make it pay for the long term.

STUDENT PROBLEM 4-3

Assume in Linda's example above that Uncle Pete's company becomes a victim of a lousy economy and ends up shutting its doors and going bankrupt in year 4. Linda's LLC ends up with an empty building.

1. Estimate the impact on the LLC's monthly cash flow while the building

sits empty and Linda scrambles to find a new tenant.

2. Assume that two options emerge for Linda's LLC. The first is to transfer the building to the bank that holds the debt and walk away from the whole deal with no residual liability. The second is to move forward with a new tenant who demands (remember, the economy is now hurting) six months of free rent and thereafter seven years of fixed, triple-net rents at 40 cents warehouse and 80 cents office. What factors should Linda consider in assessing these two options?

E. NED'S AMORTIZATION SCHEDULE

	Beginning Balance	Interest	Principal	Ending Balance
1	$200,000.00	$1,166.67	$2,793.57	$197,206.43
2	$197,206.43	$1,150.37	$2,809.87	$194,396.56
3	$194,396.56	$1,133.98	$2,826.26	$191,570.30
4	$191,570.30	$1,117.49	$2,842.75	$188,727.55
5	$188,727.55	$1,100.91	$2,859.33	$185,868.22
6	$185,868.22	$1,084.23	$2,876.01	$182,992.21
7	$182,992.21	$1,067.45	$2,892.79	$180,099.43
8	$180,099.43	$1,050.58	$2,909.66	$177,189.77
9	$177,189.77	$1,033.61	$2,926.63	$174,263.14
10	$174,263.14	$1,016.53	$2,943.71	$171,319.43
11	$171,319.43	$999.36	$2,960.88	$168,358.56
12	$168,358.56	$982.09	$2,978.15	$165,380.41
year 1 end				
13	$165,380.41	$964.72	$2,995.52	$162,384.89
14	$162,384.89	$947.25	$3,012.99	$159,371.89
15	$159,371.89	$929.67	$3,030.57	$156,341.32
16	$156,341.32	$911.99	$3,048.25	$153,293.07
17	$153,293.07	$894.21	$3,066.03	$150,227.04
18	$150,227.04	$876.32	$3,083.92	$147,143.13
19	$147,143.13	$858.33	$3,101.91	$144,041.22
20	$144,041.22	$840.24	$3,120.00	$140,921.22

21	$140,921.22	$822.04	$3,138.20	$137,783.02
22	$137,783.02	$803.73	$3,156.51	$134,626.52
23	$134,626.52	$785.32	$3,174.92	$131,451.60
24	$131,451.60	$766.80	$3,193.44	$128,258.16
year 2 end			
25	$128,258.16	$748.17	$3,212.07	$125,046.10
26	$125,046.10	$729.44	$3,230.80	$121,815.29
27	$121,815.29	$710.59	$3,249.65	$118,565.64
28	$118,565.64	$691.63	$3,268.61	$115,297.03
29	$115,297.03	$672.57	$3,287.67	$112,009.36
30	$112,009.36	$653.39	$3,306.85	$108,702.51
31	$108,702.51	$634.10	$3,326.14	$105,376.37
32	$105,376.37	$614.70	$3,345.54	$102,030.82
33	$102,030.82	$595.18	$3,365.06	$98,665.76
34	$98,665.76	$575.55	$3,384.69	$95,281.07
35	$95,281.07	$555.81	$3,404.43	$91,876.64
36	$91,876.64	$535.95	$3,424.29	$88,452.35
year 3 end			
37	$88,452.35	$515.97	$3,444.27	$85,008.08
38	$85,008.08	$495.88	$3,464.36	$81,543.72
39	$81,543.72	$475.67	$3,484.57	$78,059.15
40	$78,059.15	$455.35	$3,504.89	$74,554.26
41	$74,554.26	$434.90	$3,525.34	$71,028.92
42	$71,028.92	$414.34	$3,545.90	$67,483.01
43	$67,483.01	$393.65	$3,566.59	$63,916.42
44	$63,916.42	$372.85	$3,587.39	$60,329.03
45	$60,329.03	$351.92	$3,608.32	$56,720.71
46	$56,720.71	$330.87	$3,629.37	$53,091.34
47	$53,091.34	$309.70	$3,650.54	$49,440.80
48	$49,440.80	$288.40	$3,671.84	$45,768.97

year 4 end				
49	$45,768.97	$266.99	$3,693.25	$42,075.71
50	$42,075.71	$245.44	$3,714.80	$38,360.91
51	$38,360.91	$223.77	$3,736.47	$34,624.45
52	$34,624.45	$201.98	$3,758.26	$30,866.18
53	$30,866.18	$180.05	$3,780.19	$27,086.00
54	$27,086.00	$158.00	$3,802.24	$23,283.76
55	$23,283.76	$135.82	$3,824.42	$19,459.34
56	$19,459.34	$113.51	$3,846.73	$15,612.61
57	$15,612.61	$91.07	$3,869.17	$11,743.45
58	$11,743.45	$68.50	$3,891.74	$7,851.71
59	$7,851.71	$45.80	$3,914.44	$3,937.27
60	$3,937.27	$22.97	$3,937.27	$0.00
year 5 end				

CHAPTER 5

Time-Value-of-Money Basics

A. TIME IS MONEY

A dollar in the future is worth less than a dollar today. Today's dollar can be invested to create a positive yield, and yield is a function of time. It's a simple concept that is understood by everyone. Business owners and executives often have to make decisions that require a comparison of dollar values at different points in time. Those decisions require an application of basic concepts related to the time value of money.

Conceptually, such principles are relatively easy to understand. The complicating factor in many time-value-of-money discussions is the formulas, the equations with exponential functions that are used to calculate key numbers. Readers often get lost in trying to comprehend how particular formulas work, and soon everything seems very difficult. The key for most lawyers and executives is to ignore the formulas. Focus on the relevant concept, the numbers necessary to apply the concept, and the elements needed to produce such numbers. Leave the formulas to a calculator. Handheld financial calculators are easy to use, and online calculators (see, for example, www.calculator.net) are even easier. Simple technology has stripped away the mathematical challenges of decisions that incorporate time-value-of-money concepts. A user-friendly online calculator (www.calculator.net) was used to generate the numbers in the following illustrations in a few seconds.

B. CONCEPTS AND CALCULATIONS

1. PRESENT VALUE

Bob is a talented operating officer whom Petro Inc. badly wants to recruit. Bob and Petro have tentatively agreed to a deal that includes a $500,000 signing bonus. If Bob voluntarily leaves Petro within the first four years, he must repay $300,000 of the bonus. When Petro's chief financial officer (CFO) reviewed the deal, he didn't like the idea of Petro having to chase Bob for $300,000 if Bob has a change of heart during the first four years. As an alternative, he proposed paying Bob a $200,000 bonus on signing and a deferred $350,000 signing bonus at the end of four years. Bob's voluntary departure would be the only circumstance that would prevent payment of the deferred bonus.

Bob understands the basis of the CFO's proposed alternative. He has no concerns about Petro's capacity to pay the deferred bonus or willingness to honor its commitments. His concern is how $350,000 four years from now stacks up against $300,000 right now. After considering all variables, Bob has determined that an annual yield factor of 8 percent is fair. If he had the money now, he might be able to generate an annual yield of 8 percent. This is usually called an "interest rate," the factor used to calculate a yield going forward. But, in this case, what Bob needs to know is the present value of $350,000 four years down the road, using the eight percent as a discount factor. Think of a "discount rate" as an interest rate looking back. It is used to derive the present value of future amounts by "discounting" such amounts.

Bob's question now: What sum invested now at an annual compounded yield of 8 percent would produce a value of $350,000 in four years? Inserting the future value ($350,000), the discount factor (8 percent), and the number of time periods (four) into the online calculator generates a present value of only $257,260.[1] Bob now knows that the CFO's proposal falls far short of the original deal that would pay Bob the $300,000 forfeitable portion of his bonus upfront.

2. FUTURE VALUE

Bob and the CFO need to get their deal back on track. The CFO accepts Bob's 8 percent interest/discount factor. To find an acceptable solution, they change the underlying question. No longer would it focus on the present value of $350,000 in four years. The question would now focus on the future value of $300,000 right now. Simply stated: What would be the future value in four years of $300,000 invested now at an annual compounded yield of 8 percent?

Inserting the present value ($300,000), the discount factor (8 percent), and the number of time periods (four) into the online calculator generates a future value of $408,147.[2] Bob and the CFO settle on a deferred bonus of $410,000, each understanding that, given Bob's 8 percent yield factor, this future payment fairly equates to the payment of $300,000 right now.

3. FUTURE VALUE FROM PERIODIC PAYMENTS

Bob joins Petro and does a superb job. He has become the chief operating officer of the company (COO), is approaching his 50th birthday, and is constantly being courted by other companies. In order to provide Bob with a powerful incentive to stay with Petro, the chief executive officer (CEO) of Petro has proposed that Bob be given a supplemental retirement plan designed specifically for him.

Bob's plan would require the company to accrue on the first day of each year a $50,000 credit that would be used to fund a retirement benefit for Bob at age 65. These annual accruals (15 in total) would grow at a compounded annual

---

1. The relevant formula is $PV = FV/(1+r)^n$ where PV is the present value, FV is the future value, "r" is the discount rate, and "n" is the number of periods.

2. The relevant formula is $FV = PV \times (1+r)^n$ where FV is the future value, PV is the present value, "r" is the discount rate, and "n" is the number of periods.

rate of 7 percent. If Bob voluntarily terminates his employment with Petro before reaching age 65, he would forfeit all accrued benefits. If Bob's employment with Petro terminated before age 65 as a result of death or disability, the accrued balance at time of termination would be paid to Bob or his designated heirs, as appropriate.

When told of the CEO's proposal, Bob had one overriding question: How much will accumulate in the plan by age 65? The question requires a calculation of the future value of the annual accruals that Petro will make for Bob's benefit. This is not the future value of a fixed sum today, as was the case with Bob's deferred signing bonus. This is the future value of a series of annual accruals that occur over a fixed period of time.

Inserting the number of time periods (15), the interest factor (7 percent), and the amount of each annual accrual ($50,000) into the calculator generates a future value of $1,344,000.[3] This is the total amount that would accrue under the CEO's plan for Bob's benefit by age 65.

4. PERIODIC PAYMENT FROM A PRESENT VALUE

Bob is initially impressed with the future value of $1,344,000 that will accumulate by the time he reaches 65. But as he thinks more about the situation, he concludes that a lump sum figure at age 65 doesn't fully answer his key retirement question. He really needs to know the amount of the monthly retirement income that he and his spouse can plan on receiving during the 20 years following his retirement (from age 65 to 85).

The answer to this question requires the calculation of a future monthly benefit based on a known present value and an assumed interest factor. Given that this will be a retirement nest egg that is conservatively invested, Bob decides to use an annual interest yield of 5.4 percent from age 65 to 85. Note that the future value from the previous calculation ($1,344,000) has become the present value in this calculation because the relevant time periods have shifted from pre-age-65 to post-age-65. Inserting the present value ($1,344,000), the annual interest factor (5.4 percent), and the number of monthly payments (240) into the calculator produces a monthly payment of $9,169.[4]

5. PRESENT VALUE FROM FUTURE PERIODIC PAYMENTS

Bob is dismayed to learn that his special retirement plan will generate a monthly retirement payment of only $9,169. Considering the impacts of inflation and taxes (every payment will constitute taxable income), he figures that he is going to need much more. He wants the plan structured to pay a monthly benefit of $15,000 for the 20 years following his retirement, based on his retirement yield assumption of 5.4 percent.

The first step is to calculate the amount needed at age 65 to fund such a benefit. This is a present value calculation based on a known future payment

---

3. The relevant formula is $FV = P \times [(1+r)^n - 1/r]$ where FV is the present value, P is the periodic payment, "r" is the interest rate, and "n" is the number of periods.

4. The relevant formula is $P = (r \times PV) / (1 - (1 + r)^{-n})$ where P is the periodic payment, PV is the present value, "r" is the interest rate, and "n" is the number of periods.

stream and a given discount factor. Inserting the number of monthly payments (240), the annual discount factor (5.4 percent), and the desired monthly payment ($15,000) into the calculator produces a present value of $2,208,500.[5] This is the amount that would need to be accrued by age 65 to fund a $15,000 monthly benefit for 20 years.

6. PERIODIC PAYMENT FROM A FUTURE VALUE

Bob presents his analysis to Petro's CEO. The CEO's appreciates Bob's concerns, but wants to know how much will have to be annually accrued over the next fifteen years to accumulate a total accrued balance of $2,208,500 by the time Bob reaches age 65. This requires the calculation of a periodic payment based on a future value and a given interest factor. Note that here the present value from the prior calculation ($2,208,500) becomes the future value in this calculation because the relevant time period has shifted from post-age-65 to pre-age-65. Inserting the number of annual periods (15), the annual interest factor (7 percent), and the future value ($2,208,500) into the calculator produces a required periodic payment of $82,136.[6] This is the principal amount that Petro would need to accrue each year for the next fifteen years in order to accumulate $2,208,500 at an annual compounded yield of 7 percent.

7. ANNUITIES

In the foregoing analysis, the amount accumulated for Bob's benefit at age 65 would be paid to Bob over a 20-year period in equal monthly installments. This is often referred to as "annuitizing" a fixed sum. In Bob's case, the assumption was that Petro would calculate and pay the annuitized amount each month.

In many situations, a person decides to purchase an annuity contract from an insurance company. Such an annuity can shift investment and other risks to the company, depending on how the annuity is structured. Plus, it can eliminate the hassles of tracking and monitoring investments and mitigate temptations to deviate from an established spending program. Of course, the strength and creditworthiness of the insurance company and the specific terms of the annuity contract, including commissions paid, are always important considerations. Lawyers should have an understanding of basic annuity terms and the related vocabulary.

Immediate Annuity. An immediate annuity triggers periodic payments as soon as the contract is executed. There is no accumulation period. A sum is deposited, and the company immediately starts making payments pursuant to the terms of the annuity.

Deferred Annuity. A deferred annuity delays the commencement of payments. The owner of the annuity decides when the annuitization of the

---

5. The relevant formula is $PV = P \times ((1 - (1+r)^{-n})/r)$ where PV is the present value, P is the periodic payment "r" is the interest rate, and "n" is the number of periods.

6. The relevant formula is $P = (r \times FV) / ((1+r)^n - 1)$ where P is the periodic payment, FV is the future value, "r" is the interest rate, and "n" is the number of periods.

contract commences. The period preceding the annuitization is often called the accumulation period. The annuity may be funded with a single premium or multiple deposits to the contract at various times during the accumulation period. All yields that accumulate inside the contract are tax deferred until they are actually paid. The size of the periodic payment when annuitization commences is predicated on the balances generated during the accumulation period.

Fixed-Term vs. Life Annuity. A fixed-term annuity guarantees periodic payments for a defined period. A life annuity guarantees periodic payments for the life of the individual (often called the "annuitant") or so long as one of a designated group (e.g., husband and wife) is living. The insurance company takes an added mortality risk with a life annuity and, therefore, the periodic payments are often less than what would be received under a fixed annuity. An annuity contract may incorporate both mortality and fixed elements by requiring payments for the greater of a defined term or the life of one or more individuals. For example, the annuity contract could mandate a payout period of at least 20 years if the annuitant dies within 20 years.

Fixed vs. Variable Annuity. With a fixed annuity, the insurance company promises a guaranteed rate of return during the accumulation and annuitization periods. The investment risk is born by the company. With a variable annuity, the owner of the contract determines the investments within the contract and bears all the associated investment risks. The deferred tax benefits remain the same. Typically, the owner of a variable annuity must select from a pre-defined list of investments (often called "sub-accounts") that offer a wide range of risk/reward options.

8. INTERNAL RATE OF RETURN

Internal rate of return ("IRR") is a concept that helps compare the profitability of investments, particularly when one or more of the investments have irregular cash flows in or out of the investment. Sometimes IRR is referred to as the "economic rate of return" or "discounted cash flow rate of return." Technically, the calculation of an investment's IRR is designed to determine the discount rate at which the net present value of all amounts put into the investment (the negative cash flows) equals the net present value of payments (positive cash flows) that come from the investment. A simple example will help illustrate the function of an IRR analysis.

Let's go back to Bob, our stellar COO. Bob's neighbor has a "hot real estate" deal for Bob. Bob would invest $60,000 in year 1, $50,000 in year 2, and $40,000 in year 3. The venture is projected to start paying off in year 6. The projections show that Bob would receive $30,000 in year 6, $50,000 in year 7, $60,000 in year 8, and $120,000 in year 9 when the project sells out. Bob wants to know how the projected yield from this investment stacks up against his other more traditional investments that historically have yielded Bob an average of 7 percent annually.

Bob needs an IRR calculation that is based on the projected cash flows (both positive and negative) of the venture. An online calculator (www.pine-grove.com/) confirms that his neighbor's projected cash flows would generate an

IRR of 9.36 percent. If by chance the actual cash flow benefits (the returns in years 5 through 9) turn out to be 15 percent less than the projections, the IRR plummets to 6.5 percent. Similarly, if the annual projected payments turn out to be accurate but are delayed two years because of unforeseen obstacles, the IRR drops to 7.55 percent. With these IRR calculations, Bob is in a much better position to compare this opportunity against other available investment options.

STUDENT PROBLEM 5-1

Lauren is the sole owner of Belts Galore, Inc. ("Belts"), a successful C corporation. Morse Inc. ("Morse") has offered to buy all of the assets and business of Belts for a price that has Lauren very excited. The big obstacle is that Morse wants to buy the assets of Belts, which will trigger a costly double income tax for Lauren and her company. The tax burden would be substantially reduced if Morse bought Lauren's stock in Belts, as opposed to the assets of Belts. But such a stock purchase would result in Morse having smaller tax deductions in each of the next fifteen years (about $100,000 a year), and thus higher taxes ($35,000 a year) in each of such years. Lauren thinks that her after-tax yield from the sale will be higher if she entices Morse to do a stock (as opposed to an asset) deal by reducing the stock price by an amount equal to the present value of the $35,000 additional tax costs that Morse is projected to incur in each of the next fifteen years with a stock deal.

1. In making such present value calculation, will Lauren prefer to use a high discount rate or a low discount rate? What will Morse prefer?

2. Assume that Lauren and Morse agree that the price reduction should be based on a discount factor of 9 percent. Calculate the amount of the price reduction. I suggest using the finance calculator at www.calculator.net

CHAPTER 6

Valuing a Business Enterprise

A. THE LAWYER'S NON-ROLE

A primary objective of nearly all business owners is to continually increase the value of the business. There are many situations where a business owner wants or needs third party verification of the enterprise's value. In these situations, experts are called upon to express an opinion as to the value of the business as a going concern.

Foolish is the lawyer who attempts to value a client's business or even express an opinion on its value. It's not the job of the lawyer. It is beyond the lawyer's expertise or training. Other professionals are trained to tackle the tough job of pinning a value on an ever-evolving bundle of assets and income-generating operations. Let them take the heat. Avoid any temptation to start sounding like a valuation expert with clients.

This does not mean that a lawyer should not understand the vocabulary and basic techniques of business valuations. Such an understanding is essential to being a good legal advisor to business owners. At the most basic level, it makes intelligent conversation possible with those business owners who regularly analyze and ponder the importance of events, both internal and external, that may impact the value of the business they have devoted their working lives to building. They regularly talk of intangible asset indicators, capitalization and discount rates, EBITDA multipliers, and the like.

But the need to know goes beyond client relationships. The issue of value goes right to the heart of the planning effort in many situations. It, for example, is center stage in buy-sell planning among co-owners, new owner admission challenges, executive-based equity incentives, insurance planning, estate planning and related family planning challenges, and all exit strategy planning. Valuation challenges are always present in major transactions, including acquisitions, mergers, leveraged buy-outs, and initial public offerings. Also, business valuation issues often arise in a broad range of litigation contexts, including marital dissolutions, bankruptcies, breach of contract battles, dissenting shareholder and minority owner oppression disputes, economic damages computations, and many other situations.

While the lawyer is not the valuation expert in these situations, the lawyer's working knowledge of the relevant factors and techniques can strengthen the quality of the entire planning or dispute-resolution effort. It facilitates dialogue with the experts that may help identify or eliminate sloppy valuations. It enables the lawyer to spot unreasonable client valuation expectations. Often it makes it possible for the lawyer to assist the client in understanding the factors that impact the valuation determination and to explain the valuation to other parties who are impacted by the determination. And in most situations, it helps the lawyer lead the planning process.

Knowledge of valuation factors and techniques also can make a lawyer a much better negotiator. Most business negotiations are about value. A primary challenge in the negotiation process is to convince the other side that it is being offered a fair deal based on the values. The lawyer who is equipped to use valuation lingo and measurement techniques to make the case is often very effective. This is one situation where the lawyer can become a valuation advocate by applying favorable factors, drawing comparisons, and expressing "heat-of-battle" opinions. The difference here (and it is huge) is that the lawyer is not seeking to advise a client, but rather is seeking to prevail in a negotiation with one who is not a client. Often the lawyer who gets on a valuation soapbox in a tough negotiation is well advised to privately remind any client who witnessed the show that negotiation dialogue is no substitute for quality advice from a valuation expert.

B. Scope of the Challenge

Revenue Ruling 59-60[1] is a useful starting point in assessing the nature of the business valuation challenge. Although ancient, this ruling continues to provide relevant guidance. In the context of business valuations, it states the classic definition of "fair market value" as "the price at which the property would change hands between a willing buyer and a willing seller when the former is not under any compulsion to buy and the latter is not under any compulsion to sell, both parties having reasonable knowledge of the relevant facts." In lieu of prescribing a specific mathematical valuation formula, the ruling discusses the following factors that should be considered in arriving at a fair market value determination:

1. The nature of the business and the history of the enterprise from its inception.

2. The economic outlook in general and the condition and outlook of the specific industry in particular.

3. The book value of the stock and financial condition of the business.

4. The earning capacity of the company.

5. The dividend-paying capacity of the business.

6. Whether or not the enterprise has goodwill or other intangible value.

7. Sales of the stock and the size of the block of stock to be valued.

8. The market price of stocks of corporations engaged in the same or a

---

1. 1959-1 C.B. 237. Years later in Revenue Ruling 68-609, 1968-2 C.B. 327, the Service stated that the valuation principles of 59-60 also would apply to partnership interests.

similar line of business that have their stocks actively traded in a free and open market, either on an exchange or over-the-counter.

Although the fair market value standard has been around forever and nearly a half century ago the Internal Revenue Service provided guidance on how it should be applied in valuing business interests, serious valuation disputes routinely erupt. These disputes teach two important lessons. First, secure the services of a professional appraiser. Valuing a business interest requires judgment calls that must be made by a professional. Second, get the best appraiser available. If a dispute breaks out, the quality, reputation, and competence of the appraiser may be the ultimate deciding factor. The Tax Court, for example, has consistently refused to accept an appraisal on its face; it has followed a practice of carefully examining the underlying details and assumptions and the quality of the appraiser's analysis.[2]

Revenue Ruling 59-60 also recognized that the size of the block of stock is a relevant factor in valuing an interest in a business enterprise, specifically noting that a minority interest would be more difficult to sell. In many situations, valuation discounts become the name of the game and play an essential role in the valuation process. The two most significant discounts associated with an interest in a closely held business enterprise are the minority interest (lack of control) discount and the lack of marketability discount. The minority interest discount recognizes that a willing buyer will not pay as much for a minority interest; there is no control. The lack of marketability discount reflects the reality that a willing buyer will pay less for an interest in a closely held business if there is no ready market of future buyers for the interest. Usually both discounts are applied in valuing the transferred interest.[3] Often the two discounts total as much as 35 to 40 percent when a minority interest is being valued.[4]

Of course, publicly traded companies and closely held enterprises present different valuation challenges. A public company's value is impacted by the demand for its stock, which can be heavily influenced by general market conditions and factors that are unrelated to the company's performance. A closely held enterprise's value tends to be more closely tied to specify industry factors and the company's track record. Stockholders of public companies generally have no significant influence on how the company is managed; owners of closely held enterprises usually run the whole show. And whereas profit maximization is the premier objective in publicly traded companies, income maximization often takes a back seat to tax planning for the owners of closely held businesses.

When it comes to business valuations, nothing is easy and uncertainty abounds. William Yegge, an experienced business valuation expert and author of books on business valuation practices, summed it as follows:

> For nearly 30 years I have wrestled with the question: What is business

---

2. See, for example, Rabenhorst v. Commissioner, 71 TCM(CCH) 2271 (1996) and Estate of Kaufman v. Commissioner, 77 TCM (CCH) 1779 (1999).

3. See, for example, Dailey v. Commissioner, 82 TCM 710 (2001); Janda v. Commissioner, 81 TCM 1100 (2001); Barnes v. Commissioner, 76 TCM 881 (1998); Litchfield v. Commissioner, T.C. Memo 2009-21.

4. Id.

value? And to this day, assignment of intangible value in business remains the more perplexing task. There simply is no "pat" answer or formula. My way is neither right nor wrong, and the task is not really made easier with experience. If I have learned one common essential, it is to exercise caution in assigning intangible value throughout the whole process. There will always be reams of theory and flames of discussion, because scientific formulas developed for intangible value can do no more than "attempt" to measure the art form of human enterprise.[5]

C. ALTERNATIVE VALUATION METHODS

It helps to have a basic understanding of the various methods that are used to value a business. The most appropriate method in any given situation depends on the nature and history of the business, market conditions, and a host of other factors. Often a combination of methods is used. Following is a brief description of select methods used in valuing a business.

Book Value Method. The book value method bases the value on the company's balance sheet. It is total assets less total liabilities, using the balance sheet's historical dollar cost numbers. No attempt is made to account for the fair market value of the assets or the going concern value of the enterprise. For that reason, it is usually a poor measure of a company's real value. Its only virtue is its simplicity.

Adjusted Book Value Method. This is the same as the Book Value Method, with one important twist. Under this method, the assets are adjusted to reflect their current fair market values. The balance sheet is still the driving force, but asset values are restated. It works best in those situations where asset values are the key to the company's value. But it is a poor measure for an operating business whose value is predicated on its earning capacity and going concern value.

Capitalized Earnings Method. This is a popular valuation method when the business' value is based on the earnings capacity of the business. This method was illustrated in Chapter 3 (factor 9, page 64) in valuing Jane's catering business. In that situation, Chain's management decided that a purchase would make sense if the purchased operation would generate a pre-tax operating yield of 13 percent on the price paid for the business. This is known as the capitalization rate, the rate used to determine the purchase price based on a known income measure, usually EBITDA. The capitalization rate is the driving factor in the valuation and is usually based on the strength, stability and growth rate of the earnings of the business. A low capitalization rate reflects strong earnings and results in a higher value. The value of the business declines as the capitalization rate increase. In the case of Party Time Inc., its 20122 EBITDA ($147,250) was divided by the desired capitalization rate of 13 percent to produce a business valuation of $1,132,692. Sometimes the capitalization rate is

---

5. Yegge, A Basic Guide to Valuing a Company (John Wiley & Sons Inc. 2002).

expressed as an equivalent income multiple. They are two sides of the same coin. In Party Time Inc.'s situation, the 13 percent capitalization rate was the equivalent of an income multiple of 7.69 (147,250/1,132,692). Thus, specifying an EBITDA income multiple of 7.69 is the equivalent of specifying a capitalization rate of 13 percent.

Hybrid Method. The hybrid method, in most situations, is a combination of the Adjusted Book Value Method and the capitalized earnings method illustrated in Chapter 3 (factor 9). A value is determined under each method and then the two values are weighted to arrive at a value for the business. For example, if a determination is made to base 20 percent of the value on the Adjusted Book Value Method and 80 percent on the capitalized earnings value, an amount equal to 20 percent of the Adjusted Book Value method would be added to an amount equal to 80 percent of the capitalized earnings value. The Hybrid Method works best in those situations where the business' value is attributable to a combination of asset values and the demonstrated earning capacity of the business.

Excess Earnings Method. This method incorporates the features of the Hybrid Method, but factors in the cost of carrying the assets of the business and financing impacts. The starting point is to multiply the "Net Tangible Assets" (aggregate fair market value of the tangible assets less liabilities) by a relevant applied lending interest rate to arrive at the annual cost of carrying the assets ("Cost of Money"). The designated income measure (EBITDA, for example) is reduced by the Cost of Money, and the result is divided by the designated capitalization rate to arrive at the business' "Intangible Value." The Intangible Value is then added to the Net Tangible Assets to arrive at the total value.

Discounted Cash Flow of Future Earnings. This method calculates the company's value by looking to the future. The applicable earnings measure (EBITDA, for example) is projected to increase at a given rate for a designated period of time, such as 10 years. The present value of the projected EBITDA in each of such years is then calculated by applying a discount rate that reflects the level of risk and uncertainty associated with the business and the time value of money. The present value determinations for each of the years are then added together to arrive at the business' value. When this method it used, often it is done to confirm the reasonableness of conclusions under one or more other methods.

STUDENT PROBLEM 6-1

Refer to the financial statements of Caterpillar Inc. set forth in Section D of Chapter 2, but ignore the reference that they are expressed in millions of dollars (that is, assume they are dollars only). Calculate the company's value as of December 31, 2012 under the following methods:

A. Book Value Method

B. Adjusted Book Value Method, assuming the following assets have the following values and each other asset has a value equal to its book value:

Inventories: $ 19,500

Property, Plant and Equipment: $ 26,000

Investments in Unconsolidated Affiliated Companies: $ 7,500

Goodwill: $ 49,000

Intangible Assets: $ 8,000

C. Capitalized earnings method based on the average consolidated profits before taxes for the last three years (2010 thru 2012) and a capitalization rate of 12.5 percent (equivalent to a multiplier of 8).

D. Hybrid of B and C, with 30 percent allocated to B and 70 percent allocated to C.

E. Excess earnings method based on consolidated profits before taxes in 2012, a 6.5 percent applied lending rate, and a 12.5 percent yield rate (capitalization rate). Assume the Net Intangible Assets total $ 23,500.

F. Discounted cash flow of future earnings method based on projections of consolidated profits before taxes for the next 10 years, assuming consolidated profits before taxes increase 8 percent each year and the risk-level return requirement is 18 percent.

CHAPTER 7

Basic Microeconomics Concepts

A. FOR LAWYERS?

Most lawyers should have at least a rudimentary understanding of elementary neoclassical microeconomics concepts. These are the supply and demand concepts that are so often used to justify or explain a specific event, decision, or course of action. For those who study antitrust, such an understanding is a must. But the need to know reaches far beyond those who seek a deeper knowledge of market inefficiencies and anticompetitive conduct. It extends to any lawyer who wants a basic understanding of how certain market forces work and how many business owners approach decisions to maximize profitability. The following short discussion explains and illustrates certain key concepts and the related vocabulary.

B. THE DEMAND SIDE

The law of demand is simple: if the price of a product increases, the demand for the product will decrease. Similarly, if the price is driven down, more consumers will be drawn to the product and the demand will increase. Anyone who shops understands this basic law. Of course, there are exceptions. Some products are so essential or attractive that certain consumers will pay whatever it takes to get them. Utilities are an example. The term used to describe the demand for these products is "inelastic" – price changes do not precipitate significant demand changes. In contrast, the demand for many products is deemed to be "elastic" – a change in price will trigger a significant change in demand. Many factors can impact the elasticity of a product, including the nature of the product (is it essential or a staple?), competitive products, the availability of substitutes, the strength of the brand, fads, and a host of other potential considerations.

A demand curve is commonly used to illustrate the demand for a seller's product at different price points at a fixed point in time. It assumes the seller has sufficient information to develop the curve and make rational profit-maximizing decisions based on the curve. Exhibit 4 is an example of three demand curves. The vertical axis in each curve reflects escalating prices, and the horizontal axis reflects increases in quantities. The curve represents the quantity demand at various price points. Given the law of demand itself, the curve generally has a negative slope.

Note the differences in the demand curves in Exhibit 1. The curve in the right margin is nearly vertical to reflect an inelastic demand and strong market power. With this curve, the seller knows that it can increase prices significantly and suffer only minor losses in volume. This is the monopolist's dream. The curve in the center reflects an elastic demand and limited market power. If the seller chooses to increase the price, there will be a significant drop in demand. Consumers will either opt for competitor products or substitutes or choose to go without.

Exhibit 1
Demand Curves

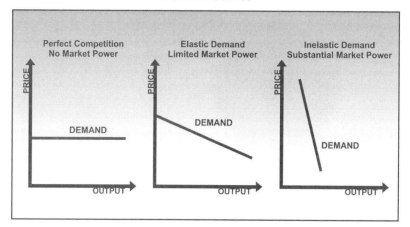

The curve to the far left reflects a state of pure competition and no market power. In this situation, the seller has no control over price because there is so much competition. The seller's entrance and exit from the market would have no impact on price. The price is established by the market and is not impacted by the seller's volume. Hence, a horizontal line is used to reflect the market price at all volumes. If the seller tries to sell at any price above the line, there will be no demand because other sellers will satisfy all demands of consumers at the market price. As described below, even in such a pure-competition condition, the model may still be used to identify the volume that will maximize profits for the seller.

In many situations, the demand curve is not a straight line. Exhibit 2 illustrates such a demand curve. As Exhibit 2 shows, at lower volumes, there may be significant market power, little elasticity, and thus a more vertical demand curve. A certain volume of customers may be willing to pay any price within a broad range to get the product. For example, it may be a niche market condition geared to a limited audience of discriminating buyers.

In order to move to higher volumes, the seller will have to compete with many more competitors or substitute products and attract customers who are far less discriminating and far more price conscious. The result is greater elasticity and a more horizontal curve at these higher volume levels.

Exhibit 2
Market Power Hypothetical Market

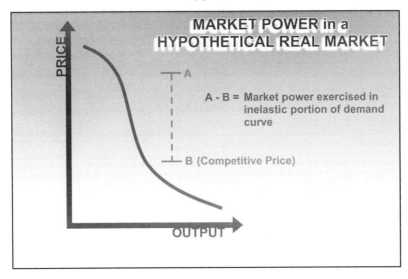

Marginal revenue is an important concept associated with demand curves. It can best be illustrated with an example. Assume that Judy has developed a new computer case and has determined that she can sell 10,000 units during a designated time frame if she prices the case at $100. Higher volumes will be realized as she lowers the price. Her findings are summarized in Exhibit 3.

Exhibit 3
Judy's Revenue Analysis

Total Unit Sales	10k	13k	16k	19k	22k	25k
Price Per Unit	$100	$90	$80	$72	$64	$57
Total Dollar Sales	1,000,000	1,170,000	1,280,000	1,368,000	1,408,000	1,425,000
Marginal Revenue Per Unit		$57	$37	$29	$13	$6

As the Exhibit indicates, a decrease in the price to $80, for example, would increase the sales volume to 16,000 units, and a price of $57 could push volumes to as high as 25,000 units. The last row on this exhibit reflects the marginal revenue per unit that would result from each price reduction and volume increase. The marginal revenue for each price change is calculated by dividing the projected increase in total sales by the projected increase in units sold (here 3,000 units).

Note, for example, that a reduction in price from $100 to $90 increases sales from 10,000 to 13,000 units and increases total revenues from $1 million to $1,170,000. This additional $170,000 of revenue translates to a marginal yield of $57 per unit (170,000/3,000) for each of the additional 3,000 units sold. The marginal revenue per unit number is far less than the sales price of $90 because all units, not just the additional 3,000 units, would be sold at the lower price of $90.

Note the impact of price and volume changes on marginal revenue per unit yields, as reflected on the last line of Exhibit 3. The marginal revenue per unit drops rapidly as prices decrease and volumes increase. This is because, as volumes increase, there is a disproportionately larger increase in the percentage of units that could be sold at higher price points. Thus, for example, as shown on Exhibit 6, a price reduction from $64 to $57 and a corresponding jump in volume from 22,000 units to 25,000 units generates a marginal revenue yield of only $6 per unit. For these reasons, the marginal revenue curve for a product (as shown on Exhibit 4) typically will descend much faster (be more vertical) than the product's demand curve.

Exhibit 4
Demand and Marginal Revenue Curves

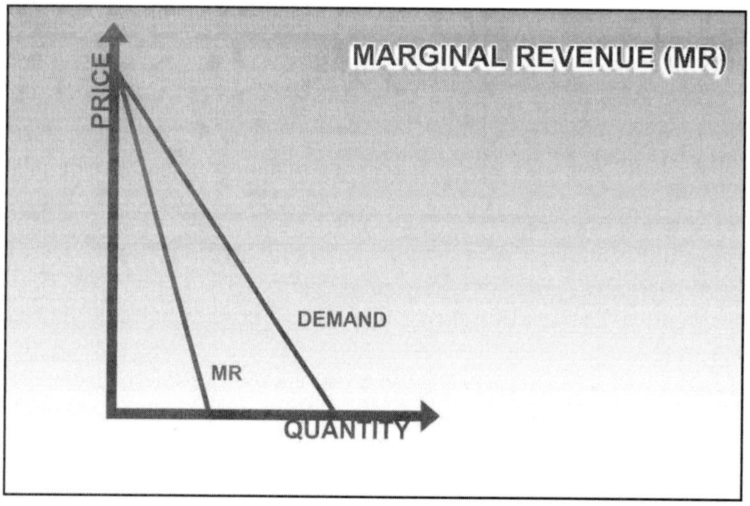

C. THE COST-SUPPLY SIDE

Let's turn to the cost side by again looking at Judy's situation. Judy first calculates her total projected costs at each volume level. These are reflected on line 6 of Exhibit 5 on the following page. Thus, for example, her costs would total $600,000 at a production level of 10,000 units and $980,000 at a projection level of 19,000 units. The average cost per unit at each production level (shown on line 5) is calculated by dividing total costs at that level by the number of units produced. Therefore, at 19,000 units, the average cost per unit is $52 (980,000/19,000).

The average cost per unit consists of two components. The first component is fixed costs, those costs that do not change as the volume increases. Examples include rent, insurance, professional fees and the like. The total fixed cost per unit drops as volumes increase because the fixed costs are spread over a greater number of units. Thus, as volumes increase, the fixed cost component will drive down the average per-unit cost.

Exhibit 5
Judy's Revenue and Cost Analysis

Total Unit Sales	10k	13k	16k	19k	22k	25k
Price Per Unit	$100	$90	$80	$72	$64	$57
Total Dollar Sales	1,000,000	1,170,000	1,280,000	1,368,000	1,408,000	1,425,000
Marginal Revenue Per Unit		$57	$37	$29	$13	$6
Average Cost Per Unit	$60	$59	$54	$52	$51	$53
Total Costs	600,000	765,000	860,000	980,000	1,120,000	1,330,000
Marginal Cost Last Unit		$52	$37	$43	$64	$78

The second component of average cost is the variable costs. These are the additional costs incurred to produce more units; they vary based on volume. Examples include raw materials, labor, and shipping expenses. The variable cost per unit at any production level is calculated by dividing the total variable costs at the level by the number of units produced.

If the variable cost per unit remains relatively constant, the fixed cost component will push average per-unit costs down as volumes increase.

But often the variable cost per unit starts to increase at higher levels that stretch capacities and trigger inefficiencies. A host of additional expenses may surface – more overtime pay, expanded rental facilities, more production errors, accelerated shipping needs, higher raw material costs, and the like.

If and when increases in the variable cost component exceed the fixed-cost-per-unit benefit, there will be an increase in the overall average cost per unit. Note in Judy's situation (line 5 of Exhibit 5) how the average cost per unit descends until the volume level hits 22,000 units, beyond which the average cost per unit starts to increase. Of course, in some situations the fixed cost component may be so dominant within the relevant volume ranges that variable expense hikes cannot trigger an increase in the average per-unit cost.

Closely related to variable cost is the concept of marginal cost. Marginal cost is the additional cost incurred to produce a single unit. Whereas variable cost focuses on the extra costs incurred to produce a designated quantity of units, marginal cost is focused on the cost of a single unit. In essence, variable cost for a designated number of units is the sum of the marginal costs for each of those units. As efficiencies kick in at higher volumes, the marginal cost per unit will decrease.

But as described above, costs may be pushed higher at certain volume levels, triggering increases in the marginal cost per unit. Line 7 of Exhibit 5 reflects Judy's marginal per unit costs at designated volume levels. Note how they descend until the volume level hits 16,000, at which point they start to increase.

Exhibit 6
Average and Marginal Cost Curves

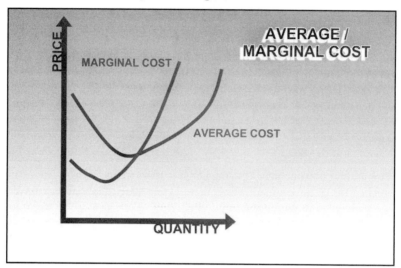

Exhibit 6 reflects average and marginal per-unit cost curves at various price and quantity levels. Note how they descend, bottom out, and then start to increase. Because marginal per-unit costs (unlike average per-unit costs) do not factor in the per-unit benefits of the fixed cost component, the average cost curve bottoms out at a higher volume level and then increases at a more modest pace. This is certainly true in Judy's situation. Compare line 5 (average cost) with line 7 (marginal cost) in Exhibit 5.

D. PROFIT MAXIMIZATION

Judy is now in a position to determine what price point and corresponding sales volume will maximize her profitability. She does this by subtracting her total costs from total revenues at each price point level. The bottom line of Exhibit 7 shows these results. It indicates that her profits will be maximized at a price of $80 and a projected sales volume of 16,000 units.

Note that this profit maximization point is the intersection of Judy's marginal revenue and marginal cost points, both $37 at the 16,000 volume level. Up to this point, each unit sale produced revenue that exceeded the cost to produce the unit, thus adding to the profitability of the enterprise. Any sale beyond this point triggers a marginal cost in excess of the corresponding marginal revenue, thereby reducing overall profits.

A monopolist with market power will always seek to maximize profits by selling up to, but not beyond, the point where the marginal per-unit cost equals marginal per-unit revenue. Graphically, this is represented by Exhibit 8, which shows the demand, marginal revenue, and marginal cost curves. The marginal cost and marginal revenue curves intersect at quantity "q" (16,000 units in Judy's situation) and price "p" ($80 in Judy's situation).

Exhibit 7
Judy's Revenue, Cost and Profit Analysis

	10k	13k	16k	19k	22k	25k
Total Unit Sales	10k	13k	16k	19k	22k	25k
Price Per Unit	$100	$90	$80	$72	$64	$57
Total Dollar Sales	1,000,000	1,170,000	1,280,000	1,368,000	1,408,000	1,425,000
Marginal Revenue Per Unit		$57	$37	$29	$13	$6
Average Cost Per Unit	$60	$59	$54	$52	$51	$53
Total Costs	600,000	765,000	860,000	980,000	1,120,000	1,330,000
Marginal Cost Last Unit		$52	$37	$43	$64	$78
Profits	400,000	405,000	420,000	388,000	288,000	95,000

↑
Maximized

Exhibit 8
Market Power Profit Maximization Price and Quantity

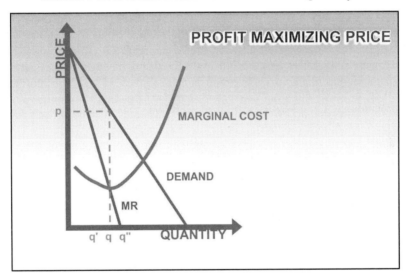

Now let's switch gears and assume that Judy has no real market power. She is in a highly competitive market with many sellers and competing products. Assume further that the established market price for a case is $64, and any attempt to sell above that price will generate no significant demand. Exhibit 9 on the following page reflects Judy's situation under this scenario.

Note that her sales price and marginal revenue will be $64 at all volume levels because her volumes will have no impact on the market price. The only real question for Judy is: What volume will maximize profits? Profit maximization will occur at that volume where her marginal per-unit cost equals the established market demand price (which is also her marginal per-unit revenue). As Exhibit 9 indicates, Judy would maximize profits by selling 22,000 units. Any unit sale beyond this point would reduce profitability by triggering marginal costs in excess of marginal revenues.

Exhibit 9
Judy's Profit Analysis with No Market Power

Total Unit Sales	10k	13k	16k	19k	22k	25k
Price Per Unit	$64	$64	$64	$64	$64	$64
Total Dollar Sales	640,000	832,000	1,024,000	1,216,000	1,408,000	1,600,000
Marginal Revenue Per Unit		$64	$64	$64	$64	$64
Average Cost Per Unit	$60	$59	$54	$52	$51	$53
Total Costs	600,000	765,000	860,000	980,000	1,120,000	1,330,000
Marginal Cost Last Unit		$52	$37	$43	$64	$78
Profits	40,000	67,000	164,000	236,000	288,000	270,000

↑

Maximized

We are now ready for a little (very little!) antitrust theory. Most now agree that the social objectives of antitrust are to promote the efficient allocation of goods and services; to prevent "deadweight loss," the loss that results when restricted output limits access to products and services; to stop "wealth transfer," the transfer of wealth from consumers to those who exercise market power to limit or restrict competitive conditions; and to promote "dynamic efficiency," the development of new products, innovations and technologies. Of far less concern, although once deemed the essence of antitrust, are desires to decentralize power and to protect market entry for individual firms. Now all have pretty much accepted the reality that big is not bad when it promotes efficiency and innovation and produces no serious signs of deadweight loss or wealth transfer. It is against these fundamental objectives that each gray issue must ultimately be tested.

The comparative profit maximization conclusions for Judy under the alternative market-power and no-market-power scenarios described above (Exhibit 7 versus Exhibit 9) demonstrate the market inefficiencies of deadweight loss and wealth transfer. With the market power to set her price, Judy will set a price of $80 and restrict output to 16,000 units in order to maximize profits. With no market power and a competitive market price of $64, she will maximize profits by producing 22,000 units. The difference in volumes under the two scenarios (6,000 units) is the deadweight loss, the units that never get to customers under the market power scenario. Exhibit 10 reflects this graphically, with "Qm" being the market power quantity (16,000 units in Judy's situation), and "Qc" being the competitive no-market-power quantity (22,000 units in Judy's situation).

Exhibit 10
Profit Maximization – Deadweight Loss

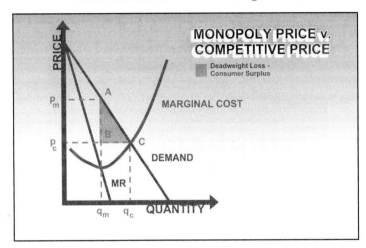

The difference in price under the two scenarios ($16 per unit) is the wealth transfer, the additional transfer of wealth from consumers to the seller with market power. Exhibit 11 reflects this graphically, with "Pm" being the market-power price ($80 in Judy's case) and "Pc" being the competitive no-market-power price ($64 in Judy's situation).

Exhibit 11
Profit Maximization – Wealth Transfer

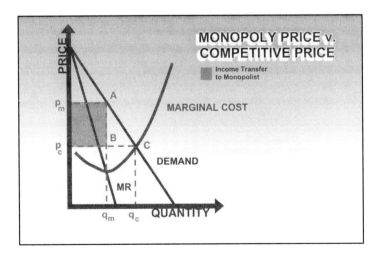

STUDENT PROBLEM 7-1

Judy, our computer case designer, has carefully studied the foregoing discussion and has some questions. Provide her answers to the following:

1. Under the market power scenario, will profits always be maximized at the volume that yields the lowest marginal cost per unit?

2. Is an average variable cost curve the same as a marginal cost curve? If not, how do they differ?

3. Under what conditions will the price of a product be the same as the marginal revenue generated from a sale of the product?

4. Will a seller with market power ever prefer a demand curve that is not highly vertical?

5. What impact will very high fixed costs have on an average cost curve?

CHAPTER 8

FUNDING THE ENTERPRISE

———

A. PUBLIC COMPANIES

Very few companies seriously consider "going public" – having their stock owned and regularly traded by a large number of public shareholders. Most businesses are just too small or not suited for public ownership and the associated regulatory hassles and horrendous expenses. The few that do succeed with an initial public offering (IPO) play in a different league and daily live with pressures, expectations and protocols that are foreign to those who run closely held enterprises.

1. PROS AND CONS OF BEING A PUBLIC COMPANY

The advantages of being a public company are compelling. The owners have liquid stock that facilitates the rapid growth and diversification of their wealth. The company has a larger, stronger capital base to fuel growth, pursue new ventures, or expand through the acquisition of other companies. The compensation paid to the corporation's executives often increases dramatically though higher salaries, bigger bonuses and stock equity incentives. There is often a perception that the prestige and presence of the entire enterprise and those who work for it has been pushed to a whole new level.

Balanced against these advantages are risks, pressures, hassles, and costs that must be carefully considered and planned for. The pressure to show strength of earnings and growth is relentless and never-ending. It's all about the short-term, the here and now. The investing public, primarily though their guardians, the brokerage community, will scrutinize results and ask the tough questions. The challenges of public disclosure and confidentiality will demand serious time and attention to avoid litigation burdens that often accompany bad disclosures or breached confidences. Accounting, audit, internal control, and regulatory reporting and compliance pressures will balloon at all levels. Management will be directly accountable to an active board of directors, partially comprising outside, independent members who will be the sole players on the all-important audit and compensation subcommittees. Sales and purchases of company stock by corporate executives will have to be publicly reported and carefully monitored to avoid securities law liability risks.

And then there are the costs – the costs to go public and the ongoing increased costs that come with being a public company. The baseline upfront costs to go public include substantial legal fees for a host of items, including preparation of the registration statement and securities law compliance, accounting and audit fees, printing costs, and various others direct fees and costs that are incurred during the launch period, which typically runs six to nine months. In a survey of 26 companies that went public during the 2009 to 2011 timeframe, Ernst & Young LLP[1] found that the companies, on average, engaged 11 third-party advisors in connection with the their IPOs, including investment bankers, attorneys, auditors, printers, D&O insurance carriers, stock transfer agents, Sarbanes-Oxley consultants, compensation advisors, investor relations firms, tax advisors, road show consultants, compensation advisors to the board, and internal audit advisors. On average, the surveyed companies spent $13 million in one-time advisory costs associated with executing the IPO. Of course, the core offering costs will typically be much less in smaller offerings. But the bottom line is always the same – the up-front costs of an IPO, which are not predicated on a successful offering, are very expensive. And beyond these direct getting-started costs are the indirect and opportunity costs of personnel and management time and the substantial commissions and expenses that must be paid to those who sell the stock in the offering.

As for the additional costs that come with being a public company, in the same survey Ernst & Young reported that new public companies, on average, incur additional ongoing costs (not related to the IPO) of approximately $2.5 million a year as public companies. Of this amount, $1.5 million is attributable to executive compensation and directors' benefits, and the remaining $1 million represents increased compliance costs.

2. GOING PUBLIC PROCESS

What does the process of going public involve? The starting point is a determination that the company is a good candidate for an initial public offering. This often requires discussions with consultants, underwriters, accountants and attorneys to assess the state of the market and the appeal of the company. The focus is on the proven ability of the company to maintain consistent growth, the experience and track records of the management team, the type of product or service offered by the company (the "hotter" the better), how the company stacks up against its competition, and whether the audit and internal control requirements for a public offering have been or can be satisfied.

Although the IPO process itself may run three or four months, usually it takes at least a year or two to prepare for the process. During this preparatory phase, the company must develop the capacities and tools to operate as a public company. These require a management team that instills confidence and has a demonstrated capacity to manage a public company, strong corporate governance procedures, qualified outside board members, proven internal control systems, solid accounting and audit histories, performance ratios that meet or beat established benchmarks and key competitors, reduced debt loads, and a

---

1. Ernst & Young IPO Cost Survey, November 2011. Ernst & Young is a global leader in assurance, tax, transaction and advisory services that employs 141,000 people worldwide.

convincing and engaging story of present and future success.

Timing is always a critical issue. Market conditions are often the most compelling factor. Smart timing creates the opportunity for an optimal yield from the offering, the development of a solid trading history after the offering, and strong upside potential for investors. Many factors can impact an IPO timing decision, including political events, interest rates, inflation projections, economic forecasts, and the performance of other companies in the same sector. Impatient gun-jumping fueled by a need for capital and an over-anxious management team can lead to poor stock prices, a disappointing or disastrous aftermarket or, in extreme situations, a complete failed offering.

A key challenge is to get an underwriter committed to the offering. Often the creatability and experience of the management team is the primary factor in attracting a quality underwriter. And, of course, size matters. Most companies who are seriously exploring a public offering have annual sales of at least $100 million. It's often impossible to reasonably justify the increased costs and regulatory burdens of being a public company when the annual sales drop much below this threshold. In select situations, an underwriter may have an interest in smaller companies that have a cutting edge product and promise sustained, extreme annual growth (say, 25 percent) for the next five years.

The registration statement is always a major challenge in an initial public offering. It must be carefully drafted to include the history of the company, details related to the market for the product or services offered by the company, how the proceeds of the offering are going to be used, the risk factors that accompany an investment in the company, the backgrounds of the officers and directors, any transactions with related parties, the identifies of any major shareholders, and more. Of course, audited financial statements must be included in the registration statement. Once completed, the registration statement is submitted to the Securities and Exchange Commission for review.

The selling begins when the registration statement is approved and the offering is effective. Usually there are multiple steps in the selling process that require constant input and monitoring from professionals who have proven IPO track records. Often a key to the sales effort is a high-quality "road show" that smartly and quickly lays out key facts and stimulates investor interest in the company. An institutional investor generally has no interest in visiting a company that it might select for its portfolio. It will want an informative presentation at a convenient (and usually private) road show meeting that gives it an opportunity to ask questions, size up management, and obtain what it needs to make an investment decision. This is the ideal time (often the only time) for the company's senior management to communicate directly with potential investors. Usually the sales presentation is carefully scripted in various formats (everything from a full-blown presentation to a two-minute pitch) to accommodate different sales opportunities.

When the offering wraps up and the money has arrived, the market reaction, governance, management, performance, disclosure, and compliance challenges of being a public company take center stage. The importance and complexity of these challenges should not be understated. They set the stage for the future and require critical advance planning.

3. PUBLIC MARKETS: FACTORS AND LINGO

A lawyer should have a basic understanding of the public markets and the terms that are commonly used to refer to various elements and strategies that are part of such markets.

a. Stock Markets

A stock market is a network of economic transactions in which buyers and sellers deal in securities that are listed on a stock exchange or that trade in private transactions. Escalating stock market prices are considered primary indicators of a strong and growing economy, an increase in business investment, and improving household incomes and consumption.

Often stock markets and the prices of specific stocks are heavily influenced by news of economic and financial developments that have no direct connection to the markets or the stocks. Rumors, press releases, announcements, political showdowns, wild speculations and many other factors can trigger massive reactions and big price swings that usually open up short-term profit opportunities for experienced investors who have the capacity and knowledge to take advantage of the situation.

A stock market crash occurs when negative economic factors precipitate a rapid loss in the confidence of the investing public, panic selling that feeds on itself, and steep declines in stock prices across the board. Famous stock market crashes include the Wall Street crash of 1929, the crash of 1973-74, the Black Monday crash of 1987, the Dot-Com Bubble Bust of 2000, and the Market Crash of 2008.

The last two crashes are painful, recent reminders of how brutal stock markets can be in destroying savings programs and retirement hopes. The Dot-Com Bubble Bust of 2000 began as some, then many, and then all concluded that the future profitability expectations of new investments were grossly overoptimistic, particularly those related to the technology and dot.com boom. Foreign capital began to disappear and stock markets crashed as spending and demand plummeted, companies quickly found themselves swimming in excess manufacturing capacity, venture capital was nearly impossible to find, and monthly investment statements became something to hide from. The tech-heavy Nasdaq Composite lost 78 percent of its value in a few short years, and even the stalwart S&P 500 got hammered, losing 49 percent of its value during the same time frame. Trillions of dollars in equity value quickly vanished in a few short years following the bubble's burst.

Slowly, the return began and then strengthened, strongly prodded by big tax cuts and the lowest interest rates most could ever remember. Foreigners fueled the recovery with serious capital, and all was back on track again until everything crashed again in 2008 and millions of investors lost big. Stock markets again recovered as the government and the Federal Reserve have kept money flowing by cutting short-term interest rates to nearly zero, driving up annual federal deficits to unprecedented trillion-dollar levels that no one could have imagined before 2009, and pumping trillions into the economy through the Federal Reserve's "quantitative easing" programs.

These measures have demonstrated that stock markets will respond to serious stimulus even as the economy continues to struggle. The big question now is whether these measures are just fueling another artificial stock market bubble that is doomed to burst and quickly wipeout major portions of all stock portfolios. What frightens many is that, as the stock market has flourished, the root causes of the 2008 crash – gross, irresponsible over-leveraging at many levels and a resulting massive drop in demand – have left us with a pitifully slow, anemic recovery, chronically high real unemployment numbers, countless business failures, no growth in real income levels, a labor force participation rate that hovers at a 40-year low, and an across-the-board loss in confidence and hope for the future.

b. Stock Exchange

A stock exchange provides a marketplace for trading securities, commodities, derivatives and other financial instruments and serves as a clearing house to ensure that shares are delivered and payments are made. The primary function of an exchange is to facilitate fair and orderly trading, the timely and efficient dissemination of pricing and other information, and the establishment of exchange rules that bind all participants. An exchange may be an electronic platform or a physical location where traders meet to conduct business on a "trading floor." Technology advances have proliferated the development of electronic exchanges.

An exchange specifies listing requirements that must be satisfied in order for a company to offer its securities on the exchange. Listing requirements can be stringent. For example, the New York Stock Exchange requires a company to have at least 1.1 million shares held by the public and a market value of public shares equal to at least $100 million and to meet specified alternative income, valuation, or asset tests. Listing requirements vary among exchanges, but significant exchanges uniformly require regular financial reports and audited financial statements.

Today, there are more than a hundred stock and derivatives exchanges, in over 140 countries. The five largest exchanges (market capitalization as of December 31, 2013) are the New York Stock Exchange (market cap in excess of $17.9 trillion), NASDAQ (market cap in excess of $6 trillion), Tokyo Stock Exchange (market cap in excess of $4.5 trillion), London Stock Exchange Group, and Euronext Exchange (market cap in excess of $3.5 trillion).[2]

c. Stock Indexes

A stock index tracks the movements of various stock values throughout

---

2. World Federation of Exchanges, January 2014 Report.

every business day. Usually one can't avoid hearing of the most popular three indexes: the Dow Jones Industrial Average (an index based on 30 stocks); the NASDAQ (which tracks thousands of stocks, many in the technology and communication sectors); and the S&P 500 (an index based on 500 stocks traded on the New York Stock exchange). Other less visible, but highly regarded, comprehensive indexes include the NYSE Composite Index (which includes all NYSE-listed stocks, including foreign stocks, American Depositary Receipts, and real estate investment trusts, but excludes closed-end funds, ETFs, limited partnerships and derivatives), the Wilson 5000 Equity Index (which represents stocks of nearly every publicly traded company in the United States, including U.S. stocks traded on the New York Stock Exchange, NASDAQ and the American Stock Exchange), and the Russell 2000 Index (which tracks 2,000 stocks traded on the over-the-counter ("OTC") market).

Stock market indexes are classified in various ways. A "world" or "global" index, such as the MSCI World or the S&P Global 100, includes large companies without regard to where they are domiciled or traded. "National" indexes, such as the American S&P 500, the British FTSE 100, or the Japanese Nikkei 225, are designed to showcase the stock market performance of a given nation and generally are the most quoted indexes.

d. Transaction Processing

The purchase or sale of a security often requires that an investor do nothing more than place a call to his or her broker or click a few buttons on a website. As simple as it is to initiate a transaction, the market structures used to price and process an order and promote orderliness and stability in the marketplace are quite complicated. Orders are processed one of two ways: through an exchange or over the counter (OTC).

An exchange centralizes the communication of bid and ask prices to all direct market participants through various means, which (depending on the exchange) may include a discrete electronic message, voice message, hand signal, or computer-generated command. When two parties reach agreement, the price of the transaction is communicated throughout the market to ensure market pricing transparency to all participants. Clearing facilities closely linked to the exchange handle the post-trade mechanics of securities and derivative orders traded on the exchange.

Over-the-counter markets deal primarily with securities that are not listed on an exchange. Dealers act as market makers by quoting bid and ask prices to other dealers and to their clients or customers, and the quoted prices may vary among different customers. Dealer communications may be by phone, mass e-mail messages, or instant messaging, and sometimes involve the use of electronic bulletin boards that post dealer quotes. In an OTC customer market, trading occurs between dealers and their customers, with dealers often initiating customer contact through electronic messages (called "dealer-runs") that list various securities and derivatives and the prices at which they are willing to buy or sell them. In an OTC interdealer market, dealers often have direct phone lines with each other that make it possible to quickly communicate with several dealers in a matter of seconds. In OTC markets, other market participants generally have no access to the details of a trade (although some OTC markets post execution prices and order sizes after the fact), and the clearing and settlement chores are handled by the buyer and seller firms. Compared to exchange markets, OTC markets are subject to fewer rules, are far less transparent, and are more likely to encounter liquidity or clearing problems.

Improved electronic trading platforms have enabled dealers and select nondealers in some OTC markets to submit quotes and execute trades directly through an electronic system. This exchange-like evolution may facilitate some multilateral trading among direct participants, but does not offer the access, transparency and settlement guarantees of an exchange.

Following are brief descriptions of a few common terms used in the trading process.

- **Bid vs. Ask Price.** The bid price is the maximum price that a buyer is willing to pay for a security, whereas the ask price represents the minimum price that a seller is willing to accept for a security. Since a transaction occurs when a buyer and seller agree on a price, the size of the gap between a stock's bid and ask price, generally referred to as "the spread," is a key indicator of how difficult it is to convert a security to cash; the smaller the spread, the greater the liquidity.

- **Market vs. Limit Orders.** A market order is an order to buy or sell a security at the best available price at the time the order is executed. Absent an availability or liquidity problem, fulfillment of the order is assured, but the price is not. A limit order specifies a maximum price for buying a security and the minimum price for selling a security. The price will not exceed the designated maximum buy price or be less than the specified minimum sell price, but there is no assurance that the order will be filled.

- **Round Lot vs. Odd Lot vs. Block Trade.** A round lot is 100 shares of a stock, or any number of shares that can be evenly divided by 100, and is considered a "normal trading unit." An odd lot is any order involving less than 100 shares. A mixed lot consists of both a round lot and a mixed lot (e.g. 250 shares). Commissions on an odd lot order may be higher due to specified minimums of a brokerage firm or the need to "bunch" the odd lot order with other orders to facilitate a trade. Online trading opportunities and resulting drops in trading commissions have made it easier and less expensive to fulfill odd lot orders. A "block trade" or "block order" is a large transaction (at least 10,000 shares but usually much larger) at a negotiated price between parties (usually institutional investors or hedge funds acting through investment banks or other intermediaries) outside of the open markets in order to reduce market impacts.

- **Upstairs vs. Downstairs Markets.** The upstairs market refers to the trading of securities away from an exchange, in the "upstairs trading room" of a brokerage firm. It's typically done between two brokers-dealers in an over-the-counter market transaction. The downstairs market refers to trading on an exchange or its electronic counterpart.

- **Brokerage Firm and Clearing Firm.** A brokerage firm initiates and negotiates orders and trades. The completion of a transaction requires a "clearing" process, which requires a matching of trades, delivery of the securities or book entry of ownership, and settlement of accounts between financial institutions. A small percentage of brokerage firms clear their own transactions. Exchanges and most firms use a separate clearing house to handle the clearing functions.

- **Confirmation and Settlement.** The execution of an order to buy or sell a security will trigger the sending of a trade confirmation by mail or email to the person who placed the order. This document is to confirm that the order was filled by the broker in accordance with the instructions given. The confirmation will typically include: the name of the security, applicable ticker symbol, and CUSIP number; total number of shares bought or sold; the cost or selling price per share; the commission paid; the trade execution date; the settlement date; the gross value of the transaction; the net value of the transaction after deducting brokerage commissions; the account number related to the trade; and order type (market or limit). Confirmations should be retained for tax and other purposes, and any detected error should be immediately reported to the broker. The settlement date is the date the transaction is completed and all payments must be made. The settlement date is usually three business days after the trade is executed for stock and bond transactions and the next business day for government securities and options.

e. Market Trading Breakers

Decades ago, the New York Stock Exchange put in place circuit breakers to reduce short-term market volatility by forcing a pause in trading and giving investors time to assimilate incoming information during a period of rapid market declines. In 2012, the SEC approved amendments to Exchange Rule 80B (Trading Halts Due to Extraordinary Market Volatility) that established new Level I, 2, and 3 trading breaks, triggered by declines in the S&P 500 index. A 7-percent decline between 9:30 a.m. and 3:25 p.m. will trigger a Level 1 break to halt trading for 15 minutes. Following the reopening, there can be no more Level 1 breaks during the day, but a 13-percent decline will trigger a 15-minute Level 2 halt. Following that reopening, there will be no more Level 2 breaks during the day, but a 20-percent drop will trigger a Level 3 halt in trading for the remainder of the day.

f. Derivatives

Financial instruments generally fall into one of three categories: equities (stocks), debt (bonds and mortgages), and derivatives. A derivative is a financial contract between two parties that derives its value from the performance of specified assets, which may be commodities, stocks, bonds, currencies or interest rates. The asset that governs the value of a derivative is generally referred to as the "underlying." There are various types of derivatives, which create different rights and obligations. Examples include:

- **Options**, where one party has the right, but no obligation, to buy or sell a specific security at a specified price (the strike price) on a specified future date;

- **Futures Contracts**, where a party is obligated to buy or sell a financial instrument or commodity at a specified price on a specified future date under a detailed standardized contract that facilitates trading on a futures exchange;

- **Forward Contracts**, where a party is obligated to buy or sell an asset at a specified price on a specified future date under a customized contract (any commodity, price, and delivery date) that is not suitable for trading on an exchange;

- **Swaps**, the exchange of one security, currency or interest rate for another, usually prompted by changed investment objectives;

- **Collateral Mortgage Obligations**, complicated financial instruments that enable investors to participate in the cash flow of a "pool" of mortgages through a special purpose entity that offers different "tranches" with varying repayment risks, interest rates, and maturities;

- **Warrants**, the right to buy securities, usually stocks, at a specified price within a certain timeframe that is longer than normal options periods and often attached as an enhancement to a bond or other financial instrument.

Derivatives generally are used for one of two very different purposes: as a risk-management tool to hedge against future losses resulting from changes in the value of the underlying commodity or financial instrument, or as a tool to accelerate speculation by quickly and efficiently obtaining a significant (and often high-risk) position in the underlying commodity or financial instrument.

Exchange-traded derivatives (ETDs) are traded on an exchange (e.g., the Chicago Mercantile Exchange), and over-the-counter (OTC) derivatives are traded through a dealer network.

g. Mutual Funds

A mutual fund is a pool of investment capital that thousands of investors, large and small, create by mutually contributing their savings. A professional manager then invests the funds in accordance with the stated objectives of the fund. The manager and all expenses of running the fund are paid out of the fund. A person can participate in some funds by investing a modest sum upfront and then adding as little as $50 or more to the account each month. A major advantage is instant diversification – each investor has a financial interest in every one of the fund's investments. Plus, the investor gets professional management and avoids the commissions and hassles of trading individual stocks and bonds. Mutual funds do not trigger double tax burdens like a regular C corporation (see Chapter 9), but their income from investments (interest and dividends) and capital gains (both long- and short- term) are distributed and taxed to those who own shares in the fund, and this pass-through tax consequence reduces the yield and requires planning.

In 2010, the U.S. Statistical abstract reported that there were over 7,500 mutual funds that managed more than $11.8 trillion. Today, mutual funds are the vehicles that most investors use to purchase interests in corporate stocks and bonds. Each fund is characterized by its investment objective, and the range of investment objectives is huge. There are blue chip stock funds, international funds, sector funds, asset allocation funds, bond funds – a lengthy list. There are families of funds, which are large groups of funds with different investment objectives offered by a single fund company. Examples include Fidelity, Vanguard and Dreyfus. A person who invests with such a fund family can easily move money from fund to fund within the family at little or no cost.

Mutual funds are classified in different ways:

- **Load vs. No-Load**. A "no-load" fund means that no commissions are being paid to someone for selling the fund's shares. A person can buy the "no-load" shares directly from the fund company or through a firm that offers "no-load" funds. "Load" funds use a part of the investment to pay a commission to a salesperson.

- **Open-End vs. Closed-End**. An open-end mutual fund, the most common, continually takes on new investment capital until the manager shuts off additional investments. There is no set maximum. At the end of each day, the fund's net asset value (NAV) is calculated by dividing the closing market value of the fund's investments by the shares outstanding. The NAV is the price at which investors buy ("bid price") fund shares from a fund company and sell shares ("redemption price") to a fund company. A closed-end fund has a fixed maximum amount of capital. Once the maximum is hit, no more capital flows into the fund, and the fund's shares are traded and valued like a stock. As such, the price of a closed-end fund's shares is a function of supply and demand for those shares at a given point in time and may trade at a discount or premium to the fund's NAV.

- **Managed vs. Indexed.** A "Managed" mutual fund is managed by a professional group that works to get the best possible return. Often one hears of funds boasting of beating the S&P 500 Index or the Dow Jones. An "Index" fund just mirrors an index. For example, an S&P Index Fund buys and holds the 500 stocks that make up the S&P 500. It'll never beat or loose to the index; it is the index. Why would one want an indexed fund? It offers some advantages. There's no need to fret over the fund manager's expertise, competence or track record. There are many fewer transactions in an index fund, so an investor pays fewer capital gains while in the fund. The total expenses of operating an index fund often are far less than a managed fund. And a person knows going in that he or she will never lose to the index.

h. Exchange-Traded Funds

An exchange-traded fund (ETF) typically tracks an index, a commodity or a group of assets, but trades like a stock and thus gives investors the opportunity to take advantage of price changes that occur throughout a day, sell short, buy on margin, and otherwise deal with the EFT as they would any stock. Thus, an EFT provides an active, experienced investor the diversification benefits of a mutual fund but with far more trading flexibility. Unlike an open-end mutual fund, ETF transactions that occur during a day are not priced by a net-asset-value calculation at the end of the day. In comparing an ETF to a closed-end mutual fund, both trade like a stock but EFT pricing generally is more transparent, less volatile, and typically will stay much closer (usually within 1 percent) to the net asset value of the fund.

ETFs have continued to grow in popularity since the 1993 release of the first ETF, Spider (SRDR), which tracks the S&P 500 index. The growth is attributable to professional investors and active traders who want low fund expenses and stock-like features and who can bear the significant brokerage commissions associated with ETF investing. This commission burden usually makes indexed mutual funds more suitable for small or passive investors. Although most ETFs are tied to an index, in 2008 the SEC authorized the creation of actively managed ETFs.

i. Hedge Funds

A hedge fund is a company, typically a limited partnership or a limited liability company, that uses professional management to invest and manage capital provided by sophisticated, accredited investors. A hedge fund differs from a mutual fund in various key respects: it is not sold or offered to the general public; it uses leveraging techniques; it invests in a broad range of liquid securities and employs a variety of investment techniques to generate positive yields whether markets are rising or falling; its managers often invest heavily in the fund; and it generally can avoid most (but of late, not all) of the oversight and other regulatory burdens applicable to mutual funds and investment companies. The word "hedge" refers to the techniques traditionally used by hedge funds to balance investments in minimizing (hedging) loss exposures, but today hedging is only one technique, not the primary focus, of the investment programs of many hedge funds.

Hedge funds typically are open-ended, permitting investors to make additions or withdrawals periodically. Additions and withdrawals are based on the fund's net asset value, which reflects the current value of the investment assets in the fund and the liabilities and expenses of the fund. Expenses include annual management fees, which typically are based on a percentage (e.g., 1 percent) of the fund's assets and performance bonus incentives.

j. REITs

A real estate investment trust (REIT) is a company (usually a corporation) that owns and often operates various types of income-producing real estate, including office buildings, shopping centers, apartments, warehouses, hotels, hospitals and more. Generally, a REIT is to real estate what a mutual fund is to stocks. It makes it possible for thousands of investors to pool their capital and enjoy the benefits of a diversified and professionally managed real estate portfolio. Many REITs are publicly traded and listed on stock exchanges. REITs are generally classified as equity (those that own real estate properties), mortgage (those that provide real estate financing), and hybrid (those that own equities and provide financing).

The REIT concept was pioneered in the United States, but has now been adopted by many countries. The result is a growing awareness and acceptance of global real estate securities, various REIT indexes (including the global FTSE EPRA/NAREIT Global Real Estate Index Series), and hundreds of public real estate companies in over 37 countries.

In the United States, REITs have their own tax provisions, found in sections 856 through 859 of the Internal Revenue Code. These provisions require that a REIT currently distribute at least 90 percent of its earnings to its shareholders, but provide the REIT with a deduction for all amounts distributed to shareholders. Thus, a REIT is able to avoid the double tax risks and burdens of a regular C corporation (see Chapter 9).

k. Common Trading Strategies and Related Terms

Following are brief descriptions of common terms used to describe various stock trading strategies. Descriptions of common terms related to bonds and bond investing are included in Section C of Chapter 4.

- **Buying Long or Long Position.** Investing in a security, currency or commodity with the expectation that the asset's value will increase over time.

- **Selling Short or Short Position.** Selling borrowed stock at the current market price with the expectation that the price will fall and the borrowed stock will be repaid at a cost that is less than the yield from the stock sale. The bet is on the downside. If the price drops, short selling produces a profit; if it rises, short selling produces a loss. The borrowed stock typically is provided by the short investor's brokerage firm that holds house or client shares that are available for lending to short sellers. The borrowed shares are essential to prevent illegal "naked" shorting, the selling of a shares that do not exist. An investor closes out a short position by "covering," the term used to describe the buying and returning of the borrowed shares. Short selling sometimes can be used to manipulate and drive down the price of a thinly traded security or can be used as a destructive piling-on strategy to enhance pressure on a stock whose price is falling. For these reasons, markets are subject to important restrictions that define when and how a short sale can occur, and some markets prohibit short selling.

- **Margin Buying.** Buying a security with borrowed funds on the bet that the yield from the investment will exceed the interest cost of the borrowed funds. Brokerage firms typically provide investors the option to borrow against the value of their existing portfolio account to finance margin buying activities. Regulations limit the amount of such borrowing. The maximum margin leverage permitted in the United States is 50 percent, a percentage that must be maintained if account values drop. Thus, a drop in an investor's portfolio value may trigger a "margin call," a demand that cash be added to the account or that account assets be sold to reduce the debt and protect the brokerage firm's loan position.

- **Call Option.** A contractual right, but not an obligation, to buy a security, commodity or financial instrument, at a fixed price (the "strike price") on or before a designated expiration date. An American call option may be exercised anytime before the expiration date; a European call option may be exercised only on the expiration date. Standard short-term stock options usually expire in 30 days, and long-term options may run as long as 30 months. The buyer of the option pays a premium for the option right and is betting that the price of the asset will sufficiently increase to generate a positive yield from selling or exercising the option. The seller of the option is willing to surrender any value in excess of the strike price for the premium received. A call option will not be exercised unless the price of the underlying asset exceeds the strike price. Thus, a call option is deemed to be "in-the-money" when the price of the underlying asset exceeds the strike price and is "out-of-the-money" until that point.

- **Put Option.** A contractual right, but not an obligation, to sell a security, commodity or financial instrument, at a fixed price (the "strike price") on or before a designated expiration date. It's the reverse of a call option. A premium is paid to protect against a decline in the price of the underlying asset. If the price does not fall below the strike price, the put will not be exercised. As with a call option, an American put may be exercised anytime before the expiration date, and a European put may be exercised only on the expiration date. The buyer of the put seeks protection against a price drop. The seller of the put is willing to take the downside risk for the premium received. A put option is "in-the-money" when the price of the underlying asset drops below the strike price and is "out-of-the-money" until that point.

- **Collar.** A strategy designed to lock-in existing values and protect against future price declines by simultaneously purchasing an out-of-the-money put option and selling an out-of-the-money call option. The put option protects against price declines, and the premium received from the sale of the call option covers all or a portion of the premium paid for the put option. A collar surrenders upside potential for downside protection.

- **Dollar Cost Averaging.** A strategy, often used in connection with mutual funds, that invests the same amount of funds periodically, usually quarterly or monthly. This form of automatic investing ignores market price swings and ensures over time that investment costs will reflect of average of a market's up and down movements.

- **Arbitrage.** A strategy to purchase a security on one market for immediate resale on another market to take advantage of price discrepancies in the markets. The goal of a pure arbitrage is to generate a profit without taking any risk. If, for example, a stock's price on an exchange is not aligned with a futures contract for the same stock, a short sale of the more expensive and a simultaneous purchase of the other could yield an instant profit with no risk. Market efficiencies generally make it impossible for retail investors to spot or capitalize on pure arbitrage opportunities, but market makers and investment firms often have program trading and other computerized systems that help generate small arbitrage yields from large investment transactions. The term "arbitrage" also is used to refer to quick, non-risk-free investment opportunities that surface before the market reacts to a significant development, such as an announcement of a merger or liquidation or an unexplained difference in two closely related competing stocks.

STUDENT PROBLEM 8-1

Jason is the founder and chief executive officer of TechMore, Inc. (TechMore), a rapidly growing company near San Francisco. Over the past five years, TechMore has developed a sterling reputation for designing sophisticated operating systems for select growth industries. It has a stable of talented designers and engineers that is growing weekly and continually expanding and improving its product offerings. Jason and four other key executives own 30 percent of TechMore's outstanding common stock, and the balance is owned by 38 wealthy investors, most of whom recently converted notes to common stock. TechMore has very little debt, annual sales that have passed the $60 million mark, solid profits that have consistently grown over the last 24 months, and an established and projected growth rate of 25 to 30 percent a year. The big issue now is whether TechMore is ripe for a public offering. Answer the following questions that Jason has raised:

1. What are the primary benefits that would be realized from a public offering?

2. What additional administrative and management burdens will be triggered by a public offering?

3. What governance and operating changes would be required to prepare for a public offering?

4. What are the cost factors of a public offering and operations following the offering?

5. How long does it typically take to prepare for and execute a public offering? What are the timing considerations and how important are they?

STUDENT PROBLEM 8-2

Assume for purposes of this problem that ABC Inc. is a public company actively traded on the NASDAQ. Consider which trading strategy may work best in each of the following situations:

1. Jennifer received common stock of ABC Inc. in a reverse triangular merger involving a subsidiary of ABC and a closely held corporation in which Jennifer was a major stockholder. Jennifer is restricted from selling her ABC stock and must structure any liquidation of the stock over an extended period. She wants a strategy that will protect her, at the lowest possible cost, from any serious decline in the market value of her ABC stock.

2. Pete's research has convinced him that the value of ABC's common stock will drop significantly over the next three to six months. He has just sold all of his ABC stock, but wants a strategy to further profit from his research.

3. George is convinced that the value of ABC's common stock will grow significantly over the next three to six months. He has a stock portfolio of roughly $1.2 million in his brokerage account, but no cash in the account. George doesn't want to sell any stock in his portfolio or add cash to his account, but he wants to secure a position in ABC, at the lowest cost, that will allow him to participate in the upside that he expects.

4. Luke, age 29, wants to start building capital for the future. He can afford to add $400 to an investment account each month and anticipates that this contribution amount will grow each year. He wants an investment vehicle that will facilitate monthly contributions, provide instant diversification across numerous stocks and sectors, generate returns that reflect market performance, and eliminate or minimize commissions, professional management fees, and other expenses.

B. CLOSELY HELD ENTERPRISES

1. START-UP CAPITAL SOURCES

Capital is usually the biggest obstacle for a new business. An idea has blossomed into a business plan, perhaps even a prototype or a few sales, but money is now needed to get the business started and fuel growth. Of course, the entrepreneur would love to secure the needed financing at the lowest possible cost. But, in most cases, cost isn't the driving factor. The challenge is availability or, perhaps better stated, the lack of available financing. This funding challenge often triggers the following key questions.

Is bank financing available?

Bank financing often is the key to growth for an established company that has a proven history of profitability. The business can leverage the bank debt by generating a return on its assets that far exceeds the interest cost of the debt. It is business 101 leverage at its best. The problem for a new business is that it lacks a proven income history and a solid asset base. Thus, absent a personal guarantee from a deep-pocket player that trumps the company's status as a start-up, bank debt usually isn't available to a new venture.

Once the business is established, bank debt often is the best and lowest cost capital source to fund growth. A business can usually obtain asset-based bank financing for most hard assets that have a market value. It is common to secure financing for up to 85 to 90 percent of creditworthy accounts receivable, 50 percent of finished goods inventories, 80 percent of the cost of the equipment (repayable in fixed installments over a period of three to 10 years), and up to 75 percent of the value of marketable real estate. If asset-based financing doesn't work or there is a need to supplement such financing, banks often provide cash flow financing (through lines of credit or short-term debt) that allow a company to borrow against its demonstrated ability to generate sufficient cash to service and repay the financing. This ability is established through factors and ratios (debt coverage, debt-to-equity, working capital, senior debt restrictions, etc.), that are built into the loan documents as conditions that continually must be satisfied to keep the financing alive.

To assist with bank financing in select situations, the Small Business Administration, the Farmers Home Administration, and other government agencies often will guarantee a bank loan to enable a business to obtain financing that it could not obtain on its own. For SBA programs, any owner of the business with an equity stake of 20 percent or more must personally guarantee the loan. Plus, there are SBA fees that must be paid, and often banks charge a higher interest rate on an SBA-guaranteed loan. Because an SBA lender's track record is important to the lender, most banks will not lend to start-up businesses that lack financial statements for two to three years and significant owner's equity in the business.

What about angel or investment fund investors?

Angel investors range from family and friends to deep-pocket individual investors who manage their own money. They can be fertile ground for the budding entrepreneur who needs capital. Angels often are advised and heavily influenced by their accountants, lawyers and other professionals, with whom the entrepreneur must deal. Some angel investors band together to develop specialized expertise, share due diligence burdens, and spread the cost of professional advisers.

Often friends, acquaintances and advisors are the only sources for finding angel investors. Many angels are well-suited for businesses that are too small for venture capital firms, but often they are unwilling or unable to help with future capital needs and sometimes become a frustrating source of complaints and naïve questions and demands.

As compared to angels, venture capital funds tend to be more sophisticated, more expensive, more demanding, and more interested in bigger deals. They often include pension funds and endowment investors, along with wealthy individual investors. Targeted annual returns of 50 to 60 percent are not uncommon hurdles when dealing with venture capital firms. These return objectives often require a firm to negotiate tough terms that give the firm control of major corporate decisions and, in select cases, the power to dictate day-to-day operational decisions.

A venture capital firm will expend a great deal of effort investigating a potential investment. Its obligations to its investors permit nothing less. A business plan targeted at venture capital firms should be concise and attempt to stimulate further interest, rather than describe the business in exhaustive detail. The amount of needed financing should be discussed without proposing or mentioning the terms of a potential deal. Generally, information that is proprietary or confidential should be left out of the document because such documents are often copied and circulated.

Seldom do venture capital firms just purchase common stock. The preferred form of investment usually is a mix of debt and equity, convertible debt, or a convertible preferred security. The firm wants a preferred position in the event of a failure and liquidation and full upside equity benefits if things play out as all hope.

Are strategic investors an option?

In the right situation, a corporate partner or strategic investor is the best option. Such investors are becoming a popular source of growth capital for many companies. Seldom will these deals work for a fresh start-up because the unknowns and perceived risks are too high. But as the business matures and the needs and benefits of more capital are more clearly defined, strategic partners can be a good source of capital. Usually the partner is looking for something more than an investment. It may want the opportunity to get an inside track on a new or evolving technology or the first opportunity to buy the company at the right time.

What is crowdfunding?

Crowdfunding is where a group of individuals collectively contribute funds to a start-up effort in response to solicitations that usually come via the Internet. There are two kinds of crowdfunding: non-equity and equity. Non-equity crowdfunding is where the contributor does not receive any equity interest for his or her contribution to the cause. The contributor's motive may be completely charitable or with the hope of receiving a tangible item (not a security) promised by the company. Kickstarter.com is one of the leading non-equity crowdfunding sponsors. A company that has a creative idea but no money can use Kickstarter in hopes of raising money to "kick start" its business.

Equity crowdfunding is a much different, and far more controversial, concept. General solicitations in 506 private offerings (described below) represent a form of crowdfunding that may now be used to target only accredited investors. The big issue is when and under what conditions will equity crowdfunding targeted at non-accredited investors ("ordinary folks" is the term many use) be permitted. There is no question that such crowdfunding will soon be legal, but, as of this writing, nobody knows exactly when it will happen.

The JOBS ("Jumpstart Our Business Startups") Act of 2012 mandated that the SEC implement rules for a new crowdfunding securities registration exemption within 270 days of the April 5, 2012 passage date. The President heralded crowdfunding as a "game changer" for "small businesses and start-ups," stating "for the first time, ordinary Americans will be able to go online and invest in entrepreneurs that they believe in."[3] In late 2013, the SEC finally issued its proposed regulations for non-accredited investor equity crowdfunding. The comment period for these regulations closed in March 2014, and this has caused many to speculate that final regulations will be released and the crowdfunding gates will open in late 2014.

The concept of equity crowdfunding scares many. Within a short time, private business ventures of all types will be using the Internet to sell

---

3. President Obama's address on April 5, 2012 at signing of JOBs Act bill.

unregistered securities to "ordinary Americans" who will have no capacity to evaluate what's being offered. All the targeted investors will see are ground floor opportunities to play like the big dogs. The maximum amount that a business can raise through this crowdfunding tool in a 12-month period is $1 million – not serious money in the world of business development. Those who have an annual income and a net worth of less than $100,000 may invest the greater of $2,000 or five percent of their income or net worth. Those who exceed the $100,000 threshold many invest 10 percent of their income or net worth up to a maximum of $100,000.

Proponents of equity crowdfunding compare it positively to buying lottery tickets. Opponents claim that the securities laws should seek to promote something greater than dumb luck gambling.

Here's the feared scenario. A budding entrepreneur with a hot-sounding business idea will use the Internet to raise, say, $450,000 from 150 investors (average investment of $3,000) who have an average income and net worth of $60,000. These 150 investors will need attending to and will soon become a nuisance. They will have questions and concerns. They will want reports and information, to be assured that everything is on track. Of course, there will be no market for the stock, but some will want out anyway because of a lost job, a sickness, or a desire for a new car. A few will file bankruptcy, and their stock will end up in the hands of a bankruptcy trustee. An investor will die, and the heirs will demand the lowdown on the investment.

Meanwhile, the $450,000 will be spent on salaries, fees and start-up expenses. Soon more money will be needed to keep the plan alive. But what savvy investor will want to partner-up with 150 needy neophytes who can't bring any more to the table? If such an investor does surface, a plan will be developed to flush out the original 150 investors at the lowest possible cost. The more likely outcome is that the entrepreneur, having consumed the money, will just move on to the next deal after advising the investing crowd that there's no more money, the plan is dead, and they may be entitled to a tax deduction for a worthless investment.

Is this fraud? It might be. It might just be incompetence, stupidity or greed. Either way, the uninformed investors end up losing. Investing in unregistered securities of start-ups is a super high-risk game that always poses serious risks of fraud, abuse, and complete loss. That's why, to date, it's a game that has been off limits to general solicitation and advertising and has been limited to sophisticated investors and those with a certain level of wealth. Many believe that it's no place for unsophisticated investors of modest means.

This assessment is not unique. In commenting on the impacts of equity crowdfunding, the President of the North American Securities Administration Association (NASAA) stated, "Congress has just released every huckster, scam artist, small business owner and salesman onto the Internet." Ralph Nader claimed that it's a "return to the notorious boiler room practices" where any start-up "can sell stock to investors like the old Wild West days with little disclosure or regulation."

Will there be any serious oversight? In announcing the passage of the JOBS act, the President stated that the SEC would play an "important role" to ensure that "the websites where folks go to fund all these start-ups and small businesses will be subject to rigorous oversight." Opponents are quick to point out that this is the same SEC that failed to spot Enron, Worldcom, Madoff, the dot-com bust, the derivative showdown banking industry, the subprime mortgage lunacy, the financial meltdown, and a host of other huge messes. How about state securities regulators helping out with oversight and regulation? There is no hope there. The new law specifically provides that the federal exemption will cut off all state involvement.

Although there are now many unknowns, it appears highly likely that, at some point in the not too distant future and for better or worse, many start-up companies will be using the Internet and social media to raise capital from large groups of small, uninformed investors.

Is "do-it-yourself" start-up funding the ultimate answer for most?

It's certainly the answer for many. The owners fund their dreams with their own resources: savings accounts, 401(k)s, credit cards, second mortgages, personally guaranteed loans, gifts from family members – you name it. It's tougher and lonelier, but it ensures 100 percent ownership and freedom from investor hassles during the early life of the enterprise. And for many, there is no other viable option to capitalize the operation until the business is up and running. A study conducted years ago concluded that 80 percent of the companies on Inc. Magazine's list of the 500 fastest growing companies were started and grown with no outside capital.[4]

2. *SECURITIES LAW REGISTRATION EXEMPTIONS AND RISKS*

How much do I need? From whom can I get it? Many business owners mistakenly assume that these two basic questions sum up the capital challenges for a start-up or thriving business. But there's a third and, in many respects, a more fundamental question: How do I do it legally?

Since the immediate fallout of the great crash of 1929, our laws have recognized that there is a big difference between selling a security and selling a used car. The former is an intangible; it's not possible to get the lowdown by kicking the tires, looking under the hood, and taking a test spin. So over the past 85 years, a body of federal statutory securities laws has developed to provide special protections for those who entrust their investment dollars with others.[5]

---

    4. Amar Bhide, Bootstrap Finance: The Art of Start-ups, Harvard Business Review (Dec. 1992) p. 109.

    5. The federal securities statutes include the Securities Act of 1933 (15 U.S.C. §§ 77a et seq.), the Securities Exchange Act of 1934 (15 U.C.C. §§ 78a et seq.), the Public Utility Company Act of 1935 (15 U.S.C. §§ 79 et seq.), the Trust Indenture Act of 1939 (15 U.S.C. §§ 77aaa et seq.), the Investment Company Act of 1940 (15 U.S.C. §§ 80a–1 et seq.), the Investment Advisors Act of 1940 (15 U.S.C. §§ 80b-1 et seq.), the Securities Investor Protection Act of 1970 (15 U.S.C. §§ 78aaa et seq.) and the Sarbanes-Oxley Act of 2002 (miscellaneous provisions of 15 U.S.C.).

All states have followed suit with their own statutory schemes.[6] The purpose of these laws is to protect the public from some of the risks inherent in investing money in intangible assets. Various means are used to accomplish this overriding purpose, including mandated disclosure requirements, industry player regulation, government law enforcement, and expanded causes of action for private litigation. Very few lawyers possess the know-how or the experience to navigate a client through the SEC and state regulatory mazes to take a client public. But a lawyer should understand the basics of this all-important body of law, be sensitive to the flags that indicate that a client is near (or far over) an important line, and know how to discuss key issues with business clients. For most businesses, the three primary securities law considerations are the registration requirements, the resale restrictions, and the anti-fraud prohibitions.

Sections 4 and 5 of the Securities Act of 1933 (the 1933 Act) establish the general requirement that any security offered for sale by an issuer, underwriter or dealer must be registered with the Securities and Exchange Commission (SEC).[7] As explained in the previous section, only a tiny fraction of businesses would ever consider going through the expense and hassle of such a registration process. For this reason, the important registration issues for most businesses in need of investors are the exemptions to the registration requirement. Is there an applicable exemption that fits so that the money can be raised without enduring the burdens of registration?

There are two big statutory exceptions that become the ball game for most privately owned businesses that want outside investors. The first is found in Section 4(2) of the 1933 Act that exempts from registration any "transactions by an issuer not involving a public offering."[8] It is commonly referred to as the "private offering exemption." The second is in Section 3(a)(11) of the 1933 Act that exempts from registration securities offered and sold only to residents of a single state by an issuer who is a resident of and doing business within the same state.[9] It is commonly referred to as the "intrastate offering exemption." Of course, the challenge is to know what it takes to qualify for one of these exemptions. To this end, the SEC has published rules that set forth specific standards for meeting the exemptions. Rules 504 through 506 of Regulation D describe three private offering exemptions; SEC Rule 147 deals with the intrastate offering exemption.[10]

Rule 504 Exemption

SEC Rule 504 allows a company to issue unregistered securities with a value of up to $1 million to an unlimited number of unsophisticated investors who purchase the securities for their own account and not for resale. The offering must be completed within a 12-month period, which starts when the first

6. Most states have patterned their statutes after the Uniform Securities Act.
7. 15 U.S.C. §§ 77d and 77e.
8. 15 U.S.C. §§ 77d(2).
9. 15 U.S.C. § 77c(a)(11)
10. 17 C.F.R. §§ 230.504 thru 230.506. The definitions and other provisions of sections 230.501-230.503 should be read in conjunction with these three rules.

investment agreement is signed by an investor. The rule itself does not mandate any specific disclosures, but the issuer must satisfy the basic antifraud provisions of the securities laws (discussed below). The rule permits general solicitation, but often this is prohibited or limited by state securities laws. Securities issued under Rule 504 are not subject to certain resale restrictions because they are not considered "restricted securities." The company must comply with the securities laws of each state in which a purchaser is a resident, and usually must file a notice with that state's commissioner of corporations or similar official. Any person who purchases a security in a Rule 504 offering should sign an investment agreement as proof of his or her investment intent and other required representations. A Form D must be filed with the SEC within 15 days after the first sale.

Rule 505 Exemption

SEC Rule 505 allows a company, within a 12-month period, to issue up to $5,000,000 worth of unregistered securities to 35 unsophisticated investors plus any number of "accredited investors." Generally, an "accredited investor" is an individual with a net worth of at least a $1,000,000 (primary home excluded) or an annual income of over $200,000 ($300,000 for a married couple) for the last two years. The definition also includes: banks and investment companies; private development companies; corporations, partnerships and trusts with assets over $5 million; and company insiders (officers, directors, and promoters). There are a number of required disclosures if any securities are sold to non-accredited investors. Advertising and general solicitations are prohibited. The securities are "restricted securities" and may not be readily resold. The company must comply with the securities laws of each state in which a person who buys the security is a resident, and usually must file a notice with that state's commissioner of corporations or similar official. Any person who acquires a security in a Rule 505 offering should sign an appropriate investment agreement. The company must file a Form D with the SEC within 15 days after the first sale.

Rule 506 Exemption

Rule 506 is the most popular registration exemption because there are no dollar limitations and (this is the big one) an exemption under 506 preempts all state securities law registration requirements. This can save a great deal of time, hassle or expense for the company that intends to raise money from investors in various states. Under Rule 506, there can be any number of accredited investors and up to 35 non-accredited investors if, and only if, each non-accredited investor (or an authorized representative) has knowledge and experience in financial and business matters and is capable of evaluating the risks of the investment. Historically, all advertising and general solicitations were prohibited under 506, but the JOBS Act of 2012 (discussed below) now permits general solicitation of accredited investors in a 506 offering if all the purchasers in the offering are accredited investors and reasonable steps are taken to ensure the accredited investor status of all investors. The company must file a form D with the SEC and with the corporation's commissioner in each state where stock is sold. Any person who buys stock in a Rule 506 offering should sign an appropriate investment agreement confirming that he or she is buying the stock for investment purposes, that there are serious restrictions on the resale of the stock, and that no attempt will be made to resell the stock without the approval of the company.

Rule 147 Exemption[11]

Rule 147 exempts from federal registration a company that sells securities in an "intrastate offering" to residents of only one state. To qualify as an "intrastate offering," the principal office of the company must be located in the state, at least 80 percent of the company's gross revenues must be derived from operations in the state, at least 80 percent of the company's assets must be located in the state, and at least 80 percent of the proceeds realized in the offering must be used in the state. The company must comply with the state's securities laws. Any person who acquires a security should sign an appropriate investment agreement containing proof of residence.

Regulation A Offerings

Regulation A provides an exemption for public offers and sales of up to $5 million of securities in a 12-month period. It is sometimes referred to as a mini-registration. Investment companies and any company subject to the periodic reporting requirements of the Securities Exchange Act are not eligible. Regulation A requires the company to file with the Securities and Exchange Commission an offering statement containing disclosures similar to those made in a registration statement, certain exhibits, and financial statements prepared in accordance with generally accepted accounting principles (audited statements are not required). When the offering statement has been reviewed and qualified by the SEC, it must be delivered to prospective investors before any securities are sold. The company is required to file reports with the SEC detailing the securities sold and the use of proceeds from those sales. But once the offering is complete (and unlike all public companies), there are no ongoing reporting requirements. Securities sold in a Regulation A offering are unrestricted and may be transferred in a secondary market transaction. Regulation A offerings are seldom used because of the $5 million limitation and the amount of work they require.

The Jobs Act of 2012 mandated that the SEC issue rules that raise the limit for offerings under Regulation A from $5 million to $50 million and exempt Regulation A offerings from state securities laws so long as the securities are offered or sold over a national securities exchange or are sold to a "qualified purchaser" (a term the SEC will need to define). The revised Regulation A will require a company to file audited financial statements annually with the SEC, and the SEC is directed to develop rules relating to periodic disclosure by Regulation A issuers.

When implemented, these changes will take Regulation A offerings to a whole new level, offering a powerful money raising option for many companies. Proposed regulations were issued for comment in December 2013, and many believe that final regulations will be issued in 2014.

---

11. 17 C.F.R. § 240.147.

JOBS Act of 2012

On April 5, 2012, President Obama signed the Jumpstart Our Business Startups (JOBS) Act with strong bi-partisan support. The Act is intended to increase American job creation and economic growth by improving access to the public capital markets for emerging growth companies. Key provisions of the Act include the following:

• The maximum number of shareholders of record that a private company can have before it must register with the SEC as a public company was increased from 500 to 2,000, so long as fewer than 500 are non-accredited investors.

• The prohibition on general solicitation and advertising in a private offering under Rule 506 of Regulation D must be removed by the SEC. As a result, the SEC now has a rule that permits general solicitation and adverting if all the purchasers in the offering are accredited investors and reasonable steps are taken to ensure the accredited investor status of all investors.

• The SEC must adopt rules that permit "crowdfunding" activities so that entrepreneurs may raise up to $1 million from a large pool of small investors, subject to limitations based on investor income levels. (See related discussion of crowdfunding above.)

• The SEC must raise the limit for offerings under Regulation A from $5 million to $50 million and exempt Regulation A offerings from state securities laws so long as the securities are offered or sold over a national securities exchange or are sold to a "qualified purchaser" (a term the SEC will need to define). The revised Regulation A will require a company to file audited financial statements annually with the SEC, and the SEC is directed to develop rules relating to periodic disclosure by Regulation A issuers. As mentioned above, proposed regulations were issued for comment in December 2013.

• **A** category of issuer called an "emerging growth company" is created under the Act. This is a company that has under $1 billion in annual revenues. The regulatory burden on such companies is eased by permitting them to include only two years of audited financial statements and selected other information in their IPO registration statement, not requiring an auditor attestation of management's assessment of internal controls for financial reporting created under Sarbanes Oxley, and exempting them from certain other accounting requirements. Also, the Act eases offering-pending research disclosure rules, marketing communication conflict-of-interest rules, and pre-filing institutional investor communication limitations. Furthermore, an emerging growth company will be exempt from shareholder approval requirements of executive compensation

Antifraud Challenges

Beyond the registration exemptions are the anti-fraud prohibitions. Section 10(b) of the Securities Exchange Act of 1934 (the 1934 Act) prohibits "the use of a manipulative and deceptive device" in connection with the purchase or sale of any security.[12]   SEC Rule 10b-5, promulgated under Section 10(b), makes it unlawful for any person, directly or indirectly in connection with the purchase and sale of a security, "to make any untrue statement of a material fact or to omit to state a material fact necessary in order to make the statements made, in the light of the circumstances under which they were made, not misleading."[13]   This rule takes all dealings in securities to a higher level. The seller has an affirmative duty to accurately state material facts and to not mislead; the buyer has a solid cause of action if the seller blows it. Rule 10b-5 and its state counterparts keep our courts packed with countless disgruntled investors who believe they were unfairly deceived when things didn't go as planned.

In offerings that are exempt from registration, the tool that is used to protect against antifraud risks is the private placement memorandum ("PPM"), a carefully prepared document that provides the necessary disclosures.   Items typically included in a PPM include:

- The name, address, and telephone number of the issuer

- A description and the price of the securities offered

- The amount of the offering (minimum and maximum amounts, if any)

- The plan and cost of the distribution of the securities

- An identification and description of the officers, directors, and advisers of the company

- A description of the company's business and products or services and any related technology

- A discussion of the market for the issuer's products and services and related competition

- A description of all risk factors, including those related to the company and those related to general market or economic conditions

- A description of how the proceeds realized from the offering will be used;

- A statement that neither the Securities and Exchange Commission nor any state securities commission has approved the securities or passed on the adequacy or accuracy of the disclosures in the PPM

- A statement describing how the offering price was determined

- A description of the company's present capital structure, prior offerings, and any outstanding stock plans or stock options

- An explicit warning that the company could become insolvent or bankrupt and any investment in the company could be a total loss

- Recent financial statements of the company (audit not required)

---

12. 15 U.S.C. § 78j.
13. 17 C.F.R. § 240.10b-5.

- Projections of future revenues, expenses, and profits or losses (optional)

- A description of the restrictions on the resale of the company's securities and the fact that no market now exists or may ever exist for the securities

- A disclosure of any contracts or agreements with management

- A disclosure of all significant contracts that the company has with third parties

- Copies of key documents related to the offering (legal opinions, Articles of Incorporation, etc.)

- An offer for investors to meet with management, tour the company's facilities, and ask questions.

Resale Restrictions

The Securities Act of 1933 does not provide an exemption for private resale of restricted securities acquired through a private placement. In order to qualify for the private placement exemption, there can be no immediate distribution or resell by the initial purchasers of the securities. For that reason, companies should take precautions to protect against resells. These precautions typically include confirming the investment intent of each purchaser, printing restrictive legends on the share certificates, issuing stop transfer instructions to any transfer agents, and obtaining representations in writing from each purchaser confirming that the security is being bought for his or her own account and not for resale or with a view to distribution.

There are options for a purchaser of restricted securities who desires to resell. SEC Rule 144[14] provides a non-exclusive safe harbor from registration for resales of restricted securities. Among other things, it imposes holding period and "dribble out" requirements. SEC Rule 144A[15] provides a separate safe harbor for resells to qualified institutional buyers. Also, the courts and the SEC have acknowledged an additional resale exception, known as the "Section 4(1 1/2)" exemption.[16] The SEC has characterized it as "a hybrid exemption not specifically provided for in the 1933 Act but clearly within its intended purpose" and has stated that it will apply "so long as some of the established criteria for sales under both section 4(1) and section 4(2) of the [1933] Act are satisfied."[17] Under this exemption, an investor holding restricted securities may resell the securities to another accredited investor who purchases them for his or her own account and not for distribution if the subsequent purchaser signs an appropriate investment letter and if the certificate issued bears appropriate legends for restricted securities.

---

14. 17 C.F.R. § 230.144.

15. 17 C.F.R. § 230.144A.

16. See SEC 1933 Act Release No. 33-6188 (Feb. 1, 1980) and Ackerberg v. Johnson, 892 F.2d 1328 (8th Cir. 1989).

17. SEC 1933 Act Release No. 33-6188 (Feb. 1, 1980). On this exemption, see Olander and Jacks, The Section 4 (1 1/2) Exemption – Reading Between the Lines of the Securities Act of 1933, 15 Sec. Reg. L.J. 339 (1988) and Schneider, Section 4 (1 1/2) – Private Resales of Restricted or Controlled Securities, 49 Ohio St. L.J. 501 (1988).

3. DANGEROUS MISCONCEPTIONS

The root cause of most trouble under the securities laws is ignorance. The client just didn't understand and didn't stop to think or ask for advice before charging ahead. There are many misconceptions that can get in the way. A challenge for the business advisor is to spot and eradicate these misconceptions before they become a problem. It's an ongoing educational effort with many business owners. Following is a brief summary of some of the most common misconceptions.

a. Big Guy Rules. Some business owners mistakenly assume that the securities laws apply only to public companies whose stock is regularly traded. It's the old "Why would the SEC want to mess with little old me?" notion. This misconception is supported by the little they read in the press (it's all focused on big companies), and the fact that none of their business owner friends have ever had to deal with the SEC. Although many securities law issues are uniquely directed at public companies and SEC efforts are focused on the public markets, the securities laws extend to any private security transaction between a company and individual investors. Size is not a prerequisite for Rule 10b-5. For most privately owned businesses, the fear is not a call from the SEC; it's a letter from a hungry plaintiff's lawyer who, armed with 10b-5 and a set of ugly facts, is making demands on behalf of unhappy investors at the worst possible time.

b. This Ain't a Security. The misconception is that the securities laws apply only to stocks. The term "security" is broadly defined in the 1933 Act to include, among other things, any note, bond, evidence of indebtedness, certificate of interest or participation in any profit-sharing agreement, and investment contract.[18] The Supreme Court has held that a "security" exists whenever money is invested in a common enterprise with profits to come solely from the efforts of others.[19] Applying this broad definition, courts have found a "security" in investment contracts involving worm farms, boats, silver foxes, oyster beds, vending machines, parking meters, cemetery plots, exotic trees, vineyards, fig orchards, chinchillas, beavers and more.[20] A flag should surface whenever a client claims or suggests that money can be raised by offering something that is *not* a "security."

c. The Safe, Dumb, Poor Crowd. Some mistakenly believe that it is "safer" to target unsophisticated investors who don't know the law and lack the means or the will to fight back if things go wrong. Plus, this group is "easier" because they don't know enough to ask the tough questions – that is, they can be fooled. This is dangerous thinking for a number of reasons. First, the most important registration exemption requires that the investors be accredited investors[21] or be non-accredited investors who are sophisticated in financial

---

18. 15 U.S.C. § 77b(1).
19. S.E.C. v. W.J. Howey Co., 328 U.S. 293 (1946).
20. See 2 L. Loss & J. Seligman, Securities Regulation (3rd ed. 1989-93) pp. 948-956.
21. Individuals are considered accredited investors if they have a net worth that exceeds $1 million (primary residence excluded) or an annual income of over $200,000 ($300,000 if married) for the most recent two years preceding the securities purchase. 15 U.S.C. § 77b(15) and 17 C.F.R. § 230.501(a).

affairs or have representatives who possess such sophistication.[22] Second, the company loses the opportunity to bring in savvy investors who may contribute their wisdom and experience in addition to their money. Third (and this is the crux), besides just being a bad thing to do, the whole purpose of the securities laws is to protect the naive and uninformed from those who peddle intangible investments that promise riches. The dumb, poor investors may lack the capacity to evaluate what is being promised; but after things go bad, it doesn't take much to find an aggressive lawyer who is willing to spec the case against a contingent fee because, given the undisputed limitations of the plaintiffs, it's a slam dunk. Smart business owners generally limit their offers to accredited investors who have experience in financial and investment matters and who can afford the loss of their investment. In rare instances, they might consider a non-accredited individual, but only if that individual is sophisticated in financial matters and is investing a sum that he or she can afford to lose.

d. Only "Really Important" Stuff. The misconception is that only the "really important" information has to be disclosed because Rule 10b-5 speaks in terms of "material facts." Often this misconception is aggravated by the notion that the important information is the bottom-line conclusions that support the business plan. So, they reason, there's no need to sweat details that may complicate the money raising effort. The determination of a "material" fact within the meaning of Rule 10b–5 "depends on the significance the reasonable investor would place on the withheld or misrepresented information."[23] The "material" standard will be met if the misrepresentation or omission "would have been viewed by a reasonable investor as having significantly altered the 'total mix' of information made available."[24] It's a very broad definition that presents a mixed question of fact and law in most cases; it is decided as a matter of law only when reasonable minds would not differ on the issue.[25] It's a mistake to assume that the materiality requirement eliminates the need to provide details. Plus, there is another hard reality that always supports the conclusion that more, not less, should be disclosed. If things go bad and a significant contributing factor to the failure was not disclosed up front, it may be impossible, looking back, to claim that that factor was not material and worthy of disclosure. The wisest and safest approach is to lay out all known risk factors and the related details.

e. My Successes Say It All. Many business owners focus only on past successes when talking track record. Failures or disappointments are forgotten or "amended" to look like successes. The misconception is that it is appropriate to paint the best possible track record, even when it involves a little fudging or selective editing. A key executive's track record is important to any investor. What one has done in the past often is the best indicator of what might happen in the future. If things go bad, an investor who first learns after the fact that this was not the key person's first failure may be shocked into action. The challenge

---

22. The all-important Rule 506 exemption requires that nonaccredited investors be sophisticated investors. 17 C.F.R. § 230.506.

23. Basic Inc. v. Levinson, 485 U.S. 224, 240 (1988).

24. TSC Industries, Inc. v. Northway, Inc., 426 U.S. 438, 449 (1976).

25. Id. at 450.

is to accurately and fairly summarize the background and experiences, both good and bad, of the key players in a way that suggests that they now possess the skills and abilities to successfully manage the proposed venture.

f. Good Advertising Is The Key. Some mistakenly assume that fundraising is all about advertising. They start a makeshift advertising campaign, only to learn that they have killed some of their best shots at a registration exemption. Although the JOBS Act of 2012 has opened up general solicitation and advertising in select Rule 506 offerings and presumably the crowdfunding world, usually the word of an exempt offering must be spread through friends, relatives and business associates.

g. Safety in Numbers. The misconception is that it is safer to have a large number of small investors, rather than one or two big players. It's based on the false assumption that a small investor will be more inclined to swallow a loss and less inclined to fight back. It ignores some basic realities. First, the size of one's investment does not govern the capacity to stomach a loss; many large players are better equipped to understand and suck up a loss than most small investors who have had unrealistic expectations from the get-go and can't afford any loss. Second, it ignores the capacity of many voices to stir each other up and to share the expense and burden of hiring a gladiator to fight their cause. Third, it ignores the burden, often horrendous, of having to respond to multiple ongoing inquiries all along the way from nervous, uninformed investors who just want to hear that all will pay off "as promised" and that there are "no problems." Finally, it ignores the significant value of binding a few key players to the effort. Inviting them into the inner circle gives the business the benefit of their advice and counsel and often eliminates any securities law exposure because they see it all, hear it all, and are part of it all.

h. Dodge the Downside. Some wrongfully assume that there is no need to talk about the potential of failure when trying to raise money. They figure that everyone knows there is risk. So why talk about it? The truth is that, from a securities law perspective, it is essential to spell out the risk factors in writing for any prospective investor. Nothing is more material than those factors that may potentially cause the business to fail. Thought should be given to risk factors that are specific to the business (competition, market condition changes, supply access, technology changes, skilled labor needs, capital and liquidity challenges, etc.) and the potential impact that general risks (e.g., interest rate increases) may have on the business. Often this is one of the most difficult tasks for business owners to embrace. As the risk factor list is committed to black and white, they begin to fear that everyone will be "spooked away." It helps to remind them that seasoned players are used to seeing such lists, and that they have all made money in ventures that started out with risk factor lists that were just as ugly as the one being created.

i. Projections Are Just Projections. The misconception is that since projections, by their very nature, are speculative, they create an opportunity to strengthen the money raising effort by painting the rosiest possible picture of how things might play out. It's little wonder that such projections have been the driving force behind many securities law claims. The use of projections should be handled carefully. They should not be viewed as an opportunity to oversell, but rather as a means of illustrating the business' potential under a defined set of reasonable assumptions. If overdone, they may create unrealistic false expectations that cause an otherwise good performance to disappoint or, worse yet, fuel a legal dispute when things turn sour. There are a few important precautions that can be taken. First, make certain that the projections are based on reasonable assumptions that are spelled out. The operative word here is "reasonable;" the assumptions should not reflect an ideal, unrealistic set of conditions. Second, the predictions should be accompanied by a cautionary statement that identifies the predictions as forward-looking statements, warns that conditions and risks could cause actual results to differ substantially from the projections, and lists specific risks and conditions that may have such an effect. The effort may allow the company, if necessary, to rely on the "bespeaks caution doctrine" that provides a defense against allegations of false and misleading forward-looking statements when such precautionary language has been used.[26]

j. "Puffing" Works. Some business owners believe that the key to "legal money raising" is "puffing" – making vague overstated generalizations that get potential investors excited. Often they have heard about cases where defendants escaped securities law liability because the court concluded that the alleged misrepresentations were nothing more than "obviously immaterial puffery."[27] Statements like "our fundamentals are strong," "our product is revolutionary and could change the world," and "the stock is red hot" have been dismissed as immaterial puffing.[28] The problem is when it goes too far. What may appear as harmless puffing can trigger liability under the securities laws if the speaker had no reasonable basis for making the statement. The court will examine whether the speaker really believed that the statement was accurate and had a factual or historical basis for that belief.[29] There is some room for harmless puffing, but in no sense is it a free pass without limits.

k. Let 'Em Be. The misconception is that investors, once they've bought in, should be free to deal with their stock as they see fit. As described above, the private offering exemption requires that the investors not be used as a device to disseminate the stock to a broader audience and thereby convert what would otherwise be a private offering into a public offering. This important factor, coupled with the obvious antifraud challenges, gives the company a huge interest in what the investors do with their stock. For this reason, as described above, it is common practice to ascertain the investment intentions of purchasers up front, to place resale restrictive legends on share certificates, to issue stop transfer

26. See, e.g., In re Worlds of Wonder Sec. Litig., 35 F.3d 1407 (9th Cir. 1994); Gasner v. Board of Supervisors, 103 F.3d 351 (4th Cir. 1996); and Nadoff v. Duane Reade, Inc., 107 Fed. Appx. 250 (2d Cir. 2004).

27. See, e.g., Grossman v. Novell, Inc., 120 F.3d 1112 (10th Cir. 1997); Raab v. General Physics Corp., 4 F.3d 286 (4th Cir. 1993); and Helwig v. Vencor, Inc. 210 F.3d 612 (6th Cir. 2000).

28. Rosenzweig v. Azurix Corp., 332 F.3d 854 (5th Cir. 2003); Vosgerichian v. Commodore Int'l, 832 F.Supp. 909 (E.D. Pa. 1993); Newman v. Rothschild, 651 F.Supp. 160 (S.D.N.Y. 1986).

29. See, e.g., Kline v. First Western Government Sec., 24 F.3d 480 (3d Cir. 1994), cert. denied 513 U.S. 1032 (1994) and In re Allaire Corp. Secs. Litig., 224 F.Supp.2d 319 (D. Mass. 2002).

instructions to those who control the stock register, and to obtain written representations from all purchasers that they are acquiring the security for their own account and not for resale or with a view to distribute the stock.

l. Cashing In Is the Easy Part.   This misconception surfaces when everybody just assumes that an acceptable exit strategy will present itself at the most opportune time. Often a business plan is developed with little or no thought given to the ultimate strategy that will be used to realize a return for the owners of the business. The organizers assume if things work out and the business becomes profitable, an opportunity will surface to cash in at the best time. No serious effort is made to research the practicality and possibility of specific exit scenarios. The details of operating the business and generating revenues have been thought through, but the broader picture is left to fuzzy notions of market options and base ignorance. This gets scary when an organizer with little knowledge starts speculating on return strategies with a potential investor who has even less knowledge. The organizer often has no specific knowledge regarding the appetite others may have for the business. The sad reality is that many business owner/managers are shocked and disappointed to discover that there is little or no market for their business. This disappointment can be magnified many times for the outside investor who draws no compensation and has assumed all along that a big payday was within reach. And then there are the baseless, overstated "going public" expectations. This sounds great to the naive investor, even though the organizer has no real clue as to what a public offering entails or requires. A primary challenge for many business owners is to develop a realistic expectation of the business' capacity to create returns for the owners. Seasoned entrepreneurs do this instinctively. Experience has taught them to always have their eye on the big picture and the entire life cycle of the business. Plus, they understand that conditions can change; what is solid and profitable today can be weak and vulnerable tomorrow. So timing is often the key when it comes to cashing in the marbles. Less experienced owners, particularly those who are wrapped up in their first effort, often fail to see, let alone focus on, the broader picture and never develop such realistic expectations for themselves and those who have entrusted them with their money. As a result, they end up in a situation where they can only disappoint.

STUDENT PROBLEM 8-3

For the past three years, Judy has been the sole owner and CEO of a corporation that manufactures and distributes a relatively expensive line of fashion baby apparel, known as "Plum," that is progressively "catching on" in more countries. The business has grown steadily, and Judy is convinced that it's time to "shoot for the stars." To make this happen, she needs $2 million of equity capital and an expanded bank line of credit that will be "doable without personal guarantees" based on the past record of the business and the new equity. Lucy is willing to give up 45 percent of the company's equity to secure the needed capital.

Judy's mother-in-law Diane, a wealthy divorced socialite who adores Judy and her line, is convinced that she can "rustle up the money" from her wealthy friends who live in various states and are "always looking for a great ground-floor deal." Judy is impressed with Diane's offer, but has a number of questions that have surfaced from her preliminary Internet reading. Please answer:

1. What securities law registration exemption will work best for Judy's company? What additional facts, if any, do you need to answer this question for Judy?

2. Is the wealth of those who might invest in Judy's company a factor to consider?

3. Can Judy use social media (e.g., Facebook) to prospect for potential investors?

4. Might equity crowdfunding be a partial or complete answer for Judy's company?

5. Does Judy need to concern herself with antifraud risks if she qualifies for a registration exemption? If so, how does she protect herself?

6. What is the best way to deal with investors who want to sell their investment in the company?

CHAPTER 9

BUSINESS ENTERPRISE TAXATION BASICS

A. THE WORLD TAX STAGE

Business owners need to be smart with taxes. The objective is to minimize government bites, consistent with other objectives, and to avoid costly planning blunders.

Smart tax planning requires more than just strategizing against a static set of rules. Changes in the rules must be anticipated and factored in. Tax planning has always favored those who can wisely anticipate a moving target. And there is little question that today, perhaps more than ever, the target is moving fast, and its path is hard to predict.

1. CORPORATE TAXES AROUND THE GLOBE

The importance of business and corporate taxes throughout the world cannot be overstated. They directly affect the stability and strength of nations and communities, the scope and quality of governmental services, and the growth and development of economies that provide jobs and markets for goods and services.

While many will forever debate the virtues and vices of the progressive globalization of the world's economy, it has triggered three tax consequences that no one can reasonably doubt. First, corporate tax rates generally have been descending as the world stage has shrunk and nations compete for capital and business opportunities to strengthen their economies, boost income levels, and broaden their tax bases. Second, while each nation is free to develop its own tax structure and rates, the impacts of a nation's tax changes can reach far beyond its borders as businesses around the globe engage in strategic, multinational tax planning to maximize after-tax yields for their shareholders. And third, movements by other nations have pushed the United States to the top of the list of developed countries with the highest corporate tax rates. Although many question the seriousness of the United States occupying this top slot, the unenviable position itself and a host of other factors, not the least of which is a sluggish economy for over five years, has prompted cries for lower corporate tax rates from voices on both sides of the political aisle. Many believe that lower U.S. corporate tax rates are inevitable.

The OECD. The Organization for Economic Co-operation and Development (OECD) is an international economic organization that includes 34 member countries. Originally founded in 1961 and headquartered in Paris, the OECD seeks to promote economic progress and world trade by emphasizing the values of democracy and free market forces and providing a mechanism for nations to share policy experiences, tackle common problems, identify best practices, and coordinate domestic and international policies. Member nations include the United States, the United Kingdom, Canada, Australia, many European countries (Germany, Switzerland, France, Italy, Portugal, Spain, and others), emerging countries (Chile, Turkey and Mexico), and others. Also, the OECD prides itself in working with major and emerging non-member countries, such as China, India, Brazil and economies developing in Africa, Asia, Latin America and the Caribbean. Taxes and tax policy are important considerations for OECD members. OECD members are forever being benchmarked against one another in evaluating tax trends, tax rates, and the breadth of tax bases.

Corporate Tax Rates. Corporate tax rates throughout the world have consistently dropped over the past 30 years. In 1981, the average corporate tax rate of OECD countries was 47.4 percent. That average dropped to 41 percent by 1990, to 32.6 percent by 2000, and to 25.5 percent by 2013. The policy decisions of key countries to lower their corporate tax rates have been significant. A few examples: the United Kingdom dropped its corporate rates from 33 percent in 1993 to 23 percent in 2013; Canada's corporate rates dropped from 42.6 percent to 26.1 percent over the past 20 years; Israel's corporate rates declined from 36 percent to 25 percent from 2000 to 2013; Italy's corporate rates declined from 52.2 percent in 1993 to 27.5 percent in 2013; Germany's corporate rates plummeted from 56.5 percent to 30.2 percent over the past 20 years.[1]

The global push for lower corporate rates has been fueled by competition for investment capital and business activity and a basic, proven realization that any reduction in government coffers directly attributable to lower corporate rates will be offset many times by increased revenues attributable to more capital and a stronger and broader economic base.

The corporate tax rate history of the United States has been very different than that of other countries. In 1993, the official OECD corporate tax rate of the United States (considering both the federal rate of 35 percent and state corporate income tax rates) was 39.8 percent. At that time, the U.S. corporate rate sat near the middle of the OECD pack, with over one-third of the OECD member countries having a corporate tax rate above the U.S. rate, and only three countries having a corporate rate that was at 9 percent or more below the U.S rate. As other countries have reduced their corporate rates over the past 20 years, the U.S. rate has remained constant. In 2013, the U.S. corporate rate was 39.1 percent, the highest of all OECD countries, nearly 14 percent higher than the average

---

1. Tax Foundation, OECD Corporate Income Tax Rates, 1981-2013, December 13, 2013.

corporate rate of OECD countries, and more than nine percentage points higher than 29 of the other 33 OECD countries.[2]

Corporate Effective Tax Rates. Often the rate of income taxes actually paid by a corporation is less than the statutory corporate rate. For example, in Chapter 2 we saw that Caterpillar Inc.'s provision for income taxes in 2012 equaled 30.7 percent of its consolidated pretax net income. The difference between this percentage and the 35 percent U.S. corporate tax rate was principally attributable to non-US subsidiaries of Caterpillar that were subject to the lower rates of other countries. The term used to describe the tax rate actually paid by a corporation is the corporate effective tax rate. This effective rate often is impacted by a host of factors (often referred to as "corporate loopholes"), including deferring or eliminating taxes on controlled foreign corporations by stockpiling profits offshore, using accelerated depreciation deductions for machinery and equipment, generating tax- free interest on state and local bonds, benefiting from special deductions for domestic manufacturing, and claiming tax credits for research and development, alcohol-based fuel production, foreign taxes paid, and more. The corporate average effective tax rate (AETR) for a given country, while accepted as a conventional and useful concept, can vary widely among countries and vary significantly from year to year based on differences in the tax base that is the denominator of the equation.

Marginal Effective Tax Rates. Closely related to the AETR is the marginal effective tax rate (METR), a widely accepted analytical tool for measuring a country's corporate tax impacts on investment and capital allocation decisions. This tool is based on the premises that the increased capital mobility across borders associated with globalization enhances the relevance of tax competitiveness, and that a country's competitiveness is hurt by taxation that undermines productivity through investment. The METR compares the pre-tax rate of return on capital with the after-tax rate of return on capital for the relevant market. If the former is 22 percent and the later 11 percent, the METR is 50 percent. A high METR is indicative of a country's capital-repressive tax structure. The United States has had the highest METR of all OECD countries since 2007 by a relatively wide margin. In 2013, the METR rate of the United States was 35.3 percent, far higher than the 19.6 percent MRTR average of all OECD countries and the METR rates for other key countries: UK - 25.9 percent; Germany - 24.4 percent; Switzerland - 17.5 percent; Australia - 25.9 percent; Canada - 18.6 percent; Israel - 15 percent.[3]

Corporate Tax Contribution to Total U.S. Tax Burden. Although the U.S. corporate income tax rate and U.S. METR have topped for years the rates of all OECD countries, many are disturbed by the relatively small percentage of total U.S. taxes that come from corporate income taxes. For example, in 2013 U.S. corporate income tax collections totaled $273.5 billion, only 9.8 percent of the $2.774 trillion in total U.S. tax collections and enough to fund federal spending for only about 28 days. Individuals' income taxes and payroll and self-employment taxes exceeded by many times total corporate tax collections. A

2. Id.
3. Tax Foundation, The U.S. Corporate Effective Tax Rate: Myth and the Fact, February 6, 2014.

review of U.S. tax collections by source over the past 40 years confirms that 2013 was not an aberrational year for corporate income tax collections. Although the percentage of total U.S. tax collections attributable to corporate income taxes was higher in select years (e.g., 15.4 percent in 1977 and 14.41 percent in 2007), the corporate tax contribution percentage has hovered in the 9 to 11 percent range for many years and stretches of years, and there is nothing to suggest that the corporate contribution percentage will increase in the future.[4]

There are various reasons to explain this relatively low corporate income tax contribution percentage. More corporations are reducing their U.S. tax burden by taking advantage of corporate tax breaks and diversifying their operations through foreign controlled corporations that are subject to lower tax rates imposed by other countries. As explained below, many closely held businesses are able to avoid all corporate taxes by electing to be taxed as an S corporation or by operating as a limited liability company or partnership that is taxed as a partnership. Such a pass-through entity pays no entity-level taxes; its income is passed through and taxed directly to the owners of the business. And there are numerous corporations that effectively eliminate or reduce to very low levels their corporate income taxes by bailing out their earnings to owners of the business through compensation and other tax-deductible payments.

2. ROLE AND CHALLENGES OF TRANSFER PRICING

For the past 80 years, countries have incorporated transfer pricing adjustments into their tax structures to curb the abuse of intercompany prices by multinational companies. If Company A, a U.S. company subject to a 35 percent tax rate, provides goods or services to Company B, a U.K. company subject to a 23 percent rate, overall taxes will be reduced as the prices that A charges B are lowered. If Companies A and B are unrelated, market forces will dictate the prices between the entities as both companies seek to maximize their respective profits. But if Companies A and B are related entities owned by the same parties, market forces cease to be relevant and often the emphasis shifts to tax savings through strategic intercompany pricing. Hence, the need for transfer pricing rules.

The current, comprehensive transfer pricing rules can be traced to a white pager published by the United States that ultimately led to the adoption of detailed regulations in 1994, primarily under Section 482 of the Internal Revenue Code. Section 482 is an ominous provision that gives the Internal Revenue Service authority to "distribute, apportion, or allocate gross income, deductions, credits or allowances between and among" commonly controlled business interests "whenever necessary to prevent evasion of taxes or clearly to reflect the income" of any such businesses. In 1995, the OECD issued a draft of transfer pricing guidelines, which were expanded in 1996 and have been adopted by many countries, including European Union countries, with little or no modification.

---

4. Congressional Budget Office, The Budget and Economic Outlook: 2014 to 2024, February 4, 2014.

The U.S. transfer pricing regulations and the OECD transfer pricing guidelines are similar in many respects. Members of a commonly controlled enterprise may set their own prices, but such prices may be adjusted by a taxing authority to conform to an arm's-length standard. Some countries, including the United States and Canada, impose special related-party reporting requirements to facilitate the review and adjustment process. As for the arm's-length standard determination, a price will meet this standard if falls within a range of prices that an independent buyer would pay an independent seller for an identical item under identical terms and conditions, where neither is under any compulsion to act. U.S. regulations and the OECD guidelines specify several methods for testing prices, establish standards for comparing third-party transactions, permit adjustments to a midpoint of an arm's-length range, and do not require a showing of an intent to avoid or evade taxes.

Tax authorities usually examine prices actually charged between related parties by comparison testing of such prices to comparable prices charged among unrelated parties. Some countries mandate a specific method of testing prices, but U.S. regulations and the OECD guidelines use a "best method" rule, which requires use of the method that produces the most reliable measure of arm's-length results. Factors that impact the best method determination are the reliability of available data and assumptions under the method, the comparability of tested and independent items, and validation of the method's results by the use of other methods.

Countries often impose significant transfer pricing penalties to encourage and force taxpayers to make reasonable efforts to determine and document the arm's-length character of their intercompany transfer prices. For example, the United States imposes a 20- percent non-deductible transactional penalty on a tax underpayment if a transfer price is 200 percent or more, or 50 percent or less, than the arm's-length price, and the penalty jumps to 40 percent if the transfer price is 400 percent or more, or 25 percent or less, than the arm's-length price.[5] In addition to these individual transaction penalties, U.S. statutes provide that a series of transactions may trigger a 20-percent net adjustment penalty if the net pricing adjustment exceeds the lesser of $5 million or 10 percent of gross receipts, and the penalty is hiked to 40 percent if the net transfer pricing adjustment exceeds $20 million or 20 percent of gross receipts. These penalties can be avoided only if the taxpayer demonstrates a reasonable basis for believing that its transfer pricing would produce arm's-length results and that appropriate documentation supporting such a belief existed at the time the relevant tax return was filed and is tendered to the IRS within 30 days of a request.[6]

B. U.S. BUSINESS ENTITY TAX CONCEPTS

1. CORPORATION TAX BASICS – Q&As

Q.1 What is a C corporation?

---

5. See, generally, IRC § 6662(e), (h) and Treas. Reg. 1.6662-6(b).
6. Id.

A C corporation is a regular corporation that pays its own taxes. It is a creature of state law, is recognized as a separate taxable entity, and is governed by the provisions of subchapter C of the Internal Revenue Code. Any corporation that does not properly elect to be taxed as an S corporation will be taxed as a C corporation.

Q.2 What tax rates do C corporations pay?

The first $50,000 of a C corporation's taxable income each year is subject to a favorable 15 percent tax rate. The rate jumps to 25 percent on the next $25,000 of taxable income. Thus, the overall rate on the first $75,000 of taxable income is an attractive 18.33 percent, far less than the personal marginal rate applicable to most successful business owners. Beyond $75,000, the rate advantage disappears as the marginal rate jumps to 34 percent. Plus, if the corporation's income exceeds $100,000, the rate "bubbles" an additional 5 percent on taxable income over $100,000 until any rate savings on the first $75,000 is lost. The impact of this 5 percent "bubble" is that any C corporation with a taxable income of $335,000 or more will pay a rate of at least 34 percent from dollar one. Earnings of a C corporation in excess of $10 million are taxed at 35 percent, and a 3 percent "bubble" applies to C corporation earnings in excess of $15 million until the rate applicable to all income is 35 percent.[7]

There are no rate breaks for a professional service organization that is taxed as a C corporation; it is subject to a flat 35 percent rate from dollar one.[8]

Q.3 What is the C corporation double tax structure?

The biggest negative of a C corporation is the double tax structure – a corporate level tax and a shareholder level tax. It surfaces whenever a dividend is paid or is deemed to have been paid. But the grief of the double tax structure is not limited to dividends; it kicks in whenever the assets of the business are sold and the proceeds distributed. It's all a result of the inherent double tax structure of a C corporation.

Q.4 What are the federal tax rates that shareholders must pay on dividends received from a C corporation?

The economic stimulus package of 2003 resulted in a compromise that reduced the maximum tax rate on "qualifying corporate dividends" paid to non-corporate shareholders to 15 percent (5 percent for low-income shareholders otherwise subject to maximum marginal rates of 15 percent or less).[9] These reduced rates applied to all dividends received from January 1, 2003 to December 31, 2012. The American Taxpayer Relief Act of 2012 (the "fiscal cliff" legislation signed into law during the final days of 2012)[10] increased this low dividend rate to 20 percent starting in 2013 for couples with taxable incomes in excess of $450,000 and individuals with taxable incomes in excess of $400,000. Plus, in 2013, the 3.8 percent Medicare tax kicked in on interest,

---

7. I.R.C. § 11(b)(1).
8. I.R.C. § 11(b)(2).
9. I.R.C. § 1(h)11(b).
10. Section 102 of the American Taxpayer Relief Act of 2012.

dividends, capital gains, and other "net investment income" to the extent that this income, when added to the taxpayer's other modified adjusted gross income, exceeds $200,000 in the case of unmarried individuals, $250,000 in the case of married individuals filing jointly, and $125,000 in the case of married individuals filing separately.

The net result is that a couple with an adjusted income of less than $250,000 or a single person with an adjusted gross income of less than $200,000 will continue to pay the pre-2013 dividend rates (a maximum of 15 percent).[11] Couples or individuals with higher incomes will pay a combined income and Medicare dividend rate of either 18.8 percent or 23.8 percent, depending on whether the new $450,000 or $400,000 thresholds are exceeded.

Q.5 How are C corporation dividends paid to C corporation shareholders taxed?

There is an attractive income tax deduction for dividends paid by one C corporation to another C corporation. The purpose of the deduction is to eliminate the potential of a triple tax on corporate earnings – one at the operating C corporation level, a second at the corporate shareholder level, and a third at the individual shareholder level. The deduction is at least 70 percent of the dividend paid to a C corporation shareholder, and increases to 80 percent for corporate shareholders who own 20 percent of the operating entity's stock and 100 percent for members of an affiliated group who own at least 80 percent of the operating company's stock.[12]

Q.6 How are tax losses of a C corporation treated?

Losses sustained by a C corporation are trapped inside the corporation. They may be carried backward or forward, but they will never be passed through to the shareholders.

Q.7 How much flexibility does a C corporation have in selecting a tax year?

A great deal. A C corporation may adopt any fiscal year to ease its accounting and administrative burdens and to maximize tax deferral planning.[13]

Q.8 Can a C corporation combine with other corporations on a tax-free basis?

Yes. A C corporation may participate in a tax-free reorganization with other corporate entities. It's possible for corporations to combine through mergers, stock-for-stock transactions, and assets-for-stock transactions on terms that eliminate all corporate and shareholder-level taxes.[14] This opportunity often is the key to the ultimate payday for those private business owners who cash in by "selling" their business to a public corporation. Cast as a reorganization, the transaction allows the acquiring entity to fund the acquisition with its own stock

---

11. I.R.C. § 1411.
12. I.R.C. § 243(a) & (c).
13. See generally I.R.C. § 441.
14. I.R.C. §§ 368, 354, 361.

(little or no cash required) and enables the selling owners to walk with highly liquid, publicly traded securities and no tax bills until the securities are sold.

Q.9 How is the gain recognized on the sale of C corporation stock taxed?

The stock of a C corporation is a capital asset that qualifies for long-term capital gain treatment if sold after being held for more than one year.[15] The problem for planning purposes is that it is usually difficult, if not impossible, to accurately predict when stock may be sold and even more difficult to speculate on what the state of the long-term capital gains break will be at that time. Too often, planning is based on the assumption that the status quo will remain the status quo. History, even very recent history, confirms the fallacy of this assumption with respect to the capital gains tax. Just over the past few decades, we have seen the gap between ordinary and capital gains rates completely eliminated, narrowed to levels that were not compelling for planning purposes, and, as now, widened to levels that get everyone excited.

Q.10 What is the Section 1045 small business stock rollover deferral option?

Section 1045 of the Internal Revenue Code permits a non-corporate shareholder to defer the recognition of gain on the disposition of qualified small business stock held for more than six months by investing the proceeds into the stock of another qualified small business within 60 days of the sale.[16] This perk can excite the entrepreneur who is in the business of moving money from one deal to the next or the shareholder who has a falling out with his or her co-shareholders and wants to exit for another opportunity.

Q.11 How is a loss recognized on the sale of C corporation stock treated for tax purposes?

Generally, any such loss is subject to all the limitations of capital losses. Thus, the loss usually is limited to offsetting capital gains or being recognized over time at a maximum pace of $3,000 a year.

There is a limited exception under Section 1244 of the Code. This exception grants individuals and partnerships ordinary loss treatment (as opposed to the less favorable capital loss treatment) on losses recognized on the sale or exchange of common or preferred stock of a "small business corporation" (generally defined as a corporation whose aggregate contributions to capital and paid-in surplus do not exceed $1 million). In order to qualify, the shareholder must be the original issuee of the stock and the stock must have been issued for money or property (services do not count).[17] This benefit often sounds better than it really is because the ordinary loss in any single year (usually the year of sale) is limited to $50,000 ($100,000 for married couples). This serious dollar

---

15. I.R.C. §§ 1221(a), 1222(3).
16. Section 1045 incorporates the Section 1202(c) definition of "small business stock," which generally requires that the stock have been issued to the original issuee after the effective date of the Revenue Reconciliation Act of 1993 by a C corporation that actively conducts a trade or business and that has gross assets of $50 million or less at the time the stock is issued. I.R.C. § 1202(c), (d) & (e).
17. I.R.C. § 1244.

limitation, together with the fact that bailout loss treatment is not an exciting topic during the start-up planning of any business, usually results in this perk having no impact in the planning process.

Q.12 May C corporation shareholders who are also employees participate in a company's employee benefit programs?

Yes. A shareholder of a C corporation who is also an employee may participate in all employee benefit plans and receive the associated tax benefits. Such plans typically include group term life insurance, medical and dental reimbursement plans, section 125 cafeteria plans, dependent care assistance programs, and qualified transportation reimbursement plans. Partners and most S corporation shareholder/employees (those who own more than 2 percent of the outstanding stock) are not eligible for such the tax benefits.[18]

Q.13 May multiple C corporations that are commonly controlled file as a single entity for federal income tax purposes?

Yes. Often it is advantageous to use multiple corporations to conduct the operations of an expanding business. Multiple entities can reduce liability exposures, regulatory hassles, and employee challenges as the operations diversify and expand into multiple states and foreign countries. While there may be compelling business reasons for the use of multiple entities, business owners often prefer that all of the entities be treated as a single entity for tax purposes in order to simplify tax compliance, eliminate tax issues on transactions between the entities, and facilitate the netting of profits and losses for tax purposes. This is permitted under the consolidated return provisions of the Code.[19] The key is that the entities constitute an "affiliated group," which generally means that their common ownership must extend to 80 percent of the total voting power and 80 percent of the total stock value of each entity included in the group.[20]

Q.14 Is the tax basis of the stock owned by a C corporation shareholder impacted by the corporation's retention and reinvestment of its earnings?

No. The basis of a shareholder's stock in a C corporation is not affected by the entity's income or losses. This can have a profound impact in a situation where a profitable C corporation has accumulated substantial earnings. Assume, for example, that XYZ Inc. has always had a single shareholder, Linda, who purchased her stock for $100,000, and that the company has accumulated $2 million of earnings over the past 10 years. Linda's stock basis at the end of year 10 is still $100,000. In contrast, if XYZ Inc. had been taxed as an S corporation or a partnership from day one, Linda's basis at the end of year 10 would have grown to $2.1 million.[21] On a sale, the difference would be a capital gains hit on $2 million. This basis step-up may be a compelling planning consideration in

---

18. The benefits are available only to "employees," a status that partners can never obtain. Although S corporation shareholders may clearly qualify as "employees," Section 1372 provides that, for fringe benefit purposes, the S corporation will be treated as a partnership and any shareholder owning more than 2 percent of the stock will be treated as a partner.

19. See generally I.R.C. §§ 1501-1504.

20. I.R.C. § 1504(a).

21. I.R.C. § 1367(a). Partners experience the same basis adjustment for accumulated earnings under I.R.C. § 705(a).

many situations.

Q.15 Are C corporations subject to an alternative minimum tax?

Large C corporations are subject to an alternative minimum tax. There are blanket exceptions for a company's first year of operation, for any company with average annual gross receipts of not more than $5 million during its first three years, and for any company with average annual gross receipts of not more than $7.5 million during any three-year period thereafter.[22] The alternative minimum tax applies only to the extent it exceeds the corporation's regular income tax liability. The tax is calculated by applying a flat 20 percent rate to the excess of the corporation's alternative minimum taxable income (AMTI) over a $40,000 exemption.[23] AMTI is defined to include the corporation's taxable income, increased by a host of tax preference items and adjustments designed to reduce certain timing benefits (i.e., accelerated cost recovery deductions) of the regular corporate tax.[24] The greatest impact in recent years has been the expansion of AMTI to include an amount which, roughly speaking, is designed to equal 75 percent of the excess of the corporation's true book earnings over its taxable income.[25]

Q.16 What are the disguised dividend traps of a C corporation?

Any payment from a C corporation to a shareholder may be scrutinized by the Service to see if the payment constitutes a disguised dividend. What's at stake is a deduction at the corporate level and an imputed taxable dividend at the shareholder level. Common examples of disguised dividends include excessive compensation payments to shareholder/employees or family members,[26] personal shareholder expenses that are paid and deducted as business expenses by the corporation,[27] interest payments on excessive shareholder debt that is reclassified as equity,[28] excess rental payments on shareholder property rented or leased to the corporation,[29] personal use of corporate assets, and bargain sales of corporate property to a shareholder.[30]

Q.17 What is the C corporation accumulated earnings trap?

The C corporation double-tax structure produces more revenue for the government when larger dividends are paid and less income is accumulated in the corporation. For this reason, the tax code imposes a penalty tax on C corporations that accumulate excessive amounts of income by not paying sufficient dividends. The tax doesn't kick in until the aggregate accumulated earnings exceed $250,000 ($150,000 in the case of certain professional service

---

22. I.R.C. § 55(e).
23. I.R.C. §§ 55(b)(1)(B), 55(d)(2).
24. See generally I.R.C. § 56.
25. I.R.C. § 56(g).
26. See, e.g., Exacto Spring Corp. v. Commissioner, 196 F.3d 833 (7th Cir. 1999); Elliotts Inc. v. Commissioner, 716 F.2d 1241 (9th Cir. 1983); and Charles McCandless Tire Service v. United States, 422 F.2d 1336 (Ct. Cl. 1970).
27. See, e.g., Hood v. Commissioner, 115 T.C. 172 (2000).
28. See the related discussion Chapter 4. Also, see generally Hariton, "Essay: Distinguishing Between Equity and Debt in the New Financial Environment," 49 Tax L. Rev. 449 (1994).
29. See, e.g., International Artists, Ltd. v. Commissioner, 55 T.C. 94 (1970).
30. See, e.g., Honigman v. Commissioner, 466 F.2d 69 (6th Cir. 1972).

organizations).[31] And the penalty tax can be avoided completely if the corporation can demonstrate that it accumulated the earnings in order to meet the reasonable business needs of the corporation.[32] There is a great deal of latitude in defining the reasonable business needs. For this reason, the accumulated earnings penalty is usually a trap for the uninformed who never saw it coming.

Q.18 What is the C corporation personal holding company trap?

The personal holding company trap is a close cousin to the accumulated earnings trap. Its purpose is to prohibit C corporations from accumulating excess amounts of investment income, certain compensation payments (the incorporated movie star or other talent), and rental income (the corporate yacht scenario). Unlike the accumulated earnings tax, the personal holding company penalty cannot be avoided by documenting reasonable business needs. If the penalty becomes a threat, remedial actions include increasing compensation payments to shareholder/employees and paying dividends. Like the accumulated earnings penalty, it's a nuisance that has to be monitored in select situations.

Q.19 What is the C corporation controlled group trap?

This trap is aimed primarily at the business owner who would like to use multiple C corporations to take multiple advantage of the low C corporation tax rates, the $250,000 accumulated earnings trap threshold, or the $40,000 alternative minimum tax exemption. If multiple corporations are deemed to be part of a controlled group, they are treated as a single entity for purposes of these tax perks, and the multiple-entity benefits are gone.[33]

Section 1563 of the Internal Revenue Code defines three types of controlled groups: parent-subsidiary controlled groups, brother-sister controlled groups, and combined controlled groups.[34] The existence of this trap requires, as part of any business planning analysis, a disclosure of other C corporation interests owned by those who are going to own an interest in the new entity that is considering C corporation status.

Q.20 What is the section 482 trap?

Section 482 is an ominous provision that gives the Internal Revenue Service authority to "distribute, apportion, or allocate gross income, deductions, credits or allowances between and among" commonly controlled business interests "whenever necessary to prevent evasion of taxes or clearly to reflect the income" of any such businesses.

Although 482, by its terms, applies to any type of business organization, its application to related C corporations who do business with each other can trigger brutal double tax consequences. All business dealings between commonly

---

31. I.R.C. § 535(c).

32. I.R.C. § 532 provides that the tax is applicable to any corporation that is "formed or availed of for the purpose of avoiding the income tax with respect to its shareholders..." Section 533(a) then provides that, unless the corporation can prove by a preponderance of evidence to the contrary, any accumulation of earnings and profits "beyond the reasonable needs of the business shall be determinative of the purpose to avoid the income tax..."

33. I.R.C. § 1561

34. I.R.C. § 1563(a)(3).

controlled entities must be carefully monitored to avoid Section 482 exposure.

Q.21 What is an S corporation?

An S corporation is a hybrid whose popularity has grown in recent years. It is organized as a corporation under state law and offers corporate limited liability protections. But it is taxed as a pass-through entity under the provisions of Subchapter S of the Internal Revenue Code. These provisions are similar, but not identical, to the partnership provisions of Subchapter K. The popularity of S status is attributable primarily to three factors: (1) accumulated earnings increase the outside stock basis of the shareholders' stock; (2) an S corporation is free of any threat of a double tax on shareholder distributions or sale proceeds; and (3) S status can facilitate income shifting and passive income generation.

Q.22 Can any corporation elect to be taxed as an S corporation?

No. There are certain limitations and restrictions with an S corporation that can pose serious problems in the planning process. Not every corporation is eligible to elect S status. If a corporation has a shareholder that is a corporation, a partnership, a non-resident alien or an ineligible trust, S status is not available.[35] Banks and insurance companies cannot elect S status.[36] Also, the election cannot be made if the corporation has more than 100 shareholders or has more than one class of stock.[37] For purposes of the 100-shareholder limitation, a husband and wife are counted as one shareholder and all the members of a family (six generations deep) may elect to be treated as one shareholder.[38] The one class of stock requirement is not violated if the corporation has both voting and nonvoting common stock and the only difference is voting rights.[39] Also, there is an important debt safe harbor provision that easily can be satisfied to protect against the threat of an S election being jeopardized by a shareholder debt obligation being characterized as a second class of stock.[40]

Q.23 What trusts are eligible to own stock of an S corporation?

Trusts that are now eligible to qualify as S corporation shareholders include: (1) voting trusts; (2) grantor trusts; (3) testamentary trusts that receive S corporation stock via a will (but only for a two year period following the transfer); (4) testamentary trusts that receive S corporation stock via a former grantor trust (but only for a two year period following the transfer); (5) "qualified subchapter S" trusts (QSSTs), which generally are trusts with only one current income beneficiary who is a U.S. resident or citizen to whom all income is distributed annually and who elects to be treated as the owner of the S corporation stock for tax purposes; and (6) "electing small business" trusts

---

35. I.R.C. § 1361(b).

36. I.R.C. § 1361(b)(2).

37. I.R.C. § 1361(b)(1)(A) & (D).

38. I.R.C. § 1361(c)(1).

39. I.R.C. § 1361(c)(4).

40. I.R.C. § 1361(c)(5). To fit within the safe harbor, there must be a written unconditional promise to pay on demand or on a specified date a sum certain and (1) the interest rate and payment dates cannot be contingent on profits, the borrower's discretion, or similar factors; (2) there can be no stock convertibility feature; and (3) the creditor must be an individual, an estate, a trust eligible to be a shareholder, or a person regularly and actively engaged in the business of lending money. For planning purposes, it is an easy fit in most situations.

(ESBTs), which are trusts whose beneficiaries are qualifying S corporation shareholders who acquired their interests in the trust by gift or inheritance, not purchase.[41] An ESBT must elect to be treated as an S corporation shareholder, in which case each current beneficiary of the trust is counted as one shareholder for purposes of the maximum 100 shareholder limitation and the S corporation income is taxed to the trust at the highest individual marginal rate under the provisions of the Internal Revenue Code.[42]

Q.24 How does a corporation elect in and out of S status?

An election to S status requires a timely filing of a Form 2553 and the consent of all shareholders.[43] A single dissenter can hold up the show. For this reason, often it is advisable to include in an organizational agreement among all the owners (typically a shareholder agreement) a provision that requires all owners to consent to an S election if a designated percentage of the owners at any time approve the making of the election. The election, once made, is effective for the current tax year if made during the preceding year or within the first two and one-half months of the current year.[44] If made during the first two and one-half months of the year, all shareholders who have owned stock at any time during the year, even those who no longer own stock at the time of the election, must consent in order for the election to be valid for the current year.[45]

Exiting out of S status is easier than electing into it; a revocation is valid if approved by shareholders holding more than half of the outstanding voting and nonvoting shares.[46] For the organization that wants to require something more than a simple majority to trigger such a revocation, the answer is a separate agreement among the shareholders that provides that no shareholder will consent to a revocation absent the approval of a designated supermajority. The revocation may designate a future effective date. Absent such a designation, the election is effective on the first day of the following year, unless it is made on or before the 15th day of the third month of the current year, in which case it is retroactively effective for the current year.[47]

Q.25 How is the income of an S corporation taxed?

The income of an S corporation is passed through and taxed to its shareholders. The entity itself pays no tax on the income,[48] and the shareholders' recognition of the income is not affected by the corporation's retention or distribution of the income. There is only one tax at the owner level. Unlike a C corporation, a distribution of cash or other assets generally does not trigger a tax at either the entity or owner level. Since there is no double-tax structure, all the C corporation traps tied to that menacing structure, including the double-taxed disguised dividend trap, the accumulated earnings tax trap, the personal holding

---

41. I.R.C. §§ 1361(c)(2), 1361(d), 1361(e).
42. I.R.C. §§ 1361 (e)(1)(A), 1361(c)(2)(b)(v).
43. I.R.C. § 1362(a). See generally Reg. § 1.1362-6.
44. I.R.C. § 1362(b)(1).
45. I.R.C. § 1362(b)(2). For potential relief on a late election where there is reasonable cause for the tardiness, see I.R.C. § 1362(b)(5) and Rev. Proc. 2004-48, 2004-2 C.B. 172.
46. I.R.C. § 1362(d)(1).
47. I.R.C. § 1362(d)(1)(C) & (D).
48. I.R.C. § 1363(a).

company trap, and the controlled group trap have no application to an S corporation. Also, the income passing through an S corporation may qualify as passive income for those shareholders who are not deemed "material participants."

Q.26 How are losses of an S corporation taxed?

An S corporation's losses also are passed through to its shareholders, subject to the three loss hurdles applicable to partnership-taxed entities that are discussed in question Q.33 below. The one hurdle that is slightly different for an S corporation is the basis hurdle. Unlike the basis of an interest in a partnership-taxed entity, the basis in S corporation stock does not include any share of the entity's liabilities. The result is that this hurdle, while generally not a big deal for partnership-taxed entities, often limits the tax benefits of losses allocated and passed through to an S corporation shareholder.

Q.27 Is the tax basis of the stock owned by an S corporation shareholder impacted by the corporation's allocation of income and losses and distributions?

Yes. An S corporation shareholder's stock basis is adjusted up and down for allocable income and losses and cash distributions, much as with a partnership.[49] There is no locked-in basis, as there is with a C corporation.

Q.28 As compared to a C corporation, is it easier from a tax standpoint for an S corporation to make distributions to its shareholders?

Yes. The tax consequences of distributing money or property from an S corporation generally are much less severe than for a C corporation. Generally distributions that do not exceed a shareholder's basis in his or her stock are tax-free, and a shareholder's stock basis is continually being increased as earnings are allocated to the shareholder.

Q.29 How much flexibility does an S corporation have in selecting a tax year?

S corporations have very little flexibility, particularly as compared to the flexibility of C corporations. Partnerships, LLCs, S corporations and sole proprietorships generally are required to use a calendar year unless they can prove a business purpose for using a fiscal year (a tough burden in most cases) or make a tax deposit under Section 7519 that is designed to eliminate any deferral advantage.

Q.30 Is it costly from a tax standpoint to convert from a C corporation to an S corporation?

A C corporation's conversion to an S corporation is far easier and less costly from a tax perspective than a conversion to a partnership-taxed entity, such as a limited liability company. But there are traps even in an S conversion for built-in asset gains, accumulated earnings, LIFO inventory reserves, and excessive S corporation passive income. Usually these traps can be avoided or managed with

---

49. I.R.C. § 1367(a).

smart planning.

2. LLC AND PARTNERSHIP TAX BASICS - Q&AS

Q.31 Are limited liability companies and partnerships taxed the same?

Generally, yes. The great bulk of partnerships and LLCs are treated as partnership-taxed entities under subchapter K of the Internal Revenue Code. However, any limited liability company or partnership may elect to be taxed as either a C corporation or an S corporation. Absent such an election, the entity will be taxed as a partnership under the provisions of subchapter K.[50] An election to be taxed as a corporation may be effective up to 75 days before and 12 months after the election is filed.[51] The election must be signed by all members (including any former members impacted by a retroactive election) or by an officer or member specifically authorized to make the election.[52]

Q.32 How is the income of a partnership-taxed entity taxed?

The income of the entity is passed through and taxed to its owners. The entity itself reports the income, but pays no taxes. The advantage, of course, is that there is no threat of a double tax. There is only one tax at the owner level. Unlike a C corporation, a distribution of cash or other assets generally does not trigger a tax at either the entity or owner level. Since there is no double-tax structure, all the C corporation traps tied to that menacing structure, including the disguised dividend trap, the accumulated earnings tax trap, the personal holding company trap, and the controlled group trap have no application to entities taxed as partnerships.

Q.33 How are losses of a partnership-taxed entity taxed?

The losses of a partnership-taxed entity also pass through to its owners. Unlike a C corporation, the losses are not trapped inside the entity.

Does this mean the owners can use the losses to reduce the tax bite on their other income? Maybe. There are three hurdles that first must be overcome, and they can be very difficult in many situations. The first and easiest hurdle is the basis hurdle – the losses passed through to an owner cannot exceed that owner's basis in his or her interest in the entity.[53] This hurdle seldom presents a problem in a partnership-taxed entity because each owner's share of the entity's liabilities, even its nonrecourse liabilities, is treated as a contribution of money by the owner for basis purposes.[54]

The second hurdle, known as the at-risk hurdle, generally limits an owner's losses to only the amount that the owner actually has at risk.[55] An owner's at-risk amount typically includes property contributed to the entity by the owner and the owner's share of the entity's recourse liabilities (those liabilities that create

---

50. Reg. §§ 301.7701-2(c)(1), 301.7701-3(a), 301.7701-3(b)(1).
51. Reg. § 301.7701-3(c)(1)(iii).
52. Reg. § 301.7701-3(c)(2).
53. I.R.C. § 704(d).
54. I.R.C. § 752(a).
55. I.R.C. § 465(a).

personal exposure for the owners).[56] Nonrecourse liabilities (those liabilities for which no owner has any personal exposure) generally do not count for purposes of the at-risk hurdle, but there is an important exception for qualified nonrecourse financing that makes it easy for many real estate transactions to satisfy the at-risk limitations.[57]

The third hurdle (and usually the toughest) is the passive loss rule,[58] a 1980s creation that is designed to prevent a taxpayer from using losses from a passive business venture to offset active business income or portfolio income (i.e., interest, dividends, gains from stocks and bonds, etc.). It was created to stop doctors and others from using losses from real estate and other tax shelters to reduce or eliminate the tax on their professional and business incomes.

Losses passed through from a passive venture can only be offset against passive income from another source. If there is not sufficient passive income to cover the passive losses, the excess passive losses are carried forward until sufficient passive income is generated or the owner disposes of his or her interest in the passive activity that produced the unused losses.[59]

Whether a particular business activity is deemed passive or active with respect to a particular partner is based on the owner's level of participation in the activity – that is, whether the owner is a "material participant" in the activity. A limited partner is presumed not to be a material participant and, therefore, all losses allocated to a limited partner generally are deemed passive.[60] To meet the "material participation" standard and avoid the hurdle, an owner must show "regular, continuous, and substantial" involvement in the activity.[61]

Given these three hurdles, it is never safe to assume that use of a partnership-taxed entity will convert start-up losses into slam-dunk tax benefits for the owners.

Q.34 Are there potential passive income benefits with a limited liability company or partnership?

Yes. Generally, taxable income is classified as portfolio income (dividends, interest, royalties, gains from stocks and bonds, and assets that produce such income), active income (income from activities in which the taxpayer materially

---

56. I.R.C. § 465(b).

57. I.R.C. § 465(b)(6). To qualify as "qualified nonrecourse financing," the debt must be incurred in connection with the activity of holding real estate, must not impose any personal liability on any person, must not be convertible debt, and must have been obtained from a "qualified person" (generally defined to include a person who is in the business of lending money, who is not related to the borrower, and who is not the seller or related to the seller).

58. See generally I.R.C. § 469.

59. I.R.C. §§ 469(a), 469(b), 469(d)(1).

60. I.R.C. § 469(h)(2).

61. I.R.C. § 469(h)(1). Under the temporary regulations, a taxpayer meets the material participation standard for a year by (1) participating in the activity for more than 500 hours in the year; (2) being the sole participant in the activity; (3) participating more than 100 hours in the activity and not less than any other person; (4) participating more than 100 hours in the activity and participating in the aggregate more than 500 hours in significant participation activities; (5) having been a material participant in the activity for any five of the last ten years; (6) having materially participated in the activity in any three previous years if the activity is a personal service activity; or (7) proving regular, continuous and substantial participation based on all facts and circumstances. Temp. Reg. § 1.469-5T(a)(1)-(7).

participates), or passive income (income from passive business ventures). Passive income is the only type of income that can be sheltered by either an active loss or a passive loss. So the passive loss rule, by limiting the use of passive losses, exalts the value of passive income. An activity that generates passive income can breathe tax life into passive losses from other activities. A C corporation has no capacity to produce passive income; it pays dividends or interest (both classified as portfolio income) or compensation income (active income). In contrast, a profitable entity taxed as a partnership or an S corporation can pass through valued passive income to those owners who are not material participants.

Q.35 Is the tax basis of the interest owned by the owner of a partnership-taxed entity impacted by the entity's allocation of income and losses and distributions?

Yes. The owner's basis in his or her partnership interest is adjusted upward by capital contributions and income allocations and downward by distributions and loss allocations.[62] Unlike stock in a C corporation, there is no locked-in basis. This can be a valuable benefit to the owner of a thriving business that retains income to finance growth and expansion. The retained earnings will drive up the tax basis of the owners' interests in the enterprise, which will result in less taxable income at time of sale.

Q.36 How much flexibility does a partnership-taxed entity have in designing special allocations among its owners?

It has tremendous flexibility. An entity taxed as a partnership may structure special allocations of income and loss items among its various owners. For example, one owner may be allocated 60 percent of all income and 30 percent of all losses. Although a C corporation has some limited capacity to create allocation differences among owners through the use of different classes of stock and debt instruments, that capacity pales in comparison to the flexibility available to a partnership-taxed entity. The same comparison holds true for an S corporation which can issue only one class of stock.

A partnership-taxed entity's allocation will be respected for tax purposes only if it has "substantial economic effect,"[63] three words that make section 704(b) and its regulations one of the most complex subjects in the world of tax. Generally speaking (and I do mean generally), an allocation that does not produce a deficit capital account for a partner will have "economic effect" if capital accounts are maintained for all partners and, upon liquidation of the partnership, liquidating distributions are made in accordance with positive capital account balances.[64]

In order for an allocation that produces a deficit capital account balance to have "economic effect," the partner also must be unconditionally obligated to restore the deficit (i.e., pay cash to cover the shortfall) upon liquidation of the

---

62. I.R.C. § 705(a).
63. I.R.C. § 704(b).
64. Reg. §§ 1.704-1(b)(2)(ii) (b)(1), 1.704-(b)(2)(ii) (B)(2).

partnership,[65] or the partnership must have sufficient nonrecourse debt to assure that the partner's share of any minimum gain recognized on the discharge of the debt will eliminate the deficit.[66]

An "economic effect," if present, will not be deemed "substantial" if it produces an after-tax benefit for one or more partners with no diminished after-tax consequences to other partners.[67] The most common examples of economic effects that are not deemed "substantial" are shifting allocations (allocations of different types of income and deductions among partners within a given year to reduce individual taxes without changing the partners' relative economic interests in the partnership) and transitory allocations (allocations in one year that are offset by allocations in later years).[68]

Q.37 How easy is it from a tax standpoint to get money out of a limited liability company or a partnership?

It's easy to get money or property out of an entity that is taxed as a partnership. The Code is structured to eliminate all taxes on distributions at both the entity and owner level. There are a few exceptions. One is where a distribution of money to an owner exceeds the owner's basis in his or her entity interest; the excess is taxable.[69] Another is where the entity has unrealized accounts receivable or substantially appreciated inventory items; in these cases, ordinary income may need to be recognized to reflect any change in an owner's interest in such assets.[70]

These easy bail-out provisions are a far cry from the harsh dividend, redemption, and liquidation provisions of C corporations, all of which are designed to maximize the tax bite at both the entity and owner levels on any money or property flowing from the corporation to its owners.

Q.38 What is the tax-free profits interest benefit available to a limited liability company or a partnership?

Often a business entity desires to transfer an equity interest in future profits to one who works for the business. An entity taxed as a partnership can do this without triggering any current tax hit for the recipient.[71] A corporation generally cannot transfer an equity interest in return for services without creating a taxable event. Note that this benefit only applies to an equity interest in future profits, not an interest in existing capital.

Q.39 What is the family partnership tax trap applicable to a limited liability company or a partnership?

Entities that are considered family partnerships for tax purposes are subject to a special trap that is designed to prevent the use of the entity to aggressively shift income among family members. If any person gifts an entity interest to a

---

65. Reg. § 1.704-1(b)(2)(ii) (b)(3).

66. Reg. §§ 1.704-(2)(c), 1.704-(2)(f)(1), 1.704-(g)(1), 1.704-2(b)(1) & (e).

67. Reg. § 1.704-1(b)(2)(iii).

68. Reg. § 1.704-1(b)(2)(iii) (b) & (c).

69. I.R.C. § 731(a).

70. I.R.C. § 751; Reg. §§ 1.751-1(b)(2)(ii), 1.751-1(b)(3)(ii), 1.751-1(g).

71. See Rev. Proc. 93-27, 1993-2 C.B. 343 and Rev. Proc. 2001-43, 2001-2 C.B. 191.

family member, the donor must be adequately compensated for any services rendered to the partnership; and the income allocated to the donee, calculated as a yield on capital, cannot be proportionately greater than the yield to the donor.[72]

In effect, special allocations to favor donees are prohibited, as are attempts to shift service income. Any purchase among family members is considered a "gift" for purposes of this trap.[73]

Q.40   Is it possible to convert a C corporation to a limited liability company or a partnership?

Technically it is possible, but usually it is prohibitive from a tax standpoint to convert from a C corporation to an entity taxed as a partnership. Such a change will produce a double tax triggered by a liquidation of the C corporation. The far better option (and often the only viable option) is to convert to S corporation status if pass-through tax benefits are desired.

3. SELF-EMPLOYMENT AND PAYROLL TAX BASICS - Q&As

Q.41   What impact does the self-employment and payroll tax have on the business planning process?

The self-employment/payroll tax is a regressive tax that is easy to ignore, but the consequences of neglect can be painful. The tax is levied at a flat rate of 15.3 percent on a base level of self-employment earnings ($117,000 for 2014) and 2.9 percent above the base. Starting in 2013, the rate jumped to 3.8 percent on a married couple's earnings in excess of $250,000 and an unmarried individual's earnings in excess of $200,000, and the new 3.8 percent rate applies to any interest, dividends, capital gains, and "net investment income" received by such taxpayers.[74] A self-employed person is entitled to an income tax deduction of one-half of self-employment taxes paid at the 15.3 percent and 2.9 percent rates.[75]

Q.42   How does the payroll tax impact employees?

An employee has one-half of the tax (7.65 percent) come directly from his or her paycheck in the form of payroll taxes. The other half is paid by the employer who, in order to stay in business, must consider this tax burden in setting the pay level for employees.

Q.43 How does the self-employment tax impact high-income taxpayers?

For high-income owners, including many business owners, the personal impact of the self-employment tax often is not significant because they are able to structure their affairs to reduce or eliminate its impact, or the base amount subject to the tax is considered small in relation to their overall earnings. The tax, by design, is structured to punish middle- and low-income workers. For 80 percent of American workers, the self-employment and payroll taxes paid on

---

72. I.R.C. § 704(e).
73. I.R.C. § 704(e)(3).
74. I.R.C. § 1411.
75. I.R.C. § 164(f).

their earnings exceed the income tax bite, often by many times.[76]

Q.44 Is the self-employment tax a factor to consider in choosing the best form of business entity to use in a given situation?

The answer is "yes" in many, but not all, situations. The form of business entity that is selected can affect the self-employment tax burden for the owners of the business. This issue is discussed in the following chapter.

Q.45 What are the self-employment and payroll tax impacts with a C corporation?

Compensation payments from a C corporation to owners or employees are subject to payroll taxes. Corporate dividends are now subject to the 3.8 percent tax to the extent a married couple's income exceeds $250,000 and an unmarried individual's income exceeds $200,000.[77] For other taxpayers, dividends are not subject to the tax. In a C corporation context, the negative trade-off is that the dividends are subject to the double income tax structure.

Q.46 What are the self-employment tax impacts with an S corporation?

The C corporation double-tax trade-off disappears for an S corporation whose earnings are taxed directly through to its shareholders. Compensation payments to an S corporation shareholder are subject to payroll taxes. But a shareholder who works for an S corporation avoids all self-employment taxes on dividends, including the 3.8 percent Medicare tax.[78] An S corporation investor who does not materially participate in the venture will also avoid any self-employment tax on dividends unless the applicable $250,000/$200,000 threshold is exceeded, in which case the 3.8 percent tax will kick in.

A question that is often asked: Can a person who is the sole owner of an S corporation and works for the entity eliminate all self-employment and payroll taxes by paying only dividends? If a shareholder renders significant services to the S corporation and receives no compensation payments, the Service likely will claim that a portion of the dividends are compensation payments subject to payroll taxes.[79] The key is to be reasonable in taking advantage of the tax loophole for S corporation dividends paid to a shareholder/employee. Set a defensible compensation level and pay payroll taxes at that level. Then distribute the balance as dividends that are not subject to any self-employment or payroll tax burden.

Q.47 What are the self-employment tax impacts with a partnership?

Section 1402(a) of the Code specifically provides that a partner's distributive share of income from a partnership constitutes earnings from self-employment

---

76. Report of the Congressional Budget Office, Economic Stimulus: Evaluating Proposed Changes in Tax Policy – Approaches to Cutting Personal Taxes (January 2002), footnote 7.

77. I.R.C. §§ 1402(a)(2), 1411.

78. If an S corporation shareholder materially participates in the venture, dividends paid to that shareholder do not fall within the definition of "net investment income" in IRC § 1411. See IRS Guidance in Reg.130507-11 (November 30, 2012).

79. See, for example, Joseph Radtke, S.C. v. United States, 712 F.Supp. 143 (E.D. Wis. 1989), affirmed 895 F.2d 1196 (7th Cir. 1990); Spicer Accounting, Inc. v. United States, 918 F.2d 90 (9th Cir. 1990); and Dunn & Clark, P.A. v. Commissioner, 57 F.3d 1076 (9th Cir. 1995).

tax purposes.[80] There is a limited statutory exception for retired partners[81] and a broader exception for limited partners, but the new 3.8 percent Medicare tax will still be applicable to the extent the triggering income thresholds ($250,000 or $200,000) are exceeded.[82] Thus, the key to minimizing the tax in a partnership structure is to fit within this limited partnership exception.

Q.48 What are the self-employment tax impacts with a limited liability company?

It may be more difficult to avoid the tax for a member of a limited liability company that has no limited partners.

The Service's first attempt to provide some guidance on the issue came in 1994 when it published its first Proposed Regulations. After public comment, new Proposed Regulations were issued in 1997, defining the scope of the limited partnership exception for all entities taxed as a partnership, without regard to state law characterizations.[83] Under the 1997 Proposed Regulations, an individual would be treated as a limited partner for purposes of the self-employment tax unless the individual was personally liable for the debts of the entity by being a partner, had authority to contract on behalf of the entity under applicable law, or participated for more than 500 hours in the business during the taxable year. The 1997 Proposed Regulations also drew criticism because LLC members who had authority to contract on behalf of the entity could never fit within the limited partner exception. The result was a statutory moratorium in 1997 on the issuance of any temporary or proposed regulations dealing with the limited partnership exception.[84]

For planning purposes, where does this history leave us now with respect to entities taxed as partnerships? Any general partner under state law must pay the tax. Any limited partner under applicable state law is probably safe. As for LLC members, any member who can fit within the 1997 Proposed Regulations' definition is justified in relying on the statutory limited partner exception. Beyond that definition, it becomes more difficult and uncertain to evaluate the facts and circumstances of each situation. The risk escalates in direct proportion to the individual's authority to act on behalf of the entity and the scope of any services rendered. Note, however, that any member will now be subject to the new 3.8 percent Medicare tax to the extent the applicable triggering income threshold ($250,000 or $200,000) is exceeded.

Q.49 Is it smart to design a plan that reduces or eliminates self-employment tax burdens for the owners of a business?

Most think it is. Of course, the payment of self-employment taxes may result in higher Social Security benefits down the road. The Social Security program, as presently structured, will become unsustainable in the future. Current benefit levels can be maintained long term only if tax rates or

---

80. I.R.C. § 1402(a).
81. I.R.C. § 1402(a)(10).
82. I.R.C. §§ 1402(a)(13), 1411.
83. Proposed Reg. § 1.1402 (a)-2.
84. Tax Relief Act of 1997 § 935.

government borrowing levels are increased to unprecedented levels. There is a strong likelihood that, at some point in the not-too-distant future, forced structural reform of the program will reduce future government-funded benefits for all except those who are close to retirement or at the lowest income levels.[85]

STUDENT PROBLEM 9-1

Linda has started a business that will generate about $200,000 of earnings each year. Linda will work full time for the business. Her plan is to withdraw $125,000 of earnings from the business each year. She will leave the remaining earnings in the business to retire debt and fund future needs of the business. Linda wants to minimize the overall tax bite on these earnings.

What will be the total entity and personal tax cost under each of the following scenarios, assuming Linda's ordinary income tax rate is 28 percent, her dividend rate is 15 percent, and the applicable self-employment/payroll tax rate is 15.3 percent on the first $117,000 of earnings and 2.9 percent on the excess? Ignore all potential state income tax consequences.

1. Linda's business is a C corporation that distributes Linda a $125,000 dividend each year.

2. Linda's business is a C corporation that pays Linda a salary of $125,000 each year for services she renders to the corporation.

3. Linda's business is an S corporation that pays Linda a $45,000 salary each year and distributes a $80,000 dividend to her each year.

4. Linda's business is a limited liability company that is taxed as a partnership. Linda owns 90 percent of the business, and Judd, an investor who does not work in the business, owns the remaining 10 percent. The LLC distributes $117,000 to Linda each year and $13,000 to Judd. Assume Judd's marginal tax rate is also 28 percent.

---

85. See generally The Interim and Final Reports of the President's Commission to Strengthen Social Security (August 2001 & December 2001).

CHAPTER 10

CHOOSING THE BEST ENTITY FORM

A. MOVING TARGETS AND COLLATERAL CONSEQUENCES

A primary planning challenge for all businesses is to select the best form of business organization. Too many mistakenly assume that this challenge is limited to new ventures. Many mature businesses have a need to re-evaluate their business structure from time to time to maximize the benefits of the enterprise for its owners.

Some perceive the "choice of entity" analysis solely as a tax-driven exercise. Although taxes are vitally important, there are many important non-tax factors that can impact the ultimate decision. The rules of the game have changed in recent years. Some factors, once deemed crucial, no longer impact the outcome. And often new issues must be factored into the mix. In most situations, the analytical process requires the owners to predict and handicap what's likely to happen down the road. They need to consider and project earnings, losses, capital expansion needs, debt levels, the possibility of adding new owners, potential exit strategies, the likelihood of a sale, the estate planning needs of the owners, and a variety of other factors. The decision-making process is not an exact science that punches out a single, perfect answer. The owners need to weigh and consider a number of factors, while being sensitive to the potential consequences of each available alternative.

A choice-of-entity analysis requires a careful assessment of all relevant factors. The following section reviews 16 of the key factors, illustrated through five case studies. Each entity option offers certain benefits and traps that may pose problems down the road. The analysis should include a review of the benefits and traps to assess their relevance to the specific situation.

Although each factor may be important, they never have equal weight in any given situation. It is not a game of adding up the factors to see which form of entity scores the most points. In many cases, one or two factors may be so compelling in the particular situation that they alone dictate the solution. But even then, the other factors cannot be ignored because they help identify the collateral consequences of the decision that is about to be made.

Also, be ever mindful that taxes are a moving target. The rules often change. What works today may make no sense tomorrow. Those who watched the eleventh-hour theatrics of the Congress and White House during the closing days of 2010 and 2012 to prevent threatened tax chaos saw that it is all about politics and inherent uncertainty. We can make predictions and try hard to assess the political winds, but uncertainty is a given that makes choice-of-entity planning more challenging and exciting.

The issue of limited liability protection for the owners of the business, once considered to be the most critical factor in the choice-of-entity analysis, is no longer included in the list of key factors. It's not that insulating the owners of a business from personal liability for the business' liabilities is no longer important; it's as important today as ever. It's absent from the critical factor list because it can be accomplished in any situation. Thus, it is a neutral consideration that no longer needs to impact the decision-making process. Even a general partner can be protected by placing the ownership interest in a limited liability company or S corporation.

B. KEY FACTORS AND CONSEQUENCES

EXAMPLE CASE ONE: JASON

Jason, a seasoned entrepreneur, plans to start a new business that will offer specialized heavy equipment moving services in the western United States. Jason will own 60 percent of the new enterprise, and the remaining 40 percent will be owned equally by two investors, buddies of Jason.

Jason will oversee the business, as he does with the other businesses that he has organized. He will not be a fulltime employee of the business. The business will initially have about 30 employees. Jason anticipates that the business will be profitable by year two, and he has advised the investors that regular distributions will be made starting in year two. Plus, if things play out as planned, there might be a potential to sell the business to a large strategic player down the road.

Jason wants an entity that will minimize all tax bites, always leave him in complete control, and avoid, to the fullest extent possible, any potential hassles with the minority owners.

The best option for Jason's new company would be an S corporation. This case illustrates six key factors.

Factor 1: Earnings Bailout

In Jason's situation, an important factor in the choice-of-entity decision analysis is the tax cost of getting earnings out of the enterprise and into the hands of Jason and the other owners. Bailing out earnings in S corporations, LLCs, partnerships, and sole proprietorships usually is no big deal. Profits generated by the business are passed through and taxed directly to the owners, so the distribution of those profits in the form of dividends or partnership distributions carries no tax consequences. In contrast, bailing out the fruits of a C corporation may trigger substantial income tax consequences, because a C corporation is not a pass-through entity.

When a C corporation bails out its earnings by distributing them to its shareholders in the form of dividends, the dividend distribution is not deductible by the corporation. The corporation pays a tax on the earnings, and the distribution of those earnings to the shareholders in the form of dividends is taxed a second time at the shareholder level. This double tax is one of the negatives of a C corporation.

For some businesses, this double tax risk is more academic than real. There are often ways to avoid it. The most common is for the shareholders to be employed by the corporation and to receive earnings in the form of taxable compensation. The payment of the compensation to the shareholders is deductible by the corporation, so that income is only taxed once, at the shareholder level. But the compensation must be reasonable for the services actually rendered. If it isn't, it may be re-characterized as a dividend. In service corporations where the services are rendered by the shareholders, stripping out all of the earnings of the business through the use of compensation payments usually can be easily justified. Since Jason and his investors will not work for the new business, the compensation bailout strategy isn't an option.

Factor 2: Self-Employment and Payroll Taxes

Self-employment and payroll taxes can be an important choice-of-entity factor in some situations. In Jason's situation, use of an S corporation may create the opportunity to save these taxes and also escape double income tax treatment by virtue of the S election.

A C corporation will not help Jason on this issue. Any compensation payments to owners of a C corporation will be subject to payroll taxes. Except to the extent the new 3.8 percent Medicare tax is applicable to those with incomes above the triggering thresholds ($250,000 or $200,000), there is no self-employment tax imposed on dividends from a C corporation, but such dividends are subject to a double income tax structure.

Similarly, a partnership-taxed entity may not work for Jason on this issue. Distributions by a partnership-taxed entity, including a limited liability company, will not escape self-employment taxes unless the owners are limited partners. If the owners are limited partners of a limited partnership, there is a statutory exception that will protect them from self-employment taxes. The same exception should work in the context of a limited liability company where the owners have no management rights in the enterprise and are not personally responsible for the liabilities of the entity. The tough situation comes when a key owner, such a Jason, wants to exercise management rights. In Jason's case, reliance on the limited partnership exception in the LLC context may create an intolerable risk, given the uncertainty of current law.

For self-employment tax purposes, a much smarter option would be an S corporation whose income is not subject to self-employment taxes when passed through to its owners. Depending on the potential size of the self-employment tax in a particular situation, this factor may be the deciding issue in some cases.

Factor 3: Tax-Free Reorganization Potential

If the business succeeds and a sellout opportunity surfaces, a corporate entity will be able to participate in a tax-free reorganization with a corporate buyer. Corporations may combine through mergers, stock-for-stock transactions, and assets-for-stock transactions on terms that eliminate all corporate and shareholder-level taxes. This benefit often is the key to the ultimate payday for those business owners who cash in by "selling" to a public corporation. Cast as a reorganization, the transaction allows the acquiring entity to fund the acquisition with its own stock (little or no cash required) and enables the selling owners to walk with highly liquid, publicly traded securities and no tax bills until the securities are sold.

A partnership-taxed entity, such as a limited liability company, cannot enjoy the tax-free benefits of a corporate reorganization.

Factor 4: Control Rights

Jason wants complete control over all business decisions with as little discussion and fanfare as possible. A corporation, either C or S, or a limited partnership automatically offers this type of ultimate control in favor of the majority, absent a special agreement to the contrary. Minority corporate shareholders often have no control rights; the majority elects the board of directors, and the board has the authority to manage the affairs of the corporation. Limited partner status and the benefits associated with that status (i.e., liability protection and freedom from self-employment taxes) mandate little or no control. For the majority player who wants control of all the reins, the idea of easily getting it all "the normal way" can be appealing.

Limited liability companies and general partnerships are different only in that the control rights need to be spelled out in an operating agreement among the owners. In some cases, the fear is that the need for a single operating agreement may result in more dialogue, more negotiation, and more compromise. Minority owners may see that there is no "standard" or "normal" way of locking in voting requirements and that the agreement can be crafted to address the control concerns of all parties.

Once minority expectations are elevated, the majority players' options become more difficult. One option, of course, is to throw down the gauntlet and demand ultimate majority control. Beyond the personal discomfort of having to overtly make such demands, the demands themselves may fuel suspicions, undermine loyalties, or, worst case, trigger the departure of a valuable minority player. The alternative option is to build into the operating agreement "mutually acceptable" minority rights.

Factor 5: Sellout Tax Hit

Many who start a new business are not focused on selling out down the road. But this factor can be extremely important in selecting the right form of business organization. If this factor is neglected, a business owner may find that, when it comes time to cash in, there is an added tax burden that could have been avoided.

If Jason's business flourishes and its assets are ultimately sold within a pass-through entity, such as an S corporation, partnership or LLC, the gains realized on the sale of the assets are taxed to the owners in proportion to their interests in the business. After those taxes are paid, the owners are free to pocket the net proceeds. Bailing out of a C corporation may carry a significant additional tax cost. A simple example illustrates the impact.

Assume Jason started a C corporation with a $250,000 investment, that the assets in the company have a present basis of $750,000, and that the company is worth $3 million. It's now time to cash in. The buyer does not want to buy the stock, but is willing to pay $3 million for the assets in the business.

The C corporation would sell the assets for $3 million to the buyer, and the corporation would recognize a $2.25 million gain – the difference between the $3 million purchase price and the corporation's $750,000 tax basis in the assets. After the corporation pays a corporate income tax on the gain, the balance of the proceeds would be distributed to the shareholders, who would pay a capital gains tax on the difference between the amount received and their low basis in the stock. The threat of this double tax at the time of sale is a major disadvantage for many C corporations.

Beyond this double tax impact, other important elements of this sellout factor should be considered. First, if a C corporation accumulates earnings within the corporation over an extended period of time, those accumulations do nothing to increase the shareholders' tax basis in their stock. If a shareholder sells stock down the road, the shareholder recognizes capital gains based on the shareholder's original cost basis in the stock. In contrast, if the business organization is operated in a pass-through entity, such as an LLC, an S corporation, or a partnership, the earnings accumulated in the business will boost, dollar for dollar, the owner's tax basis in his or her stock or partnership interest. So if the owner sells the stock or partnership interest, the earnings accumulated within the enterprise reduce the tax bite to the owner. This is a significant consequence, and it should not be ignored if the business plans to accumulate earnings in anticipation of a sale at a future date.

A second consideration is that, if a C corporation already has substantial value, it is not easy to convert to a pass-through entity and eliminate the threat of double tax. The business cannot make the conversion just before the sale and expect the tax benefits of an S election. Usually, it takes a significant period of time (up to 10 years) to wind out of the double-tax threat.

When all these factors are thrown into the mix, the S corporation looks attractive to Jason with respect to this sellout factor. As a pass-through entity, it eliminates the double tax hit and provides the basis booster for all earnings that are reinvested in the business. Plus, as a corporate entity, it offers the potential of tax-free reorganization benefits.

Factor 6: Passive Income Potential

If Jason uses a pass-through entity, such as an S corporation or an LLC, the income allocated to the owners who are not material participants in the business (a given in this situation) will be passive income that can be offset by tax losses, including passive losses. Even if the income is not distributed to the owners and is retained in the business to finance growth, the owners' losses from other activities can be used to reduce the tax bite on the business income. This capacity to use real estate and other passive losses of the owners to reduce current taxes on income from profitable activities often enhances the reinvestment of earnings in a profitable pass-through entity to finance growth.

By comparison, if the business is operated as a C corporation, there is no way that the income of the business, whether retained in the business or distributed to the owners, can be sheltered by passive losses that the owners generate from other activities. The bottom line is that, for many income-producing enterprises, those owners who are not employed by the business (and perhaps the business itself) will be much better off with a pass-through entity.

EXAMPLE CASE TWO: SUE AND JOYCE

Sue and Joyce are planning to form a new business that will offer specialized catering services. They will be the sole owners (in equal shares), and they will both work full time for the business. They will start out with eight other employees, but anticipate that the employee base could grow to 50 or more as they expand into neighboring markets.

They project that the business will need to reinvest $50,000 to $100,000 of earnings each year to finance growth and expansion. They will bailout the rest of the earnings as compensation income for the long hours they both will put into the business.

Sue and Joyce can't imagine ever selling the business and doubt anyone would be willing to pay much for it. The business is a means for them to each pursue a passion and earn a nice living along the way. It will be their careers. They want to maximize any fringe benefits for themselves.

The best option for the new company that is being organized by Sue and Joyce is a C corporation. This case illustrates three additional choice-of-entity factors.

Factor 7: Owner Fringe Benefits

Sue and Joyce's desire for employee fringe benefits may be a compelling factor in selecting a business form. There are a number of fringe benefits that are available to shareholder/employees of a C corporation that generally are not available to owner/employees of a pass-through entity, such as a partnership, LLC, or S corporation.

The significance of these fringe benefits depends on their importance to the particular owners. Investor owners could care less; employee owners, like Sue and Joyce, often view them as big deals. Each owner needs to assess whether the tax advantages of the fringe benefits are attractive enough to impact the choice-of-entity decision.

The most significant fringe benefits available to shareholder-employees of C corporations include group-term life insurance plans under Section 79, medical-dental reimbursement plans under Section 106, Section 125 cafeteria plans,[1] and dependent care assistance programs under Section 129.

Factor 8: The Bracket Racket

Only a C corporation offers the potential that the tax rate applied to the net income of the business may differ from the income tax rate applied to the owners of the business. All other entities (S corporations, LLCs, partnerships and sole proprietorships) are not separate taxpaying entities. Income earned by these entities is passed through and reported by the owners in proportion to their interests in the business. A C corporation may create an income-splitting opportunity – to have the income retained in the business taxed at a rate lower than the rates paid by the owners. In Sue and Joyce's situation, the different rate structure might be used to their advantage.

C corporations have a tiered graduated rate structure. This structure imposes a low 15-percent tax rate on taxable income up to $50,000 and a 25 percent rate on taxable income between $50,000 and $75,000. So if Sue and Linda can keep the corporation's taxable income to less than $100,000 each year, these low corporate rates will produce a significant bottom line tax savings. If this reinvested income was passed through to them, it is likely that the income tax rate would be at least 28 percent and perhaps more, and payroll taxes would be on top of the income tax hit. This bracket differential can be a significant factor when the numbers are in these ranges.

Note that the potential negative consequences of a C corporation are no big deal in this situation. Sue and Joyce will avoid all double tax fears by bailing out all available earnings as deductible compensation. The C corporation accumulated earnings tax, personal holding company tax, and alternative minimum tax pose no threats. The locked-in stock basis and other sellout costs are not a factor because Sue and Joyce have no plans to sell.

Note also that this potential bracket rate advantage does not apply to personal service C corporations because they are subject to a single-tiered tax bracket of 35 percent. For this reason, a personal service C corporation usually will be better off stripping the income out as compensation on a tax-deductible basis. A personal service corporation is defined as any corporation that meets two tests: a function test and an ownership test. The function test requires that the corporation perform substantially all of its services in the fields of health, law, engineering, architecture, accounting, actuarial science, the performing arts or consulting. The ownership test requires that substantially all of the stock be held directly or indirectly by employees who perform services in one of those fields. For example, the typical medical professional corporation will be a personal service corporation. Generally, there are no tax advantages to accumulating earnings in a personal service C corporation because of the high, flat tax rate structure.

---

1. A section 125 cafeteria plan may be adopted by a partnership, LLC, or S corporation, but S corporation shareholders holding two percent or more of the corporation's stock, partners of the partnership, and members of the LLC cannot participate in the plan. C corporation shareholders may participate so long as no more than 25 percent of the nontaxable benefits selected within the cafeteria plan go to key employees. Subject to the 25 percent limitation, C corporation shareholders can take full advantage of the tax benefits of the plan.

Factor 9: Tax Year Flexibility

Most C corporations may select any fiscal year for tax reporting purposes. Thus, use of a C corporation will give Sue and Joyce an opportunity to select a tax years that simplifies and accommodates their accounting and that may provide a tax deferral potential. Partnerships, LLCs, S corporations and sole proprietorships generally are required to use a calendar year unless they can prove a business purpose for using a fiscal year (a tough burden in most cases) or make a tax deposit under Section 7519 that is designed to eliminate any deferral advantage. C corporations that are personal service corporations may adopt a fiscal year with a deferral period of no more than three months, but the minimum distribution rules applicable to such personal service corporations under Section 280H substantially reduce any tax deferral potential.[2]

The income tax deferral potential of a C corporation that is not a personal service corporation is a fairly simple concept. Consider a manufacturing corporation that is owned by its key employees and that uses a calendar year for tax reporting. Its projected taxable income for 2014, its first year of operation, will be $240,000, and it will earn that income proportionately in each month during the year. For 2014, the choice for the owners of the corporation is to either report the income in the corporation or pay all or a portion of it to themselves as deductible compensation payments. With either approach, all of the $240,000 of taxable income will be reported in the 2014 tax returns of the owners or the corporation.

If the same corporation elects to use a fiscal year ending on March 31, a one-year deferral can be achieved on $180,000 of the $240,000 of taxable income. This is accomplished by having the corporation file a short-year return ending March 31, 2014, reporting $60,000 of taxable income. The remaining $180,000 earned during the last nine months of 2014 is reportable in the fiscal year ending March 31, 2015. But during the first three months of 2015, the owners pay themselves bonuses totaling $180,000 plus any income earned by the corporation during those three months, thus zeroing out the corporation's tax liability for the fiscal year ending March 31, 2015. These bonuses are deducted from the corporation's income for the fiscal year ending March 31, 2015, but are not reported by the calendar year shareholders until they file their 2015 returns on April 15, 2016.

The ability to use this technique is limited by the normal reasonable compensation standards. Plus, the deferral impact is often watered down by withholding and estimated tax payment requirements. But the technique is fairly common and is a legitimate means of deferring taxes.

EXAMPLE CASE THREE: CHARLES

Charles plans on buying and operating a large apartment complex. Charles will put up 10 percent of the equity capital, and the other 90 percent of the equity will come from four outside investors. The business will obtain debt financing equal to nearly four times the total equity capital, and is expected to generate

---

2. I.R.C. §§ 444(b)(2), 280(H).

substantial taxable losses during the first five years of operation, fueled in large part by big depreciation deductions.

Charles wants an entity that will allocate 99 percent of the losses to the investors, award him with 50 percent of the profits after the investors have recouped their investment, and, to the maximum extent possible, free him from minority owner hassles and contractual negotiations and dealings with minority owners. He wants total control. Plus, he would like to protect the investors from any self-employment taxes.

Charles is going to need a partnership-taxed entity, either a limited liability company where he is the sole manager, a limited partnership where his investors are limited partners and his wholly-owned LLC or S corporation is the general partner, or a limited liability limited partnership (if available under applicable state law). Of these options, the limited partnership may make it easier for Charles to nail down his absolute control rights and reduce any self-employment tax risks for the investors. But any of the approaches will work with some quality planning.

This case illustrates three additional choice-of-entity factors.

Factor 10: Different Ownership Interests

As Charles' deal illustrates, often owners want to structure different types of ownership interests in the entity. Income rights, loss rights, cash flow rights, or liquidation rights may need to be structured differently for select owners to reflect varying contributions to the enterprise. With a C corporation, different types of common and preferred stock may be issued to reflect varying preferences. An S corporation is extremely limited in its ability to create different types of equity ownership interests. It is limited to voting and non-voting common stock, all of which must have the same income, loss, cash flow and liquidation rights.

Partnerships and limited liability companies offer the most flexibility in structuring different equity ownership interests. These partnership-taxed, pass-through entities can customize and define the different interests in the entity's operating agreement. Although the design possibilities are almost unlimited, all allocations of profits, losses and credits will be respected for tax purposes only if the allocations are structured to have "substantial economic effect" within the meaning of section 704(b).

In Charles' situation, there's a clear need to use one of these flexible partnership-taxed, pass-through entities to create different types of ownership interests. This is particularly true in situations where one group of owners is providing capital and another is providing management services and expertise.

Factor 11: Loss Utilization

Like many organizers of businesses that are projected to generate losses in the early years, Charles wants to ensure that such losses are funneled to the tax returns that will trigger the highest tax savings. The threshold issue is whether the losses should be retained in the entity or passed through to the owners.

Losses generated by a C corporation are retained in the corporation and carried backward or forward to be deducted against income earned in previous or future years. Losses sustained by S corporations, LLCs, partnerships and sole proprietorships are passed through to the business owners. When losses are anticipated in the initial years of a business, using a pass-through entity may generate a tax advantage if the owners have other taxable income against which those losses can be offset, within certain limitations. The advantage is that the losses may produce immediate tax benefits.

In planning to pass through losses to the owners, never lose sight of the fact that the losses, even if passed through, may produce no immediate benefit if one or more of three loss limitation hurdles described in Chapter 9 get in the way. The at-risk and passive loss hurdles usually are not impacted by the type of pass-through entity selected.

The basis hurdle is different in this regard. The general rule is that losses generated by a pass-through entity are unavailable to an owner of the entity to the extent that the cumulative net losses exceed the owner's basis in the entity. For example, if an investor puts $50,000 into an S corporation, that owner's basis in the S corporation stock is $50,000. If the S corporation generates a loss of $150,000 in the first year and finances the loss through corporate indebtedness, the S corporation shareholder may only use $50,000 of the loss against his or her other income. The other $100,000 is suspended because it exceeds the owner's stock basis. It is carried forward to be used in future years if and when the basis is increased. In contrast, if the indebtedness is incurred in an entity taxed as a partnership, the indebtedness will increase the partners' basis in their partnership interests under the provisions of Section 752, and the basis limitation will no longer be a factor in assessing the current tax value of the losses.

Factor 12: Real Estate

The choice-of-entity analysis is usually impacted by the presence of real estate. The fact that most real estate tends to appreciate over time has powerful consequences for planning purposes. First, it permits the owners to take advantage of a fiction in the Internal Revenue Code – depreciation cost recovery deductions that are based on the premise that real estate improvements lose their value over time. Second, it sometimes facilitates the use of nonrecourse debt because lenders are willing to make loans that are secured only by the value of the real estate. The nonrecourse debt eliminates the loss basis hurdle for any entity taxed as a partnership and escapes the at-risk hurdle by virtue of the "qualified nonrecourse debt financing" exception that is applicable only to real estate.[3] And third, it is never prudent to subject the appreciation of the real estate to the double tax structure of a C corporation. As a general proposition, appreciating real estate should be kept out of C corporations. Plus, income from real estate activities that is passed through to the owners generally is not subject to the self-employment tax.[4]

Given these consequences, real estate usually warrants its own entity, and in

---

3. I.R.C. §§ 752(a), 465(b)(6).
4. I.R.C. § 1402(a)(1). The tax will apply to anyone who receives rental income in the course of a trade or business as a real estate dealer.

nearly all situations that entity should be a partnership-taxed entity.

EXAMPLE CASE FOUR: JURDEN INC.

Jurden Inc. is a successful C corporation poised to explode. It has five shareholders, all successful business investors. The plan for the next five to ten years is to aggressively reinvest earnings to create a global presence and then sell out to a strategic buyer at the right time. The shareholders want to shed the C status now. They want the future tax benefits of a pass-though entity, including the stock basis booster for all reinvested earnings and the elimination or serious reduction of double tax bites at time of sale.

Jurden Inc's only option, as a practical matter, is to covert to an S corporation. This case illustrates a controlling choice-of-entity factor for many.

Factor 13: C Corporation Conversion Flexibility

As a C corporation, Jurden Inc. has only one option that makes sense. If it converted to a partnership structure or an LLC, a gain on the liquidation of the corporation would be triggered at both the corporate and shareholder level at time of conversion – a disastrous scenario. The corporation would recognize a gain on all its assets, and the shareholders would recognize a gain on the liquidation of their stock. The tax costs of getting into a partnership or LLC pass-through entity usually are too great to even think about.

The only practical answer for Jurden Inc. is an S corporation. At the present time, a C corporation may convert to an S corporation without automatically triggering the type of gain that would be triggered on a deemed liquidation of a C corporation.

The S corporation conversion, while clearly the preferred choice in most situations, is not a perfect solution and may trigger additional tax costs at the time of the conversion and later down the road. If, for example, the corporation values its inventories under the LIFO method, the corporation must recognize as income the LIFO reserve as a result of the S election conversion. Also, the conversion will not eliminate all threats of double taxation. If a C corporation converts to an S corporation and liquidates or sells out within 10 years after the election, the portion of the resulting gain attributable to the period before the election will be taxed at the corporate level as if the corporation had remained a C corporation. If the C corporation had accumulated earnings and profits before the conversion, the shareholders may end up with taxable dividends after the conversion. A completely clean break from C status often is impossible. But in most situations, these tax consequences of conversion can be managed and do not provide a basis for rejecting a conversion to S status that otherwise makes sense.

EXAMPLE CASE FIVE: PETER

Peter has developed a business plan for creating and exploiting a series of new Internet games that promise the potential of a huge success. He has attracted the attention of various investors, none of whom want their personal tax returns exposed to any venture and all of whom want to see Peter's unique talents showcased and exploited through a public company at the right time. The plan is to reinvest all business earnings so that Peter can build the business as fast as possible.

Peter is going to want a C corporation. This case illustrates three additional choice-of-entity factors, two of which usually are controlling when they apply.

Factor 14: Going Public Prospects

When a company is funded with outside capital and the plan is to go public at the first solid opportunity, the C corporation often is the mandated choice. The interests of the outside investors and the potential of going public trump all other considerations. Usually the audited track record of the company leading up to the offering is best reflected in the same form of entity that will ultimately go public, which is a C corporation in nearly all cases.

Factor 15: The "Not My Return" Factor

This factor is a consideration that sometimes preempts everything else. It refers to the owner who has no interest in anything that will implicate or complicate his or her personal tax return. Some just cannot accept the concept of having to personally recognize and pay taxes on income from a pass-through entity that has never been (and may never be) received in the form of cash. Others are spooked by the accounting and audit risks. The thought that their personal tax return and their personal tax liability could be directly impacted by the audit of a company managed by others is too much to bear. Still others are adamant about keeping all personal matters as simple and as understandable as possible. A stack of K–1 forms flapping on the back of their returns is not their concept of simple. When this factor cannot be eliminated, the only option is a C corporation that offers the benefit of complete "separateness."

Factor 16: Reinvestment Growth

Like many, Peter hopes to grow his company by reinvesting all earnings. In recent years, the tax rate differential between individual taxpayers and a C corporation has not been significant. Both have topped out at a maximum rate of 35 percent. So the choice-of-entity analysis has not turned on the potential to reinvest after-tax earnings and grow the business.

But that all changed in 2013. The American Taxpayer Relief Act of 2012 (the "Fiscal Cliff" legislation signed into law during the final days of 2012)[5] increased individual ordinary income tax rates to 39.6 percent starting in 2013 for couples with taxable incomes in excess of $450,000 and individuals with taxable incomes in excess of $400,000. Plus, in 2013 the 3.8 percent Medicare tax kicked in for couples with a modified adjusted gross income in excess of $250,000 ($200,000 for individuals). The net result is that a successful business owner who is allocated profits through a pass-through S corporation or LLC could end up paying federal taxes at a combined income and Medicare rate of 43.4 percent. In contrast, political leaders on both sides of the aisle and the Obama administration have suggested that top corporate tax rates should be reduced to the 25 to 28 percent range to remain competitive with other countries.

---

5. Section 101 of the American Taxpayer Relief Act of 2012.

The result is that we could end up with a condition that we haven't had for decades – a mammoth gap between top individual rates and top corporate rates.

For a company looking to grow with reinvested earnings, such a huge rate differential between individual and corporate rates may compel use of a C corporation. The difference between reinvesting 56 cents on every earned dollar and reinvesting 75 cents, when compounded over five or ten years and adjusted for leveraging differences, may impact a business' capacity to finance growth by as much as 100 percent or more. As the push for such a rate differential intensifies, this may emerge as the newest and most dominant choice-of-entity factor for businesses that need to grow.

FACTOR SUMMARY AND CONCLUSION

A review of these 16 factors in a given situation will help in choosing the best form of business entity and understanding the primary and collateral consequences. One conclusion is fairly obvious: The C corporation is a very different creature from the other forms, all of which are pass-through entities. Therefore, often the starting point is to take a hard look at the C corporation as an alternative. If it fails to pass muster (and it will in many situations), the alternative pass-through entity forms will need to be evaluated.

STUDENT PROBLEM 10-1

Sam leads a group of five wealthy investors who are going to form a new manufacturing company. They anticipate that the company's profitability will steadily grow, starting at $350,000 in year one and growing to $2.5 million a year within five years. None of the owners will work fulltime for the company, but Sam will oversee the operations and serve as a liaison between the owners and key managers. The owners plan to reinvest all profits to quickly expand the business and then to sell to a strategic buyer as soon as possible. It's possible that any sale of the business might be structured as a tax-free reorganization that would provide the owners with stock in a public company. The owners want a structure that will fuel growth by minimizing taxes, limit liability exposure, and ensure that each owner has equal control in future decisions.

What entity form would you recommend? Explain your reasoning and any alternatives that Sam and his colleagues might want to consider.

STUDENT PROBLEM 10-2

Betty is an entrepreneur who has developed a business plan for creating and exploiting a new flash-type Internet application. Betty will be the sole owner, but will spend very little time in the business. The inspiration and driving force behind the business will be Justin. In addition to Justin, the business will have six employees who will fulfill contracts with companies that want and need the technology. Betty anticipates that the business will be profitable from the get-go and that she will withdraw profits on a regular basis. She wants to have a separate entity for business purposes that will minimize taxes and not expose her personal assets and other businesses to the risks of this business. What form of entity do you recommend? What additional facts would you like to have?

STUDENT PROBLEM 10-3

Lou has plans to form a new company that will design and build custom luxury motor coaches for celebrities, professional athletes, and wealthy couples who fear planes and want to be driven in ultimate luxury. He has secured equity financing from five wealthy investors, who collectively have agreed to put up $6 million to finance the first eight coaches. The "deal" with these investors is that (1) Lou will get a salary of $250,000 a year; (2) the investors will get their investment money back before any additional distributions; (3) Lou will then be paid the $200,000 that he has invested to develop the initial plans; and (4) profits then will be distributed 30 percent to Lou and 70 percent to the investors. Any losses will be allocated 99 percent to the investors and 1 percent to Lou. Lou wants to ensure that he always has complete control of all business decisions, an investor cannot get out once he or she has acquired an interest in the business, and taxes are minimized.

You represent Lou. What entity form would you recommend? Explain your reasoning and any alternatives that Lou might want to consider.

STUDENT PROBLEM 10-4

Duke, Joan and Alice are going to form a new company that will provide web and app design and construction services. They will be the sole owners and will be employed full time by the business. They anticipate adding eight to ten support employees over the next three years as the business ramps up. Projections indicate that the business will need to retain approximately $90,000 of earnings for each of the next five years to finance growth. The balance of the earnings will be withdrawn by the three owners to fund their lifestyles and capital accumulation efforts.

The owners view the business as a career income vehicle, not an entity that will be sold at some point in the future. Their primary objectives are to create a collegial working environment, maximize income and benefits for themselves, and minimize taxes. What form of entity do you recommend? What additional facts would you like to have? Explain your reasoning and any alternatives that the owners might want to consider.

INDEX

References are to pages.

References are to Pages

References are to Pages